Frustrated Majorities

Democratic elections do not always deliver what majorities want. Many conclude from *frustrated majorities* a failure of democracy. This book argues the opposite may be true – that politicians who represent their constituents sometimes frustrate majorities. A theory of issue intensity explains how the intensity with which different voters care about political issues drives key features of elections, political participation, representation, and public policy. Because candidates for office are more certain of winning the votes of those who care intensely, they sometimes side with an intense minority over a less intense majority. Voters who care intensely communicate their intensity by taking political action: volunteering, contributing, and speaking out. From questions like whose voices should matter in a democracy to whose voices actually matter, this rigorous book blends ideas from democratic theory and formal political economy with new empirical evidence to tackle a topic of central importance to American politics.

Seth J. Hill is Professor of Political Science at the University of California San Diego.

T0381697

POLITICAL ECONOMY OF INSTITUTIONS AND DECISIONS

Series Editors

Jeffry Frieden, *Harvard University*
John Patty, *Emory University*
Elizabeth Maggie Penn, *Emory University*

Founding Editors

James E. Alt, *Harvard University*
Douglass C. North, *Washington University of St. Louis*

Other books in the series

Alberto Alesina and Howard Rosenthal,
Partisan Politics, Divided Government and the Economy
Lee J. Alston, Thrainn Eggertsson and Douglass C. North, eds.,
Empirical Studies in Institutional Change
Lee J. Alston and Joseph P. Ferrie,
Southern Paternalism and the Rise of the American Welfare State:
Economics, Politics, and Institutions, 1865–1965
James E. Alt and Kenneth Shepsle, eds.,
Perspectives on Positive Political Economy
Josephine T. Andrews,
When Majorities Fail: The Russian Parliament, 1990–1993
Jeffrey S. Banks and Eric A. Hanushek, eds.,
Modern Political Economy: Old Topics, New Directions
Yoram Barzel,
Economic Analysis of Property Rights, 2nd edition
Yoram Barzel,
A Theory of the State: Economic Rights, Legal Rights,
and the Scope of the State
Robert Bates,
Beyond the Miracle of the Market: The Political Economy
of Agrarian Development in Kenya
Jenna Bednar,
The Robust Federation: Principles of Design
Charles M. Cameron,
Veto Bargaining: Presidents and the Politics of Negative Power
Kelly H. Chang,
Appointing Central Bankers: The Politics of Monetary Policy
in the United States and the European Monetary Union

(continued after the Index)

Frustrated Majorities

How Issue Intensity Enables Smaller Groups of Voters to Get What They Want

SETH J. HILL

University of California San Diego

CAMBRIDGE
UNIVERSITY PRESS

CAMBRIDGE
UNIVERSITY PRESS

University Printing House, Cambridge CB2 8BS, United Kingdom

One Liberty Plaza, 20th Floor, New York, NY 10006, USA

477 Williamstown Road, Port Melbourne, VIC 3207, Australia

314–321, 3rd Floor, Plot 3, Splendor Forum, Jasola District Centre, New Delhi – 110025, India

103 Penang Road, #05–06/07, Visioncrest Commercial, Singapore 238467

Cambridge University Press is part of the University of Cambridge.

It furthers the University's mission by disseminating knowledge in the pursuit of education, learning, and research at the highest international levels of excellence.

www.cambridge.org
Information on this title: www.cambridge.org/9781009167680
DOI: 10.1017/9781009167697

First published 2022

A catalogue record for this publication is available from the British Library.

ISBN 978-1-009-16768-0 Hardback
ISBN 978-1-009-16767-3 Paperback

Contents

Figures

Tables

Theorems

xiii

Acknowledgments

A book project has its origins many years before it is published, and authors owe more debts than they can hope to repay. Let me use this space to offer thanks to the many who have supported me.

My interest in political science began as an undergraduate when I was introduced to the rewards of scholarly research by Linda L. Fowler and Dean Spiliotes. My journey continued as a graduate student at UCLA where many faculty and fellow graduate students inspired me. I want to thank my UCLA mentors John Zaller, Jim DeNardo, Miriam Golden, and especially Lynn Vavreck and Jeff Lewis. Lynn and Jeff have been my advocates time and time again and no words can express my gratitude to them. I am so fortunate to continue to count them as friends and colleagues. I also thank my fellow Bruin travelers, Matt Atkinson, Mac Bunyanunda, Liz Carlson, Kim Dionne, Ryan Enos, Richard Goldberg, Brian Law, James Lo, Gid Lukens, and Matt Spence for instruction and laughter.

I was fortunate to gain a postdoctoral appointment at Yale with Alan Gerber and Greg Huber. I learned from Alan and Greg how to write and publish articles and gained first-hand experience in survey, lab, and field experimental methods. I thank fellow post-docs Dave Doherty and Conor Dowling for teaching me the ropes and making me feel welcome professionally and personally from day one. At Yale, the Institution for Social and Policy Studies is a vibrant intellectual community that serves as a great example for newly minted academics.

The University of California San Diego provides an amazing setting for new assistant professors to get work done. I want to thank the Department of Political Science for its dedication to supporting junior faculty.

I am grateful to the many colleagues there who show me how to succeed in this profession. I would also like to thank the UC San Diego Library for research support and access to their collections.

For the incredible task of reading the full manuscript, I am grateful to Taylor Carlson, Gary Jacobson, John Bullock, Anthony Fowler, Dan Hopkins, Greg Huber, Sam Kernell, Chris Tausanovitch, Lynn Vavreck, and Chris Warshaw. I also benefited from three anonymous readers who evaluated the book with exceptional care. Their feedback has dramatically improved the argument and writing of the book. I thank Rob Dreessen, Erika Walsh, and the staff at Cambridge University Press for making the publication process smooth.

I have also benefited from feedback on this project at conferences, seminars, and through individual correspondence. I thank seminar audiences at the Annual Meetings of the American Political Science Association, BYU, Stanford, UCSD, USC Price School, and Yale. For feedback large and small, I thank Avi Acharya, Nageeb Ali, Pam Ban, Mike Barber, Dan Butler, Steve Callander, Liz Carlson, Jamie Druckman, Justin Fox, Sandy Gordon, Andy Hall, Hans Hassell, Michael Herron, Sean Ingham, John Jackson, Kapil Jain, Korhan Kocak, Thad Kousser, Seth Masket, Mike Olson, John Patty, Molly Roberts, Christina Schneider, Ken Shotts, Branislav Slantchev, Sharece Thrower, and David Wiens.

Finally, I want to thank those who have provided the backbone of support for this endeavor. My parents, brothers, step-parents, step-siblings, in-laws, and extended family have provided a lifetime of intellectual exploration. My children make me want to become the best version of myself. I hope that this book shows them that, with perseverance, even large goals become reality.

Finally, to my wife, my best friend and co-traveler, thank you. You have never hesitated in your support and encouragement. You have never complained about the hours I put in. Your daily embrace of all that life has to offer inspires me, and I hope this book makes you proud.

PART I

FRUSTRATED MAJORITIES, ISSUE INTENSITY, AND POLITICAL ACTION

I

Majoritarian Politics and Minority Interests

The very essence of democratic government consists in the absolute
sovereignty of the majority.
  Alexis de Toqueville (1835 [2013], *Democracy in America*, Chapter XV)

There is no maxim in my opinion which is more liable to be misapplied,
and which therefore more needs elucidation than the current one that the
interest of the majority is the political standard of right and wrong.
  Letter From James Madison to James Monroe, October 5, 1786.

From January 2012 to January 2017 the price of housing in Reno, Nevada
surged. The median sale price of single-family homes increased from
$135,000 to $302,000, and average apartment rental rates increased by
33 percent from about $825 to more than $1,100 per month (Reno Realty
Blog 2021; City of Reno n.d., Fig. 2, May 30, 2018 Planning Commission
staff report). Population growth and housing was a key issue facing the
City Council in 2017. As part of an effort to increase the supply of rental
housing, the Council voted unanimously on October 25 to direct staff
at the city's Community Development Planning Commission to develop
revisions to the city code that would allow the building of Accessory
Dwelling Units (ADU) on most single-family lots.

ADUs – "granny flats" – are smaller residential dwellings built adjacent
to larger homes. ADUs had been banned in Reno since a 2005 morato-
rium by the City Council, but escalating residential prices motivated the
Council to revisit that decision. Proponents hoped that ADUs, as part of a
multifaceted approach to housing, would provide an additional housing
opportunity with lower construction costs than new housing (City of

Reno, n.d.). City Planning Commissioner Marshall stated that the goal of the ordinance would be to "provide a long-term stable rental market."

What appeared to be a simple statutory revision to increase housing supply ended up delayed, doctored, and then denied. A small number of voters with intense opposition to ADUs contacted their representatives, attended events, and spoke at public meetings. What had been a unanimous 2017 City Council directive to draft the ordinance became a unanimous 2018 City Council rejection of the policy change. What happened?

Following the October directive, Planning Commission staff solicited input from architects and the community and fielded a survey on the city web site. They presented a report on their findings along with a draft ordinance to a public meeting of the City Planning Commission on March 21, 2018. The staff report noted some negative community feedback: Residents had expressed concern about vacation rentals and the impact of ADUs on the character of communities, parking, sanitation, and public safety (City of Reno, n.d., March 21, 2018 staff report).

At the March 21 meeting, city planning commissioners asked questions about ADUs and requested amendments to the ordinance to strengthen regulation of design and location. Nonetheless, they remained supportive. They voted unanimously to move forward and directed staff to revise the ordinance. Eight community members spoke or submitted comments at the meeting, six in support and two in opposition (City of Reno, n.d., March 21, 2018 minutes).

Planning staff presented a revised ordinance to the Commission on May 30. The revisions narrowed the type of lots on which ADUs would be allowed, increased regulations about design and setback, and prohibited use as short-term vacation rentals. Even with the revisions, commissioners expressed concern and voted unanimously for staff to investigate new issues and make additional revisions to be presented at a future meeting. Sixteen community members spoke or submitted comments at the meeting, three in support and thirteen in opposition (City of Reno, n.d., May 30, 2018 staff report and minutes).

On September 19, staff presented new research and a new draft ordinance to the Planning Commission that made further requirements for ADU construction such as a property survey prior to permitting. Although supportive of ADUs in principle and grateful to staff for their efforts, commissioners expressed even stronger skepticism about ADUs than at the May meeting (City of Reno, n.d., September 19, 2018 staff report and minutes). Commissioner Gower concluded, "[T]he Master Plan we just adopted ... says our infill strategy as a city is to concentrate growth in downtown areas, to corridors, to areas of mixed use development. It says nothing about increasing the density in existing residential areas." Ninety-one community members spoke or submitted comments in opposition to the ordinance versus ten in favor. In a surprising reversal of their initial support, the Commission voted unanimously at the meeting to recommend the City Council deny the ordinance. The proposal then moved to a City Council meeting scheduled for November 28 where the Council would make a final determination.

At the City Council meeting, the mayor and most council members expressed skepticism about ADUs. One hundred sixty-six community members spoke or submitted comments at the meeting, 20 in support of ADUs and 146 opposed (City of Reno, n.d., November 28, 2018 minutes). Council Member Brekhus stated support for the ordinance and made a motion to table the item until the new year so that staff could have time to investigate outstanding concerns. The motion to table was defeated five to two. The Council then denied the ordinance in a unanimous vote.

Both the City Council and the City Planning Commission had originally endorsed revising Reno rules to allow the construction of ADUs. Yet, within the span of 13 months, support turned to skepticism and then unanimous opposition. While I do not have data on the balance of support for ADUs among Reno voters, no public comment from any commissioner or council member recorded in meeting minutes indicated a belief that a majority of their constituents opposed ADUs.

What is clear is that a small number of opponents of ADUs made their voices heard more than did supporters. They attended public meetings, spoke and submitted comments, and contacted their representatives on the issue.

Might the efforts of ADU opponents have flipped the support of Planning Commissioners and City Council members? If so, why would politicians who sought policies to relieve a housing crunch felt by thousands of their constituents bend to the pressure of what appears to be a small group of voters? More generally, when would office-seeking politicians side with a small minority of voters on an issue with potential gains to a much larger majority?

* * *

Elected representatives do not faithfully deliver policies desired by majorities of their constituents. Even when winning office requires a plurality of votes in elections and enacting new laws requires a majority of votes in the legislature, majorities in the electorate sometimes do not get what they want. These are majorities frustrated. Frustrated majorities in representative democracies worry many observers of politics, including scholars of representation and political pundits.

Some scholars and pundits suggest that special interests cause politicians to frustrate majorities. They argue that interest groups funnel campaign contributions and other benefits to politicians in exchange for policy benefits. They argue that political parties lean on their legislators to pass policies favored by members of their coalition. They argue that former legislators become lobbyists and use their connections to nudge policy toward the needs of clients. They argue that the well-to-do participate in political venues outside of elections to tilt policy away from the common good of average citizens.

These explanations imply that if we only removed special interest perversions of the democratic process, electoral competition would select representatives who work in the public interest. Policy progress would be had and majorities satisfied.

Other scholars and pundits suggest that politicians frustrate majorities because voters aren't up to the task of motivating representation. They argue that voters are insufficiently informed, that they make electoral choices contrary to their interests, and that non-issue considerations such as blind loyalty to political parties undermine good democratic citizenship. They argue that failures of representation follow from failures of voters.

These explanations imply that if only voters would pay attention to public affairs, would participate in politics and turn out in elections, and would vote based on issue and policy considerations, then electoral competition would select representatives who work in the public interest. Policy progress would be had and majorities satisfied.

I argue in this book that both of these explanations are incomplete. Regulating campaign finance does not eliminate frustrated majorities. Removing or reforming political parties does not eliminate frustrated majorities. Prohibiting lobbying does not eliminate frustrated majorities. Voters need not be ignorant, incompetent, nor have excessive attachments to political parties for majorities to be frustrated.

I offer a theory that suggests when and why democratic elections alone can cause ambitious politicians to side with minorities over majorities. Existing explanations let voters off the hook. In fact, competent, informed voters choosing between ambitious uncorrupt politicians in competitive elections can still frustrate majorities. Majoritarian elections can represent minority interests and maintain policy opposed by electoral majorities without the influence of pressure politics and without incompetent voters failing to enact political accountability.

How do majoritarian elections represent minority interests? Differences in voter *issue intensity* cause frustrated majorities. Some voters simply care more (and quite possibly a lot more) about any given issue than do others. At elections, voters must choose between candidates or parties. Each candidate or party represents a combination of issue positions and characteristics. Voters must decide how to trade off issue positions and characteristics they like from those that they do not. In making that trade-off, voters who care intensely about an issue (or characteristic) more likely favor a candidate or party they agree with than do voters who care about that same issue (or characteristic) but less intensely. Candidate and party issue positions, therefore, more influence the choice of voters who care intensely about an issue than influence the choice of voters who care less intensely about the same issue.

Because politicians can be more sure of the votes of those who care intensely than of the votes of those who care less intensely, it is sometimes in the electoral interest of politicians to side with an intense minority against a less-intense majority. When a minority cares enough more about an issue than the majority, vote-seeking politicians expect to win more votes proposing the policy preferred by the intense minority than they expect to win proposing the policy of the less-intense majority. Majority rule is not necessarily implied by fair majoritarian elections.

My argument that majorities can be frustrated through electoral competition alone connects to voter welfare and the meaning of democracy. Many argue that frustrated majorities imply voters getting short shrift or even that frustrated majorities mean that democracy is broken. I suggest that politicians simply chasing the majority on every issue would not necessarily generate government that delivers what is best for all voters. Instead, policy set with intense minorities over less-intense majorities on some issues can, in some cases, be best for the full electorate. We ought to be cautious before objecting to a setting where an intense minority is willing to forego representation on some issues in exchange for representation on the issue they most care about.

I am not the first to suggest that issue intensity might be an important part of democratic politics. The media and popular analysts of elections use similar concepts to describe the politics of, for example, abortion or gun rights. It is not an uncommon intuition that voters who care passionately about an issue might be more likely to get what they want. Ideas such as "single-issue voters" and "issue publics" describe voters who care intensely about one issue. The theory of political "pluralism" uses the idea of issue intensity to understand how different groups compete to win political control over public policy. And the political science of congressional politics circles similar ideas. For example, Fenno (1978) reported:

> It is not the omniscient constituent armed with information on all their votes that concerns [members of Congress]. It is the individual or group armed with information and feeling deeply aggrieved about one vote or one cluster of votes that is most worrisome. "There isn't one voter in 20,000 who knows my voting record," said one member, "except on that one thing that affects him." (p. 142)

The theoretical scaffolding relating electoral competition to issue intensity, representation, issue publics, and single-issue voters, however, is missing important support. Both intuition and political science leave unanswered important questions about the operation of intensity. For example,

1. When do politicians go against majority preferences? Do single-issue voters always get what they want, or do other factors influence their success?
2. Might intensity explain policy in some issue areas but not others?
3. If voters believe that politicians cater to intense voters, do some voters pretend to care intensely so that they get what they want?
4. How do politicians distinguish voters who care intensely and will follow through on that intensity from voters who might end up acting on other issues or abstaining from politics?

This book presents my attempt at a careful theoretical argument about the operation of issue intensity in majoritarian elections. What I call "intensity theory" blends ideas from democratic theory and political economy with empirical evidence from behavioral political science to help us understand frustrated majorities, electoral competition, intensity of preference, political participation, and representation. Let me briefly summarize the theory.

1.1 THE ARGUMENT

Votes are the currency of elections, and politicians who want votes pursue voters. Politicians pursue intense voters with vigor, because voters who care intensely offer more votes in return for policy attention. When a minority of sufficient size and intensity opposes a less-intense majority, politicians who want to win votes favor the interests of the intense minority.

Why do voters vary so widely in actions taken in the realm of politics? Because some care intensely about political issues and incur costs to communicate their intensity to politicians. Choosing to incur costs informs politicians where the highest return of votes to policy resides. Both majority and minority voters who care intensely sometimes choose costly action so that politicians know how much they care.

In other words, variation in who cares, how much they care, and the size of majorities and minorities leads some voters to incur costly political action, leads other voters to abstain from action, and leads politicians to sometimes propose policy against the known preferences of an electoral majority.

Intensity theory explains stylized facts from empirical political science. First, the theory explains why majoritarian outcomes are not a necessary consequence of electoral competition in majoritarian systems. I define majorities "frustrated" when elected representatives choose a policy position known to be opposed by a majority of voters even though the alternative would have majority support. Intensity theory builds off existing theories of electoral competition over multiple issues to show when and why those politicians ambitious only to win votes would choose to side with minorities over majorities.

The intensity theory explanation of frustrated majorities helps answer questions begged by scholars who claim that representation is broken in America. Recent book titles in political science make clear that many equate government delivering policy favored by a minority as conclusive evidence of a democracy broken. Representatives are *disconnected* from and *unresponsive* to their constituents (Fiorina and Abrams, 2009; Achen and Bartels, 2016). An economic elite has *hijacked* the political agenda (Witko et al., 2021). Page and Gilens (2017) append a question mark to the existence of democracy in their book *Democracy in America?* and introduce their topic *What has gone wrong*, "Large majorities of Americans favor specific measures that would be helpful. Yet our national government often appears to ignore the wants and needs of its citizens. (3)" Hacker and Pierson (2020, pp. 12–13) worry about "creeping countermajoritarianism" where a "more and more determined minority" resists the will of the majority, "distorting democracy."

Intensity theory shows, in contrast, that a representative democracy that sometimes frustrates majorities does not indicate a system broken or undemocratic. Frustrated majorities do not require extraordinary influence of campaign finance or organized interests.[1] Frustrated majorities do not require politicians drawn from unrepresentative parts of the citizen population (Besley and Coate, 1997; Carnes, 2018) nor that voters ignore their policy interests due to identity (Lenz, 2012), distractions (Hacker and Pierson, 2020), or incompetence (Achen and Bartels, 2016). Frustrated majorities need not follow from institutional anachronisms (Krehbiel, 1998; Howell and Moe, 2020) nor a decline in civic life (Skocpol, 2013).

Instead, policy might sometimes be set with minorities over majorities through the simple dynamics of electoral competition. Politicians, seeking only votes, might choose to risk losing some votes from a less-intense majority to be more certain of winning the votes of a minority that cares intensely. And this might be a good democratic outcome.

This is not to say that the factors proposed by others to influence political outcomes or cause frustrated majorities are irrelevant. Rather, I argue that electoral competition untainted by factors such as these, as sometimes idealized by others, would not necessarily end frustrated majorities or deliver majority rule.

Policy is not *always* set with intense minorities. Intensity theory explains when politicians ignore an intense minority and side with a less-intense majority.

Intensity theory also explains why citizens sometimes engage in costly political action such as making campaign contributions, volunteering, voting in party primary elections, or participating in protests. Because intensity is hard to observe, voters incur costs through political actions to communicate to politicians how much they care. The theory thus explains *which* voters choose to take costly political action and with what *magnitude of cost*. I show that even members of the majority sometimes choose to take costly action.

Theories of costly signaling (Jervis, 1970) inform my arguments about voters' use of costly political action to communicate issue intensity. Just as corporations might make campaign contributions to signal how

---

[1] The list of scholars arguing that campaign finance distorts democracy is too long to summarize. For recent examples, see Page and Gilens (2017, chapters 5 and 6), Hertel-Fernandez (2019), or Witko et al. (2021).

much they care about an issue (Gordon and Hafer, 2005), voters might volunteer for political organizations to signal how much they care about an issue.

The intensity explanation of costly political action helps us understand the consequences of institutional reforms related to political participation. In the empirical part of this book, I show that reforms to campaign finance and primary elections have muted consequences anticipated by intensity theory.

Intensity theory also offers explanation for other patterns of democratic politics and electoral competition. It explains why many moderate or non-ideological citizens appear ambivalent on all but a few issues – issue publics – but nonetheless incur costs to participate in politics. It clarifies why issue voting might be central to electoral choice but hard to measure. It might also provide a new perspective on intra-party politics.

To explain change in policy, many students of democracy focus on changes in size of majority. When a majority becomes large enough, politicians represent their interests. Intensity theory instead shows that change in intensity can induce change in policy even holding constant the size of minority and majority. If the intensity of the minority decreases or the intensity of the majority increases, politicians can change policy from siding with the minority to siding with the majority. If the intensity of the minority increases or the intensity of the majority decreases, politicians can change policy from siding with the majority to siding with the minority.

Intensity theory brings under one theoretical umbrella vote choice in general elections and acts of political participation such as voting in primary elections and making campaign contributions. It helps explain how lobbyists and interest groups appear to have influence through pressure politics even though a system with ambitious politicians pursuing votes seems to suggest lobbying should not sway politicians from what voters want. The theory also implies that opinion surveys that do not ask how voters balance representation on one issue for representation on another might miss a key aspect of electoral democracy.

Intensity theory describes voters as an active and creative part of the electoral process rather than responding to a fixed menu of candidates or parties (Sniderman, 2000; Sniderman and Bullock, 2004). Voters are not simply a mathematical function taking candidates or parties as fixed inputs and returning a vote choice. Instead, their pre-election actions

TABLE 1.1. *Main result on politician policy proposals from analysis of mathematical model*

| | | Majority | |
		Costly action	No action
Minority	Costly action	Policy with majority	Policy with minority (Frustrated majority)
	No action	Policy with majority	Policy with majority

Note: Equilibrium depends on parameter values characterized in Proposition A.2.

influence the policy platforms of politicians by communicating what voters value. Politics is a back-and-forth interactive process between voters and politicians.

The key dynamics of intensity theory are the size and intensities of preference of electoral minorities and majorities. The combination of size and intensity determines whether politicians propose policy with a minority over a known majority and whether and which voters choose to engage in costly political action. Even when all voters and all politicians know what the majority wants, policy is still sometimes set with the minority.

In other words, frustrated majorities follow from electoral competition and intensely-held political preferences and do not require capture, mischiefs of faction, misinformation, incompetence, or corruption.

I formalize the argument of intensity theory into a mathematical model and use game theory to characterize the patterns of behavior for strategic actors. The results of the model describe when politicians choose to frustrate majorities in pursuit of votes and when voters choose political actions with certain costs and uncertain benefits. The model also allows me to describe when setting policy with an intense minority improves utilitarian social welfare over a system of majority-rule.

I summarize in Table 1.1 the main result of my analysis of the mathematical model. The cells of the table indicate the best policy for politicians to propose as a function of the costly action incurred by members of the majority (column) and members of the minority (row). Politician policy depends upon which groups in the electorate take or abstain from costly political action.

When neither the majority nor the minority take political action, politicians infer that neither care intensely about the issue and so propose policy with the majority. If the majority takes costly action to communicate intensity, politicians side with the intense majority no matter their belief about the intensity of the minority. If, and only if, the minority takes action to communicate to the politicians that they care intensely and the majority does not do politicians propose policy with the intense minority.

1.2 SCOPE

The setting of the theory is electoral competition in a representative democracy. To simplify analysis and highlight the logic of the theory, I make five assumptions that generate a model of electoral competition that would appear to favor the majority. These assumptions favor the majority by setting aside the usual explanations for frustrated majorities such as pressure politics and incompetent voters.

The first assumption of the mathematical model is that candidates aim to maximize votes received at the election using the tool of policy platforms. I assume candidates are not themselves motivated by policy or other factors outside of the election. This allows me to show that policy can be set with an intense minority even when politicians have no extra-electoral considerations pushing them away from majorities.

Second, I assume that vote choice responds to the policy platforms proposed by candidates on average but that other electoral factors make vote choice an imperfect function of policy. These other factors can represent a host of inputs the science of elections has demonstrated relevant in other work such as party identification or retrospective evaluation of the economy. These other factors make elections unpredictable because individual vote choice is not simply a deterministic function of one policy – probabilistic voting.

Third, voters vary both in what they want and in how much they value each want. The theory's scope is limited to political issues that divide the electorate such that some voters support one policy while others support another. On each issue that divides the electorate and on each side of that issue, some in the electorate might care more about the issue than others. This magnitude of care is the voter's issue intensity.

Fourth, I assume candidates know on which side of the policy issue each voter falls but do not know how much each voter cares to obtain their preference on the issue. In other words, candidates know voter policy positions but do not know voter intensities. This assumption is not necessary to generate frustrated majorities but is necessary to generate instrumental costly political action.

Fifth, voters are rational in the sense of taking actions in instrumental pursuit of goals. Voters have agency over what political actions to take and which candidates to support and use all information at their disposal to decide how much time to volunteer for campaigns and how many political contributions to make. This allows me to show that frustrated majorities arise when voters rationally pursue policy interest with knowledge, intention, and competence without need for voter action skewed by psychological identities or ineptitude.

The theory focuses directly on intensity in electoral competition with as little clutter as possible. Although this approach abstracts away from many inputs to political outcomes, parsimony allows broad connections and conclusions. Intensity theory shows how non-majoritarian policy outcomes, political participation, electoral competition, political diversity in a society, and vote choice can be brought together under one theoretical umbrella. My admittedly ambitious hope is to foster conversation between scholars of participation, elections, representation, political economy, and legislative politics.

Parsimony in a theory, however, is a two-sided coin. While it allows intensity theory to travel to multiple domains, it also means intensity theory will not account for all empirical phenomena. I abstract away from the intra-party politics that nominate candidates for office. I set aside social influences on political action and the commitment problem of candidates promising one thing in a campaign but implementing something else once in office. Finally, the theory takes as fixed voter preference and voter issue intensity. In practice, either preference or intensity might be influenced by other actors, a point I speculate about in the conclusion.

I hope to convince readers that what is gained in generality is worth what is lost in specificity. To readers who find themselves reacting with, "But what about this aspect of electoral competition?" as they learn my argument, I ask for your patience. Integrating ideas about intensity from democratic theory with empirical results from behavioral political science with mathematical models of electoral competition and costly signaling from formal political economy requires simplification, abstraction, and trade-offs. These traditions each have much to offer, and I hope to provide an example about how they can benefit each other in synthesis.

While my narrative speaks of competition over policy issues, there is nothing in the theory that requires public policy be the subject of electoral competition. One might also apply intensity theory to intense preferences over other activities or expressions undertaken by representatives in office. For example, a voter might care intensely that they are represented by a candidate who shares their ethnicity, religion, or class background.

1.2.1 Institutional Setting

I consider republics, such as the United States of America, where elevation to office goes to the candidate who wins the most votes. This leads to a simple contrast between what the majority wants and what the majority gets. Other institutional arrangements, such as proportional representation or super-majoritarian requirements, would change the parameters of the theory and model and might change some of the qualitative results.

Issue intensity as I conceive of it here, however, is consequential in any electoral institution where candidates or parties compete for the votes of electors with varying intensities of preference. Candidates or parties whose aim is to win more votes consider how policy platforms translate to votes. When intense voters care more about an issue such that their votes are more responsive to policy than the votes of less intense voters, any vote-seeking actor will consider the trade-off of siding with a smaller but intense interest and siding with a larger but less-intense interest. In fact, autocratic leaders navigating interests in their states also likely consider differences in intensity.

I focus on the setting of a binary social choice. This sets aside the complications when groups must make choices with more than two alternatives (Arrow, 1951). Without the two-choice constraint, there are many settings where there is no reasonably-defined majority to frustrate.

1.2.2 Purpose of Theory

Political scientists do not agree about the function of theory, and many use theory without explicit definition of its purpose. I want to briefly clarify my view of the connection between the theoretical exposition and empirical analysis I present in this book.

My goal for the first part of the book is to bring issue intensity front and center and execute an analytical inquiry into how, when, and where intensity has consequences for political action, electoral competition, and representation. Dedicated focus on one feature or a subset of all features can help us make sense of complicated social phenomena. Models such as the game-theoretic mathematical models in this book are abstract representations that help us investigate and refine our understanding of the non-empirical elements (e.g., concepts, mechanisms) of our theories.

Johnson (2018), for example, argues that models are best thought of as "fables" to be used as a technology for interpretation. A fable is "a narrative stripped of many literary niceties (e.g., character development) and driven primarily by plot." Johnson sees models as narratives stripped of complexity to "facilitate our talking to one another, fruitfully, about recurrent, complex, often unobservable processes."

The purpose of Aesop's fable of "The Lion and the Mouse" is not to instruct children how to act if they ever find themselves as a lion or a mouse in the circumstances of the fable, but instead to illustrate a broader lesson applicable in many contexts. Similar to fables, when models work they help others make sense of many different events.

My goal is to translate the abstract concept of "issue intensity" into a concrete representation that then allows us to reason from a general theory to particular political phenomena. My theory starts with some basic assumptions and then proceeds to trace the consequences of these assumptions in the strategic interaction of voters and candidates in electoral competition.

I hope to show how intensity theory can help you think about frustrated majorities, electoral competition, representation, and political action in new ways. I hope that its simplicity makes it useful to generate new empirical research and that subsequent extensions and revisions can promote general knowledge of political systems.

1.3 ORGANIZATION

I organize the book to first present theory and argument and second offer evidence in support of the theory's value. Chapter 2 presents existing political science theory and evidence on issue intensity, pressure politics, representation, frustrated majorities, and electoral competition and suggests an opportunity for synthesis. Intensity makes an appearance in many literatures of political science but, in my view, is insufficiently central in the political science of elections.

Three chapters form the theoretical Part II of the book. Chapter 3 presents the basics of intensity theory and introduces the modeling approach. I present six ingredients that serve as a foundation for the theory and then introduce the basics of a mathematical model. The model considers the interaction between voters who care about policy to different degrees and candidates seeking to capture their votes. I provide initial intuition for why candidates are sometimes better off siding with an intense minority over a less-intense majority even if their only goal is to win votes at the election. I show why my result departs from the benchmark of the median voter theorem.

Chapter 4 presents results from expanding the mathematical model of Chapter 3 into a full game-theoretic representation of the theory. I leave the mathematical analysis to an appendix and present accessible results from that analysis in the main text. I present the logic of frustrated majorities through a model of electoral competition where candidates know the intensities of each of three distinct voters. I then investigate the consequences of candidates not knowing the intensity of voters, showing that in response voters sometimes engage in costly political action to communicate their intensity and increase the chance that their policy preference gains representation.

I present two model results of scientific interest. In both, high-intensity voters choose political action and expression of personal cost because candidates learn information relevant to vote choice from action and expression. In both, candidates propose policy with a high-intensity minority when the candidates believe that the minority cares sufficiently more about the policy than does the majority. In one result, only voters in the minority who also care intensely engage in costly political action while voters in the majority always abstain from action. In the second, both minority and majority voters who care intensely take costly action to communicate how much they care to the candidates, while low-intensity voters of both the minority and the majority abstain from action.

In Chapter 5, I consider challenges to and implications of the results from Chapter 4. Again I present the mathematical analysis in an appendix and use the chapter to present findings accessible to those untrained in mathematical models of politics. I first show that the results hold when the electorate has more than three voters and when the size of the minority varies from small to nearly-even with the size of the majority. This analysis also shows that the intensity of the minority must increase as the size of the minority decreases in order for candidates to prefer to side with an intense minority over a less-intense majority.

I then sketch out a solution to the free-rider problem in large electorates connected to the theory of global games. Finally, I present a welfare analysis of the model results. I show that when the minority cares sufficiently more about policy than the majority, the electorate as a whole can sometimes be better off with a frustrated majority. If the minority gains more from policy than the majority loses, on average total social welfare is higher, with the possibility of candidates siding with the minority even with the deadweight loss of costly political action.

The electorate as a whole can be better off with a frustrated majority if the minority cares enough more about the issue than the majority. It is important to note, however, that better off here is in a utilitarian sense where we balance the wants of some citizens against the wants of others. The majority, however, is strictly worse off than under simple majority-rule. Non-utilitarian definitions of justice might not come to the positive conclusion that the electorate as a whole is better off. Other definitions would not come to the positive conclusion of the utilitarian analysis.

Many of the theoretical results draw on a separately-published journal article (Hill, 2022a). That essay serves as a technical presentation of the mathematical model and includes more detailed analysis. I aim for the book to make this technical logic clear to a wide audience and to show the value of the theory through new empirical applications.

In Part III of the book, I present empirical evidence first in support of the policy consequences of intensity, second, in support of the operation of intensity theory, and third, that shows intensity theory offers new understanding about costly political action beyond existing theory. Chapter 6 summarizes the contribution and connection to the theory of the four empirical chapters that follow.

In Chapter 7, I present case histories from the politics of biotechnology and firearm regulation that demonstrate a key argument of intensity theory, that politicians sometimes side against the known preferences of majorities when they believe a minority of voters care sufficiently more about the issue than the majority. In each case, politicians set policy with an intense minority against the expressed preferences of majorities. I also offer suggestive evidence with the first case that when the relative intensity of the majority increased over time, policy moved toward the interests of the majority.

Chapter 8 provides evidence for a key assumption of intensity theory, that vote choice responds more for voters who care intensely about policy. I introduce a new method to account for factors of vote choice and show that the issues about which voters care most intensely explain vote choice above and beyond other factors such as party identification.

Chapters 9 and 10 present evidence that those with intense preferences incur costly political action to communicate their intensity to politicians. I show that intensity theory provides predictions for voter response to institutional reforms to campaign finance and primary elections. In each chapter, the evidence is consistent with these unique predictions.

In Chapter 9, I show that voters in Seattle, Washington responded to a new opportunity for low-cost political contributions ("Democracy Vouchers") with empirical patterns more consistent with intensity theory than other theories of political participation. Very few voters chose to use the vouchers, and residents who did use vouchers did not decrease their level of monetary contributions. This is consistent with a motivation to incur a specific level of cost in pursuit of communication of intensity.

In Chapter 10, I show that when American states reform their institutions of nomination from closed partisan primaries to open or non-partisan primaries, individual citizens increase monetary contributions to political candidates. I interpret this response as evidence that high-intensity voters increase their costly actions when the previously-available costly action of participating in a closed primary election is removed. I also present evidence in support of this mechanism in contrast to alternative theories.

Chapter 11 offers a restatement of the argument and its contributions, a recipe to apply intensity theory to future or hypothetical electoral competition, and a discussion of five possible additions to received wisdom on electoral competition and representation that follow from the argument and evidence of this book. These additions offer ideas about how to interpret frustrated majorities with respect to the operation of democracy, the source of power for interest groups and special interests, the construction of candidate and party platforms, the meaning of responses to opinion surveys, and the dynamics of interaction between voters and candidates during elections.

2

The Political Science of Representation, Elections, and Intensity

The best lack all conviction, while the worst Are full of passionate intensity.
William Butler Yeats, "The Second Coming"

[D]emocracy is characterized by minority rule and majority acquiescence ... a system of freely contending factions. That people with common interests should be allowed to freely attempt to sway government policy is, in fact, democracy's whole point.
John Mueller (1999, pp. 152–153)

Voters with intense interests engage with the political process in many policy areas. Opponents of abortion picket reproductive health clinics (Luker, 1985). Supporters of civil rights march in protests (Wasow, 2020). Neighborhood residents attend local planning board meetings to oppose commercial or residential development (Einstein, Glick, and Palmer, 2019). Supporters of gun rights call their legislators and make their voices heard at candidate events (Lacombe, 2021).

Intensity of preference is a topic of inquiry in many research communities of political science. In this chapter, I suggest that two basic empirical facts have motivated academic attention toward understanding the dynamics of intensity in politics. Despite attention in various literatures, however, I argue that intensity has not been sufficiently analyzed as a central feature of electoral competition and that this may have hindered our understanding of these basic facts.

The chapter is organized to present two basic facts, summarize current explanations of those facts, suggest that current political science theories of elections might benefit from more attention to intensity of preference, discuss intensity in existing political science, and, finally, argue for a synthesis.

2.1 BASIC FACT ONE: FRUSTRATED MAJORITIES

The first basic fact about American politics is what I call frustrated majorities. Political scientists and observers have long wondered about the apparently limited responsiveness of the American government to majority support in public opinion. Why do we sometimes see representatives decline to deliver what majorities of voters seem to want? Political scientists aim to quantify this "democratic deficit" and measure its causes.

My definition of "frustrated majorities" follows from the observations of others. On some political issues it is widely agreed, or at least not widely disputed, that a clear majority of the public expresses support for a policy position that is not reflected in law. This majority is frustrated because the politicians empowered to represent them do not enact what the majority seems to want. It is not necessary for individuals to actually feel "frustrated" in the sense of frustration as emotion. Instead, frustrated means that the preferences of a clear majority are not reflected in the law of the land.

These terms merit unpacking. First, "widely agreed " or "not widely disputed" means that most observers, even from different political perspectives, have a common belief that a majority expresses the unrepresented policy position. These observers, importantly, include politicians. Actors may differ on what to do about the belief of the unrepresented majority, but the belief is widely shared. Few would dispute that the majority supports the unrepresented position unless they have some countervailing incentive to obfuscate – such as having decided to side with a minority.

Second, "clear majority" means a definite majority supports the policy that is not enacted. This is not 48 percent plus some undecideds who might later be persuaded. It is not even a bare 50 percent. The majority is sufficiently greater than 50 percent that all agree it constitutes the most common policy view in the public.

Third, "express support for a policy position" means that, when asked, a citizen would indicate support and, if empowered to act, would implement that policy position absent countervailing considerations.

2.1.1 Public Opinion Evidence of Frustrated Majorities

What evidence suggests frustrated majorities in American politics? The evidence usually falls in one of two classes. First, on many issues the policy implemented by legislatures and government is not the policy that a majority supports when measured by answers to questions in opinion surveys. Second, the laws as written contrast assumptions about what voters should want.

Public opinion evidence of frustrated majorities goes back to the rise of behavioral political science in the 1950s. Miller and Stokes (1963) pioneered such a comparison, generating a result that has been replicated countless times since in political science scholarship: while what citizens say they want in surveys correlates with how their representatives vote in legislatures, correspondence is far from one-to-one. On many issues, majorities of citizens, either nationwide or within specific legislative districts, express support in a survey for a policy position not reflected in the law enacted by their representatives.[1]

For example, Lax and Phillips (2012) find that across 39 policies in the American states, majorities are often frustrated. They write, "Roughly half the time, opinion majorities lose – even large super-majorities prevail less than 60% of the time. In other words, state governments are on average no more effective in translating opinion majorities into public policy than a simple coin flip (149)" and "Even for majorities of 70%, only 57% of policies are congruent (153)." Hertel-Fernandez (2019) and Witko et al. (2021) argue that corporate and monied interests are behind citizen majorities not getting what they want at both the state and federal levels.

Ansolabehere and Jones (2010) present evidence that voters hold notably more centrist views on the policy issues facing Congress than the votes cast by their representatives. Other scholars explore the nature of incongruence. Gilens (2005) and Page and Gilens (2017) argue that policy responds more to wealthy minorities than to majorities of the electorate and that majorities often do not get the policies they want. Gerber and Lewis (2004) show that fidelity of state and congressional legislators to median voter preferences in California declines with the heterogeneity of voter preferences in the district.

---

[1] There is likely bias in our society toward giving attention to issues where a majority is clearly frustrated. Naturally, when policy is set with a solid majority, it is not a feature of political conflict and less likely covered in the news media, scholarship, or academic instruction.

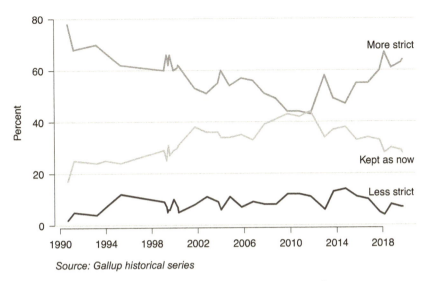

Source: Gallup historical series

FIGURE 2.1 Frustrated majorities: Restrictions on firearms
"In general, do you feel that the laws covering the sale of firearms should be made more strict, less strict or kept as they are now?"

I compiled public opinion time-series on three policy questions as examples of frustrated majorities. Figure 2.1 presents a time-series of public opinion on laws covering the sale of firearms taken by the Gallup polling organization in polls from 1990 through 2019. Gallup asked Americans, "In general, do you feel that the laws covering the sale of firearms should be made more strict, less strict or kept as they are now?"

But for a single poll from October 2011, the plurality view for 30 years has been to make laws more strict. For 24 of the 30 years, a majority of respondents expressed support for stricter laws.

Figure 2.2 presents a similar pattern of public opinion on preferential hiring by race from the American National Election Studies (American National Election Studies, 2016b). Representative samples of Americans were asked, "Are you for or against preferential hiring and promotion of blacks?" from 1986 through 2016. Opposition to preferential hiring was consistently greater than 70 percent during this time period. Support reached its peak in 2016 at 26 percent.

Figure 2.3 presents a third example of public opinion suggesting frustrated majorities. Gallup asked respondents, "Do you think the U.S. government is doing too much, too little or about the right amount in terms of protecting the environment?" from 1992 through 2019.

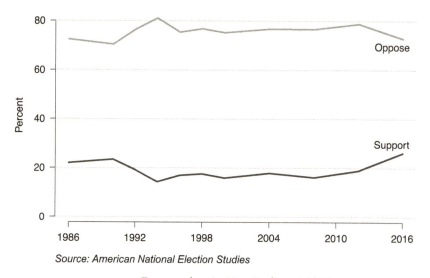

Source: American National Election Studies

FIGURE 2.2 Frustrated majorities: Preferential hiring

"Some people say that because of past discrimination blacks should be given preference in hiring and promotion. Others say that such preference in hiring and promotion of blacks is wrong because it gives blacks advantages they haven't earned. What about your opinion – are you for or against preferential hiring and promotion of blacks?"

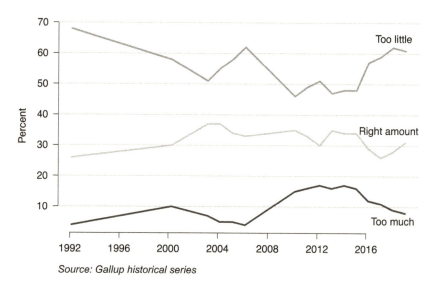

Source: Gallup historical series

FIGURE 2.3 Frustrated majorities: Environment

"Do you think the U.S. government is doing too much, too little or about the right amount in terms of protecting the environment?"

For these 27 years, the opinion "too little" was always a plurality and was a majority opinion in 11 of the 16 individual polls.

Figures 2.1–2.3 exemplify the public opinion evidence drawn upon by many scholars to conclude a democratic deficit. While I have argued elsewhere for caution in drawing strong conclusions from such survey responses (Hill and Huber, 2019), pluralities and often majorities express opinions over many decades that are not fully reflected in law. Firearm restrictions are loosened rather than strengthened. Preferential recruitment and hiring continue in government and private settings. Government programs to protect the environment do not expand.

2.1.2 Political Evidence of Frustrated Majorities

Public opinion is not the only piece of evidence scholars draw upon to suggest frustrated majorities. The second class of evidence for a democratic deficit involves reasoning about the likely beneficiaries of specific government policies. Are benefits provided by the laws as written and implemented likely to accrue to majorities of the population or to specific minorities? Scholars argue that special interests in the realm of trade (e.g., Schattschneider, 1935) and employee unions (Anzia and Moe, 2015) gain targeted benefits from government at the expense of majorities.

More generally, a long line of scholarship has aimed to measure and explain the costs of special interest politics (e.g., Tullock, 1967), where well-organized small groups gain government policy to their benefit at the expense of apathetic or uninformed majorities. Bartels (2008) and Hacker and Pierson (2011) argue that policies in the realm of taxes and spending favor the wealthy over the poor and middle class.

2.2 BASIC FACT TWO: POLITICAL PARTICIPATION VARIES ACROSS THE POPULATION

A second basic fact of American politics is that citizens vary considerably in their engagement with politics. In a representative democracy, citizens empower those who make laws through elections. Voting is the primary act of engagement with politics, but many other opportunities exist for citizens to take actions to influence or contribute to politics. Citizens can make campaign contributions, participate in political rallies, volunteer for candidates or parties, write letters to their representatives, attend public meetings, or advocate to friends and neighbors.

Political scientists have struggled to explain the basic fact that population participation in politics is neither universal nor rare. Instead, individuals vary in their participation across a spectrum from not at all to heavily involved. At one end of the spectrum, many eligible citizens do not even register to vote. At the other end, many citizens not only vote in every election but also spend extensive time and resources to interact and engage with the political process. Why do citizens fall at many locations along this spectrum of engagement?

Variation in engagement is difficult to explain because the likely impact of individual political action on political outcomes is so small that the costs to act in politics – costs of time, money, transportation, opportunity – are almost surely greater than the benefits of their likely impact on the candidate selected to govern (Downs, 1957). Because it so unlikely that actions make a difference, a standard prediction is that rational citizens should abstain from any costly political action (Palfrey and Rosenthal, 1985), with some exceptions for those who might benefit from concentrated government benefits or hurt from concentrated costs (Wilson, 1995).

Yet many citizens take costly political action in every election cycle. In fact, many take actions more costly than alternative actions of (apparently) equal consequence to the election. "Nearly two-thirds of persons who receive an unsolicited ballot in the mail before election day choose to return their ballot in-person, rather than through the less costly and more convenient U.S. Postal service" (Menger and Stein, 2020, p. 196). Also, see my analysis in Chapter 9.

Part of the variation in participation is relatively consistent across time and space. Leighley and Nagler (2014) continue the work of others (e.g., Schattschneider, 1960; Verba, Schlozman, and Brady, 1995), showing that political participation is more common among the more educated, the more wealthy, and those with more resources.

In 2018, for example, Current Population Survey census data showed that around three in four citizens with a post-graduate degree voted in the midterm election compared to less than three in ten with less than a high school diploma (McDonald, 2019). Similarly, three of four aged 60 and above voted in 2018 compared to just more than three in ten of those aged 18–29. Wide variation in political acts is not limited to turnout. Nearly 40 percent of 2012 campaign donors had incomes greater than $100,000 as compared to about 16 percent of 2012 voters (Hill and Huber, 2017).

TABLE 2.1. *Explanations of frustrated majorities*

1. Politicians are captured by special interests.
2. Politicians and candidates for office systematically misperceive what voters want.
3. Voters are not competent to enact electoral accountability.
4. Voters do not understand their own self-interest.
5. American lawmaking institutions require super-majorities.

TABLE 2.2. *Explanations of variation in costly political action*

1. Voters have intrinsic motivation or gain consumption value from costly political acts.
2. Voters do not understand their own self-interest.

2.3 CURRENT EXPLANATIONS

Political scientists offer a variety of explanations of frustrated majorities and variable political participation. I summarize these explanations in Tables 2.1 and 2.2 and then classify the explanations into categories.

2.3.1 Captured Politicians and Misperceptions

One class of explanation for frustrated majorities is that politicians are captured by non-majoritarian interests. In this story, incumbent office-holders either care about things beyond reelection or seek resources needed for reelection in exchange for frustrating majorities. Politicians might deliver non-majority policy in exchange for campaign contributions.[2] Politicians might have personal policy preferences that contrast with the wants of their constituents (Besley and Coate, 1997; Carnes, 2018). Politicians might desire power and influence within the legislature or a political party (Thomsen, 2014). Finally, politicians might hope for lucrative lobbying business after they leave office.

Particularly if combined with voters who fail to act in their own interests, these competing demands on the legislator's attention can push public policy and frustrate majorities.

---

[2] "American politics is fundamentally corrupted by money, which wealthy people can deploy to block any major egalitarian actions" (Page and Gilens, 2017, p. 49).

A second class of explanation is that politicians and candidates for office systematically misunderstand what voters want. Recent political science suggests that candidates for office, political staff, and policy experts hold biased perceptions of what the public wants (Mildenberger and Tingley, 2017; Broockman and Skovron, 2018; Hertel-Fernandez, Mildenberger, and Stokes, 2019). For example, Broockman and Skovron (2018) conclude that politicians "dramatically overestimated their constituents' support for conservative policies." These studies suggest that politicians make policy with a misperception of what voters want, resulting in policy outcomes that do not reflect majority preferences.

2.3.2 Voters Act against Self-Interest

A third class of explanation, of similar prominence as captured politicians, is that voters fail to act in their own interest. This failure leads to poor representation – frustrated majorities – and evinces as wide disparities in political participation and political action.

The story goes that voters fail in their electoral behavior because they are not competent to engage in "issue voting." Issue voting is an assumed strategy for voters to get what they want out of government. Under issue voting, voters understand what they want, learn the positions of competing candidates for office, and make a choice between candidates based on which candidate offers a platform of issues closer to what they want.

Decades of research in public opinion calls into question voter aptitude for issue voting. Scholars of public opinion find that respondents do not appear to know what they want. Answers to questions about their preferences over political issues seem unstable (e.g., Zaller and Feldman, 1992), unconstrained (Converse, 1964), and manipulable (e.g., Rahn, 1993; Lenz, 2012). Citizens respond to cues from political elites and partisan and group identities in responses to opinion survey questions about preferred policies (e.g., Zaller, 1992; Lenz, 2012).

Additional research suggests that voters' policy attitudes and vote choices follow from symbolic attitudes and attachments more than from self-interest (Sears et al., 1980). Citizens give group-congenial survey responses in ignorance of or against own interests – e.g., "cheerleading" (Bullock et al., 2015) – and respond with large magnitude to group cues in survey experiments (Rahn, 1993). If electoral choice follows from symbols rather than policy, it lessens the incentive for candidates to invest in policy.

Finally, surveys find only limited correspondence between where the candidates actually stand on the issues, what the voters claim to have wanted, and the candidate selected in the election. Citizens "neglect policy information in reaching evaluations" even when they are exposed to it, instead using "the [party] label rather than policy attributes in drawing inferences" (Rahn, 1993, p. 492). Citizens "react mechanically to political ideas on the basis of external cues about their partisan implications" and "typically fail to reason for themselves about the persuasive communications they encounter" unless those communications are extremely clear (Zaller, 1992, p. 45).

A second story of voters not acting in their own interests is that voters know what they want but their wants do not follow their own interests – Marx's idea of "false consciousness." Instead of promoting their own interests, which would lead to majority policy, voters side with minority interests. Because the majority of voters side with minority interests, politicians promote the (minority) policy that the majority of voters endorse. Voters might have false consciousness because they are deceived, distracted, or uncertain about what public policy is in their own interest.

Voters acting contrary to their instrumental policy interests are also commonly used to explain heterogeneous political participation. Because the costs of political actions are greater than the benefits, to explain widespread political participation political science has turned to explanations that do not depend on individual instrumental contribution to political outcomes. In the words of the arch-proponents of the rational actor approach to understanding politics, costly political participation must influence "parameters of the utility function for which the magnitude is independent" of contribution to the election outcome (Riker and Ordeshook, 1968, p. 27).

Most existing political science interprets costly actions and expressions through intrinsic psychological motivations rather than strategic consideration of the action's relationship to political outcomes. Textbooks, for example, suggest that participation in political activities follows not from "coldly rational" decision-making but from "[m]oral incentives, the personal satisfaction of active self-expression" (Kernell et al., 2019, p. 573) or because "the political culture's emphasis on rights and liberties encourages Americans to contact their public officials and to protest government activities" (Fiorina et al., 2011, p. 175) or that "[t]he sharing of ideology is [an] important nonmaterial benefit" (Ansolabehere et al., 2018, p. 568).

2.3.3 Institutions Frustrate Majorities

A fourth class of explanation for frustrated majorities is institutional. American public policy is thought subject to "status quo bias," where moving policy from its current value takes a greater level of support and effort than does maintaining the status quo. Krehbiel (1998) provides a careful examination of how the institutions of the federal government such as the filibuster and separation of powers generate super-majoritarian roadblocks to policy change. These roadblocks often frustrate legislative majorities from enacting policy. Howell and Moe (2020) argue that the institutional design of the US Congress directs member attention toward parochial special interests rather than the common good.

* * *

The explanations above are not implausible but might not be satisfying for two reasons. First, the explanations often assume the consequence. Four of the five explanations for frustrated majorities above assert that one or more actors in the political system act against their own interests.

How could we argue with an assertion that voters do not get what they want because they – or politicians – do not pursue what they want? To me, "because voters or politicians fail to act in their own interests" is not a satisfying scientific answer to the question "why are majorities frustrated?" If we assume that actors do not pursue their own goals, we can explain any outcome. A stronger explanation assumes actors usually try to attain what they want with competent intention but that sometimes the dynamics of politics frustrate their goals.

Two explanations hold that voters do not act in their own interest either because they do not invest in knowing what they need to know or because they have false consciousness. Two other explanations have politicians acting against their own electoral interests, either by delivering policy to special interests at some risk of penalty by electoral majorities or failing to understand what their constituency wants, again at some risk of electoral penalty.

The institutional explanation, too, might not be fully satisfying. Political institutions can be changed and so are endogenous to the political interests of actors in that system (Riker, 1982). An institutional explanation for frustrated majorities, then, requires some explanation for why the majoritarian actors within the system do not reform those institutions.

In fact, the use of the super-majoritarian filibuster in the United States Senate has been recently curtailed. The 2013 move to majority vote on executive and non-Supreme Court judicial nominations was followed in 2017 to majority vote to confirm Supreme Court nominations. Both reforms demonstrate that majorities can change institutional procedures.

Second, the explanations above seem to sidestep one of the central theories of political science, *the electoral connection*. While I do not claim that actors always follow their own interests, as long as actors sometimes pursue interests, the electoral connection provides strong reason to suspect that policy should represent the interests of the electorate. Ambitious candidates for office seek out opportunities to inform voters where the incumbent's representation falls short. Frustrated voters can increase their political activity or organize to elect candidates more representative of their interests.

2.4 BUT, THE ELECTORAL CONNECTION

The most common political science theory of how elections influence political outcomes is the electoral connection. Scholars investigate how the electoral process in representative democracies influences the policies enacted by elected representatives. Central questions include which individuals gain power at elections and how those individuals make choices once in office.

The logic of the electoral connection is clear. In a representative democracy, competitive elections provide incentives for ambitious politicians to implement beneficent public policy. James Madison (it is generally believed) wrote in *Federalist 57*,

The elective mode of obtaining rulers is the characteristic policy of republican government. The means relied on in this form of government for preventing their degeneracy are numerous and various. The most effectual one, is such a limitation of the term of appointments as will maintain a proper responsibility to the people. (Federalist 57, 1788)

Political science theories of the electoral connection follow in the logic of *The Federalist*. Elections generate accountability because incumbents must take their record to the electorate and stand before voters on a fixed schedule (well-read examples include Downs, 1957; Key, 1966; Mayhew, 1974; Fiorina, 1981). Ambitious challengers sift through the incumbent's record and make a best case for voters to remove that incumbent. Competitive elections on a fixed schedule generate the electoral connection. In their textbook on congressional elections, Jacobson and Carson (2015, p. 236) write:

> [Congress] is a representative assembly because its members are chosen in competitive popular elections, and if voters do not like what the members are doing, they can vote them out of office. Voters can hold representatives accountable for their actions as long as members care about their own reelection or their party's future, and nearly every member does. Representation is an effect of electoral politics; the electoral process determines the kind of representation Congress provides.

The existing explanations of frustrated majorities appear to be inconsistent with the electoral connection. Even if politicians are captured by special interests, they cannot offer favors to these interests without winning election to office. Even if current politicians misperceive what voters want, ambitious candidates for office have incentives to learn what voters want to gain an advantage in elections over politicians who misperceive. Even if voters are poorly informed about politics, ambitious candidates for office have incentives to collect information relevant to voters and invest in delivering it to the electorate.

The electoral connection says that, because candidates need to win election to act on the different political goals they might have, elections force candidates to appeal to voters (Mayhew, 1974). Extra-electoral influences must take a back seat to the electoral needs of politicians.

The electoral connection as a theory of representation is widely accepted in political science. Today, the debate surrounds the operation and effectiveness of the electoral connection. How do voters choose between candidates? What signal is generated by the aggregation of voter choices into election outcomes, and how do candidates respond?

2.5 THEORIES OF ELECTIONS

Scholars have proposed different theories of elections to understand *which* wants of voters are connected to representatives through elections. Each theory follows a similar structure. Voters have things they value in candidates for office. Candidates present themselves to voters, and voters then use what they value and what they believe about the candidates to determine which candidate they prefer. The theory of this book will follow this general formula while also allowing voters some proactive influence on candidate positions.

Theories of elections vary in what they assume voters value, in how they assume candidates react to what voters value, and in how voters evaluate trade offs between candidates. I now briefly summarize three widely read theories of elections on the operation of the electoral connection in American politics with an eye toward how each interacts with intensity of political preference and what each might imply about frustrated majorities.

2.5.1 Rational Actor Theories

Rational actor theories of elections consider voters choosing from a menu of candidates as analogous to consumers choosing from a menu of products. Each consumer has demand for certain features of products and each product has a profile of features. Each voter has demand for certain policies or characteristics of candidates and each candidate has a profile of policies and characteristics. Just as consumers choose the product with the largest advantage of benefit over cost, so voters choose the candidate who delivers the largest advantage of benefit over cost.

How voters evaluate tradeoffs between different policies and candidate characteristics is the challenge for rational actor models. If a voter values business experience as well as the candidate's position on welfare programs, it is not obvious how they would choose between one candidate with business experience advocating a less preferred position on welfare programs and one candidate without business experience advocating a more preferred position on welfare programs.

Some models make the simplifying assumptions that candidates and voters can each be summarized by a single point on a liberal–conservative ideological dimension (e.g., Downs, 1957, ch. 8; see Fowler et al., n.d. for evidence that this assumption is often reasonable). The voter chooses the candidate whose location on this dimension is closest to their own. If the voter's ideology is conservative, a conservative candidate is closer to them on the dimension than a liberal, and this relative proximity generates their vote choice for the conservative.

The Downsian model has been extended in many different directions from more than one dimension of policy (e.g., Enelow and Hinich, 1984) to having one candidate whose non-policy characteristics are universally preferred (Groseclose, 2001) to varying whether voters choose the closer candidate deterministically or with some randomness (e.g., Davis and

Hinich, 1968). Not all rational actor models need follow the spatial Downsian approach (e.g., Ferejohn, 1986).

2.5.2 Retrospective Theories

Under retrospective theories of elections, voters do not weigh the policy platforms of candidates as in rational actor models. Rather, voters look backwards – retrospectively – at the performance of the current incumbent. They vote for the incumbent if outcomes have been sufficiently good and vote for the challenger if not. Performance might be evaluated on policies implemented (Key, 1966), on economic or foreign outcomes (Key, 1966; Kramer, 1971), or the issue of evaluation might depend on what candidates discuss during the campaign (Vavreck, 2009).

Retrospective theories can be read as rational actor if voters use retrospective evaluation to predict future behavior (e.g., Downs, 1957; Fiorina, 1981; Ferejohn, 1986; Fearon, 1999). Retrospective voting is less consistent with rational actor if voters react with negative emotion to poor outcomes (e.g., Huber, Hill, and Lenz, 2012) rather than weighing the costs and benefits of the competing candidates for office.

2.5.3 Social-Psychological Theories

Social-psychological theories of elections assume voter judgments about political candidates rely on heuristics about how those candidates relate to broader constructs in the minds or social experiences of the voter. Voters associate candidates with political parties (e.g., Campbell et al., 1960) or social groups (e.g., Berelson, Lazarsfeld, and McPhee, 1954) in order to make sense of political choice. The stable constructs of parties and groups influence their evaluation of political objects and, thus, structure vote choice.

2.6 THEORIES OF ELECTIONS AND FRUSTRATED MAJORITIES

Under many rational actor and retrospective theories, it would appear candidates have little incentive to frustrate electoral majorities. Vote-maximizing candidates in rational actor theories craft policy platforms to win as many votes as possible. This incentive generates the famous median voter theorem, but centripetal incentives are also present in more complicated rational actor models with multiple dimensions, stochastic voting, or candidates who care about both winning office and implementing policy (e.g., Calvert, 1985).

Incumbent politicians under retrospective theories should also avoid policy that majorities might evaluate unfavorably. At the least, incumbents should not actively pursue polices that lead to conditions at the next election that a majority of the electorate would dislike. Further, challengers under retrospective theories have incentive to persuade a majority of the electorate that the incumbent has failed to deliver for the majority (Vavreck, 2009).

Social-psychological theories are ambiguous about candidate incentives with respect to policy. At the least, however, these theories suggest that elections on average should not empower candidates supported by small minorities. Further, large numbers of independents and skeptical partisans (Klar and Krupnikov, 2016) suggest candidates must appeal to broader swaths of the public to win election.

2.7 TOWARD AN ANSWER FROM THE POLITICAL SCIENCE OF INTENSITY

The theories of elections, along with the broader theory of the electoral connection, suggest against frustrated majorities. If elections connect voters to representatives, then majority elections should generate majority policy. Yet frustrated majorities stand as a basic fact of America's representative democracy. Why might frustrated majorities arise?

My answer is that frustrated majorities come from differences in issue intensity. Intensity leads ambitious candidates for office to sometimes propose policy with minorities and sometimes with majorities. Voters caring to different degrees about policy is a key ingredient to what policy candidates choose.

I next show how intensity (or synonymous research constructs using different wording) arises in the political science of democratic theory, interest groups and lobbying, trade politics, legislative representation, public opinion, and political parties. I also discuss how the potential influence of intensity is reflected in the practice of politics. Intensity, however, makes less of an appearance in theories of elections than in other subfields of political science. It merits similar attention.

2.7.1 Democratic Theory

Democratic theorists have considered the consequences of intense political preferences for both normative democratic outcomes and practical democratic process. For example, in chapter 4 of *A Preface to Democratic Theory* (1956), Robert Dahl considers the "intensity problem."

He attributes "one of the bloodiest civil wars in the history of Western man" (p. 98) to intense preferences on the question of slavery extension to newly admitted states. Dahl noted the "crucial problem" when "the minority prefers its alternative much more passionately than the majority prefers a contrary alternative" (p. 90) and concluded that intensity is a central challenge for any Madisonian republic.

Mayo (1960) argues for a theory of democracy with a strong preference for majority rule. One of his democratic principles is that when representatives disagree on an issue, "reflecting, however roughly, the divisions among the electorate, ... the decision goes to the majority" (p. 166) of the representatives. While Mayo acknowledges the problem of an intense minority, unlike Dahl he dismisses the challenge as unlikely to undermine representation:

[T]he dilemma is an imaginary one, without political relevance. Intensity of feeling – often an acute political phenomenon – has abundant opportunity to make itself felt in the many political processes which are open. It does not take much to convince the lukewarm and wavering and so reduce the majority to a minority. The place for intensity of feeling is in the give and take of politics – in campaigning, lobbying, etc.; the principle does not require that every 50 per cent plus one of the representatives should immediately enact its lukewarm wishes against a strongly emotional opposition. No party or politician gets caught in such a ludicrous trap. (pp. 178–179)

Mueller (1999) offers an interpretation of democracy where frustrated majorities do not indicate failure of representation. His argument is that democracy is not a system that aggregates preferences in a specific fashion such that a given system can be judged democratic (or not) by its outcome. Rather, democracy is a system where the outcome can be freely influenced by those who care to try, including minorities. He is comfortable with a minority winning out over a more apathetic majority. "[D]emocracy is a form of government in which individuals are left free to become politically unequal" (p. 147).

Ingham (2019) turns the intensity problem on its head by arguing that intensity is a solution to the social choice problem of majority cycles. Ingham proposes that representative democracy can be thought to generate popular control when majorities can trade off policy representation on issues they care more about for representation on issues they care less about. Posner and Weyl (2018) argue that democracy should move away from one-person, one-vote institutions toward voting institutions that recognize difference in intensity across issues. They suggest voters be endowed with a budget of "voting credits" to use across issues so that differences in intensity can be reflected in collective decisions. A similar institution has been suggested for committee and legislative settings in formal democratic theory (Casella, 2005).

2.7.2 Formal Democratic Theory

Formal democratic theory aims to characterize the welfare consequences of democratic systems through mathematical models. In that tradition, Davis and Hinich (1966) present a model of policy formation through electoral competition with an arbitrary number of policy issues. When voters have heterogeneous quadratic preferences over policy, they show that a beneficent dictator with a utilitarian decision rule chooses policies "to be the average of the preferred positions of the individuals in the population" (p. 180). While they do not use these words, their model shows that a utilitarian dictator weights policy toward those who care more intensely.

Davis and Hinich (1966, theorem 3.1) show that with more than one policy electoral competition under reasonable assumptions provides strong incentives for candidates to propose policy at the mean of the electorate.[3] This policy maximizes Benthamite social welfare.

The Davis and Hinich (1966) result is an early example of a set of mathematical models of probabilistic voting. These models generically find that candidate policy platforms are sensitive to variation in the preference intensity of voters (e.g., Coughlin and Nitzan, 1981; Lindbeck and Weibull, 1987; Banks and Duggan, 2005; McKelvey and Patty, 2006; Bouton et al., 2021). The theoretical contribution of this book can be read as a simple and accessible version of this result combined with voters using costly political action to communicate intensity to candidates.

A key input to the analysis of formal democratic theory is whether voters select candidates as a deterministic function of candidate policy platform or whether vote choices are stochastic. That is, under deterministic voting a voter is certain to select the candidate whose policies they finds more appealing. Under stochastic – or probabilistic – voting, the vote is not perfectly determined. Instead, there is some probability the voter selects the candidate whose policies they finds less appealing. For

---

[3] See Patty (2002) for a discussion of the consequences of different candidate motivations in elections.

example, there might be a 10 percent chance they vote for the candidate whose policies they finds less appealing because of idiosyncratic tastes for candidate characteristics separate from policy.

2.7.3 Legislative Representation

The political science of representation has circled the intensity problem in work both classic and contemporary. Much of this work argues that legislators do not aim to simply mirror majority public opinion in their district. Rather, legislators think about what actions might be most important to different individuals and groups in their constituency. Groups that care more about the issue might require extra attention in the legislator's decision calculus.

Many argue that the representative task as undertaken by members of the United States Congress is to anticipate how each action might translate into votes at the next election. As Key (1961) argues, a legislator worries about "what the response of his constituency will be in the next campaign when persons aggrieved by his position attack his record" (p. 499). When some constituents care more about specific issues, the translation of legislator actions on those issues to vote share might be greater for those constituents than for others.

Richard Fenno shadowed members of Congress to understand their decision-making and noted that members were particularly attuned to constituents when those constituents cared deeply on an issue. When discussing how members build and maintain electoral coalitions, Fenno wrote about one member:

The "strongest supporters" in his organization did not support him because they knew him or had had any previous connection with him. The bond was agreement on the central issues and on the importance of emphasizing the issues. Fenno (1978, 94)

It is not simply agreement on "central issues" but an agreement that the member would emphasize those issues. Presumably supporters wanted emphasis on issues they cared most about rather than issues they cared least about.

The Fiorina (1974) monograph on representation of diverse constituencies also suggests that intensity is a crucial input to politics. The theory is that representatives and candidates group the various interests of their constituency into a small number. There might be a union-member group, a small-business group, and an environmentalist group. On each decision, the member considers which groups fall on each side of the issue and then weights their decision to the size and intensity of each group. Fiorina's theory suggests variation in intensity consequential to legislative choice.

Arnold (1990) also argues that members of Congress weight the policy views of their constituents by size and intensity. When evaluating a potential course of action, Arnold argues that members estimate which of their constituents will be attentive to the action and its consequences, the probability of which depends on the incidence and timing of costs and benefits. They combine two estimates into a decision about the action. First, they estimate the direction and intensity of preference of the attentive constituency about the action itself. Second, they estimate how the attentive constituency might respond to the future consequences of the action.

Arnold echoes the challenge of Dahl's intensity problem:

Seldom do legislators face two opposing groups that feel equally strongly about an issue. Citizens differ in the intensity with which they hold particular preferences, and this intensity affects the likelihood that citizens may alter their opinions of legislators on the basis of legislators' positions or actions. Those who feel intensely about an issue may tolerate little deviance from their preferred path, whereas those who have more moderate preferences may never notice what a legislator is doing. All else equal, legislators follow the preferences of those who feel most intensely about an issue ... [however, s]ufficient size can often swamp the impact of other attributes, such as intensity. (pp. 83–84)

As in Fiorina (1974), legislators must navigate the size and intensity of divergent preferences in the constituency. Sometimes, the greater size of a less intense group suggests representing that interest while other times a smaller group with greater intensity gains representation.

Also in the legislative setting, Bawn and Koger (2008) argue that legislators can vary the effort they put toward passing a bill to reflect how intensely they feel about that issue compared to other issues. Wawro and Schickler (2006, ch. 2) argue that pre-1917 dilatory tactics in the US Senate were costly behaviors used to communicate how intensely senators felt about the bill being obstructed.

Griffin and Newman (2008) evaluate representation of minority interests in the American republic. They consider three definitions of representation to use as benchmarks. The "pluralist" standard of representation is that "intensely held preferences ought to be specially represented, even when those preferences are in the minority" (p. 20). Indeed, they find (Chapter 6) that racial and ethnic minorities are relatively well-represented by this standard, gaining near equal representation to the majority on issues of high salience to the individuals in that minority.

2.7.4 Interest Groups, Lobbying, and Pressure Politics

Intensity makes an appearance in the literatures on interest groups, lobbying, and pressure politics. For example, Schattschneider (1960) writes, "organized special-interest groups are the most self-conscious, best developed, most intense and active groups" (p. 30) and "[s]pecial-interest organizations are most easily formed when they deal with small numbers of individuals who are acutely aware of their exclusive interests" (p. 35). Wilson (1995) argues that interest group politics vary by the incidence of concentrated versus distributed costs, concentrated versus distributed benefits, and incidence of participation.

Some formal political theory has also considered the consequences of concentrated versus distributed costs and benefits. Weingast, Shepsle, and Johnsen (1981) suggest that political institutions generate inefficient distribution of public policy because of a political disconnect between costs and benefits. Bueno De Mesquita et al. (2003) argue that political conditions and institutions determine when a leader sides with a minority over a majority with implications for duration of political survival.

Anzia (2012) shows how low-turnout off-cycle elections can benefit special interests. Using teacher salary data from school districts in Texas, Anzia shows that when school board elections move from off-cycle (odd-year elections or elections in non-November months with fewer offices on the ballot) to concurrent with higher-turnout on-cycle general elections (when many other offices are on the ballot), teacher salaries increase around one percentage point less than under off-cycle elections.

Anzia's evidence suggests that special interests are most influential when they comprise a larger proportion of the electorate. Put another way, it shows that the electoral connection conditions the influence of special interests.

Baron (1994) and Grossman and Helpman (1996) study settings where both lobbyists and voters influence candidate policy platforms. Their models assume that vote share is responsive to the candidates' relative campaign expenditures. Demand for these expenditures allows lobbyists to offer political contributions in exchange for policy favors. Note, however, the conclusion that contributions influence policy follows the assumption that expenditures can sway voters against their own policy interests, i.e., they assume expenditures hinder the electoral connection.

Intensity is of particular interest to scholars of the politics of foreign trade (e.g., Schattschneider, 1935). For example, the model of trade protection in Grossman and Helpman (1994) does not explicitly incorporate intensity, but different interest groups have different elasticities of welfare to trade protection.

2.7.5 Public Opinion

Responses to public opinion survey questions indicate that citizens are ambivalent about most policy issues. Some respondents, however, do ascribe importance to or find salient one or two issues (e.g., Rabinowitz and Macdonald, 1989; Krosnick, 1990). Scholars group respondents motivated by the same issue into "issue publics." Issue publics are thought to care about policy on that issue of interest but to otherwise discount or ignore candidate positions on other issues. Academic research on "single-issue voters" can be read as an application of issue publics to elections (e.g., Conover, Gray, and Coombs, 1982; Bouton et al., 2021).

Other work analyzes issue salience and heterogeneity in voter preferences using public opinion data (e.g., RePass, 1971; Rivers, 1988). To the extent that salience is similar to issue intensity, the sum of this work suggests that individual vote choice is influenced by variation in issue intensity.

While many opinion scholars suggest that self-interest on policy issues is not an important input to vote choice, consideration of issue publics yields evidence that issue opinions do relate to vote choice. For example, Fournier et al. (2003) find that the issues voters report as important are more strongly related to vote choice than issues reported as less important. Ansolabehere, Rodden, and Snyder (2008) show that purging issue opinions of measurement error significantly increases the correlation between issue preferences and vote choice.

Gerber et al. (2011) find that respondents admit that on some issues they are uncertain what policy would be best. These same respondents report being less likely to penalize politicians for positions on those issues about which they lack confidence. Iyengar et al. (2008) find that when presented with a menu of information about candidates, voters are more likely to review candidate information on issues they deem important. Their experiment provides behavioral evidence that citizens value knowledge about candidate platforms on the issues they most care about. Chapter 8 of this book provides more evidence that issues of intensity influence vote choice.

2.7.6 Political Parties

The UCLA school of parties (Cohen et al., 2008; Bawn et al., 2012; Masket, 2016) argues that political parties are "best understood as coalitions of interest groups and activists seeking to capture and use government for their particular goals" (Bawn et al., 2012, p. 571). Policy goals, they argue, motivate these interest groups more than policy motivates the remainder of the electorate. They term these motivated interest groups "policy-demanders." Different policy-demanding groups come together to form a coalition, work out policy differences before the election, and then nominate candidates committed to their policy platform. The authors argue that this policy platform is not the platform best designed to appeal to the electorate. In my phrasing, policy-demanders care more intensely about their interests than do others in the electorate.

2.8 INTENSITY IN THE PRACTICE OF POLITICS

The influence of intense interests is not limited to the scholarship of political science. Political practice and institutions in the United States have many features that implicitly acknowledge Dahl's intensity problem:

In the state of Nevada, for example, initiatives to amend the state constitution require passage in two consecutive general elections.[4] Because not every voter participates in every election, this requirement means that constitutional amendments cannot happen when an intense minority turns out in only one otherwise low-turnout election.

Four other states require that ballot initiatives not only receive more yes than no votes but also that the count of yes votes is greater than a threshold defined outside of the initiative. Affirmative votes must attain 30 percent of the total votes cast in the election in Massachusetts, 35 percent in Nebraska, 40 percent in Mississippi, and 50 percent in Wyoming (see National Conference of State Legislatures, 2012).

The 10th Circuit Court of Appeals upheld extra-majority rules with specific reference to preventing cooptation of the initiative process by special interests, writing:

[W]e believe the State of Wyoming has a legitimate and reasonable interest in seeing that an initiated measure, for example, is not enacted into law unless it is approved by a majority of those voting in the general election in which the

---

[4] Nevada state constitution, Article 19, Section 2, www.leg.state.nv.us/Const/ NVConst.html.

initiated measure is being considered. If Wyoming wants to make it "harder," rather than "easier," to make laws by the initiated process, such is its prerogative, and, in our view, does not violate the First Amendment. A state understandably wants to minimize abuse of the initiated process and make it difficult for a relatively small special interest group to enact its views into law through an initiated measure. (James P. Brady et al. v. Diana J. Ohman, 105 F.3d 726, 1998)

Political campaigns also take actions that seem to acknowledge differences in intensity. Campaigns with limited budgets usually target outreach to voters they believe are most likely to turn out in the relevant election. In the business, these voters are sometimes called "four of five" or "five of five" voters, in reference to the count of the last five elections in which they cast a ballot. Campaigns are less likely to try to contact three, two, one, or zero of five voters. A candidate for California Secretary of State in 2014 reported that his mailers "were not going to people who don't vote in primaries" (Hill and Kousser, 2016, p. 415)." Another reported having "sent out two direct mail pieces to Republican voters who turn out frequently in primaries."

2.9 THEORIES OF ELECTIONS, INTENSITY, AND A SYNTHESIS

Theories of elections do not attend to the importance of intensity as much as I believe they should. None of the rational actor models to my reading explicitly model variation in the intensity with which voters care about policy. The weights for each dimension in multi-dimensional spatial models are related (Davis and Hinich, 1966; Enelow and Hinich, 1984). However, those weights are often assumed constant across the electorate rather than allowed to vary at the level of the voter. The model of Vavreck (2009) allows campaign messaging to influence the salience of issues. Here again, however, salience is fixed in magnitude across the electorate once influenced by the campaign.

Davis and Hinich (1966) allow intensity to vary across groups in the electorate, but intensity is either zero or large, not low or high. The mathematical model I present below might be read as in the tradition of these rational actor models of politics with the extent of heterogeneity on intensity as a parameter of the model.

Retrospective models do not explicitly consider intensity. Because the level of performance that an incumbent needs to deliver to do "well enough" to win reelection is not specified, it is possible that variation across voters in how much they value government outcomes maps into retrospective voting. To my knowledge, this is not a feature of retrospective voting to date explored. Finally, social-psychological theories do not explicitly model intensity as inputs to vote choice. Although there is some work on issue publics and single-issue voting, it has garnered much less attention than one might think given the potential importance of intensity.

The political science of democratic theory, formal democratic theory, legislative representation, pressure politics, public opinion, and political parties suggests that intensity can influence policy, but the mechanism is not always clear. If the electoral connection generates representation so that intensity operates through elections, when and why would elections frustrate majorities?

To explain frustrated majorities and variation in costly political action, I synthesize the political science of intensity with the political science of elections in the argument of this book termed "intensity theory," where political actors pursue their interests. The electoral connection remains front and center in the theory. The theory and model explain when and why candidates side with minorities over majorities and why voters choose different levels of costly political action. While intensity theory cannot explain all aspects of a complex political system, it offers new understanding for these two basic facts of electoral democracy.

PART II

ARGUMENT

An Intensity Theory of Electoral Competition

3

Sketching a Theory of Intensity and Electoral Competition

[T]hose who care deeply about preventing more and more gun violence will have to be as passionate, and as organized, and as vocal as those who blocked these common-sense steps to help keep our kids safe. Ultimately, you outnumber those who argued the other way. But they're better organized. They're better financed. They've been at it longer. And they make sure to stay focused on this one issue during election time. And that's the reason why you can have something that 90 percent of Americans support and you can't get it through the Senate or the House of Representatives.

President Barack Obama, April 17, 2013.

Different voters have different preferences. On each issue, some voters care intensely while others care only modestly. Politician beliefs about how much different groups care has consequences for policy platforms. Obama argues that representatives believe a minority opposed to firearm regulation cares much more intensely about the issue than the majority and that this intense minority votes on that issue at each election. The greater intensity of this minority, according to Obama, generates a frustrated (super-)majority.

Firearm regulation is one of many issues that representatives must confront. It is likely that on different issues there is a different balance of high-intensity and low-intensity voters. Sometimes, high-intensity voters are in the majority. On these issues, vote-seeking politicians would side with the high-intensity majority. On other issues, however, a majority cares only modestly while a minority cares intensely.

Obama suggests that legislators side with the high-intensity minority on the gun issue, but he does not explain *why*. When and why would legislators side with a high-intensity minority? Does it depend on size of majority or on level of intensity? When will majorities be frustrated and when satisfied? Answering these questions is the first goal of intensity theory.

The second feature of intensity theory is that, while candidates for office want to know which voters care more or less about issues, that knowledge is difficult to come by. Intensity is hard to observe. It is not a fixed characteristic of voters that candidates can measure with a physical instrument. Rather, how intensely a voter cares about an issue can only be approximated with reference to observable phenomena such as what voters say or do.

Unfortunately for candidates, if voters know politicians act based on *beliefs* about who cares intensely, even voters who care modestly would like politicians to believe they care intensely. If a politician simply asks voters if they care intensely about an issue, absent other incentives the voter might indicate they care intensely when in fact they do not.

If intensity is hard for politicians to observe and a key input to vote choice, both high-intensity voters and candidates for office benefit from a technology that communicates intensity. I argue that such a technology exists in the diverse array of costly political actions and expressions available to voters. By costly political actions and expressions, I mean actions and expressions with certain costs yet uncertain benefits. The voter must pay costs to take actions and expressions no matter the outcome of electoral competition. Such actions and expressions include acts of political participation, such as monetary contributions to candidates or volunteering for campaigns, and expressions costly to make, such as socially-inappropriate public statements.

High-intensity voters sometimes choose to engage in costly action or expression that low-intensity voters would not so that candidates know that they are high-intensity. Obama exhorts those he agrees with to take action, to be "as passionate, and as organized, and as vocal" as the intense minority. A second goal of intensity theory is to explore *when* high-intensity majority or minority voters choose to take costly political action and expression and the consequences of these choices.

In the remainder of this chapter, I walk through the how and why of a theory of issue intensity and electoral competition. In the next chapter, I present the results of a mathematical model of this theory. The mathematical model uses the tools of game theory to more carefully answer when and why legislators side with a high-intensity minority and when and why high-intensity majority or minority voters choose to incur costly political action or expression in pursuit of policy goals.[1] This effort, I hope, builds a theoretical scaffolding around the operation of issue intensity and its interaction with electoral competition and representation.

3.1 FOUNDATION OF A THEORY

What would a theory of issue intensity and electoral competition look like? I believe the theory should help us understand politics in new ways while remaining consistent with widely recognized characteristics of electoral competition and representation. I combine widely recognized empirical regularities with simplifying assumptions as the foundation for the theory. If the theory is wildly inconsistent with empirical regularities of politics or requires a complex combination of assumptions to work, I suspect it would be less useful. However, if the theory is consistent with first principles, relatively parsimonious, and provides new understanding of intensity of preference, frustrated majorities, electoral competition, and political action, intensity theory might be usefully employed in the scientific study of politics.

Six ingredients serve as a foundation for the theory. Each ingredient has been sometimes used by other theorists of electoral democracy, representation, and accountability and so I don't believe readers will find them unusual. I summarize these six ingredients in Table 3.1.

The first ingredient for intensity theory constrains the setting. Intensity theory considers a representative democracy where candidates for office compete for the votes of individual electors.

Second, candidates care only about winning as many votes as they can at election. Any actions taken or any costs incurred by candidates follow from the goal to maximize votes received.[2] Neither personal policy views nor other political implications of the policy proposal influence candidate platforms. Candidates care only about votes at the election.

The assumption of vote-seeking candidates allows me to set aside the possibility that candidates frustrate majorities not for electoral considerations but because they have personal preferences or other extra-electoral motives for policy. This allows me to show that simply pursuing votes

---

[1] I address the place of party identification in the next chapter.

[2] I focus on maximizing vote share as is common in many models of elections, although it is not generically equivalent to maximizing the probability of winning the election (Patty, 2002).

TABLE 3.1. *Ingredients of intensity theory*

1. Representatives gain power to set policy through plurality elections. (Representative Democracy)
2. Candidates care only about winning votes at election. (Vote-seeking Candidates)
3. Voters select candidates on policy and idiosyncratic factors. (Probabilistic Voting)
4. At the time candidates write platforms, they do not know who will win the election. (Electoral Uncertainty)
5. Candidates know what each voter wants, but not how much they want it. (Candidate Uncertainty)
6. Voters choose how much to engage in costly political action. (Voter Agency)

in a plurality election can sometimes lead to policy favored by a known minority (following the literature on probabilistic voting).

Third, vote choice depends upon the policies proposed by candidates and other factors. The other factors make vote choice uncertain even though, all else equal, voters are more likely to select candidates who propose policies that they prefer (vote choice is probabilistic). This unpredictability of vote choice can represent a host of other features of the electoral environment such as the state of the economy, foreign entanglements, political identities such as party identification, and idiosyncratic, unpredictable political tastes.

Fourth, candidates do not fully understand the electoral consequences of the idiosyncratic factors of vote choice. From the candidates' perspective, the election outcome is uncertain. Candidates work with the tool they do control – policy proposal – to maximize votes received.[3]

Fifth, candidates know the policy position of each voter but do not know the intensity of each voter. Candidates know what voters want but do not know how much they want it. This assumption is not meant to necessarily reflect the reality of every election, where candidates probably do not know the policy position of each voter. Rather, the assumption serves to show that even when candidates know with certainty what

---

[3] To the extent candidates influence the electoral consequences of other factors (e.g., Vavreck, 2009), the distribution of idiosyncratic factors might favor one candidate over the other.

policy position is favored by a majority of voters, they might still choose to side with an intense minority over the majority.

Because the votes of high-intensity voters respond more strongly to policy positions than the votes of low-intensity voters, candidates want to know who is high- and low-intensity as they craft campaign platforms. High-intensity voters also want candidates to know they care intensely to increase the chances candidates set policy at their preference. Candidate uncertainty about intensity is not required for frustrated majorities but is required for costly political action.

Low-intensity voters still want policy at their preference even though they care less intensely. Because low-intensity voters know policy proposals might depend upon candidate beliefs about voter intensity, they would like candidates to (incorrectly) believe that they care intensely – or, equivalently, believe high-intensity voters are low-intensity. Because candidates cannot accurately observe voter intensity, obfuscation can be of benefit to low-intensity voters.

The sixth and final ingredient to intensity theory is that voters choose how many political actions to take and what political statements to express. I am specifically interested in actions and expressions that are publicly observed by candidates and costly to the individual. By publicly observed, I mean that candidates (or their staff) learn which voters take which actions and make which expressions. By costly, I mean that, first, the voter must pay some cost to take the action before the election and, second, the subsequent benefits to that action might not outweigh the costs.[4]

Costly political actions might include campaign contributions, volunteering, participation in nomination politics, or attending rallies or public meetings. Expressions include yard signs, campaign stickers, social media posts, or other public statements. Each voter gets to choose how many costs, if any, to incur from political action and expression. One voter might make $500 in contributions, volunteer for 30 hours for a candidate, and display a yard sign. A second voter might make no contributions, abstain from volunteering, and make no public display about politics.

---

[4] For those familiar with game theory, the fifth and sixth ingredients generate a setting of asymmetric information with intensity private information that I model as a signaling game.

3.1.1 Observability of Intensity

The fifth ingredient of the theory merits discussion. Can candidates for office know when the minority cares more than the majority? Dahl (1956) suggested candidates cannot observe intensity: "In no conceivable way, then, can we directly observe and compare the sensate intensities of preference of different individuals" (p. 99). Schattschneider (1960), too, suggested that individual interests can be only inferred, not measured:

> We have made progress in the study of politics because people have observed some kind of relation between the political behavior of people and certain wholly impersonal data concerning their ownership of property, income, economic status, professions and the like. All that we know about interests, private as well as public, is based on inferences of this sort. (p. 25)

Arnold (1990) argued that legislators *estimate* for each course of action the incidence of costs and benefits (which are the inputs to his definition of intensity of preference) to members of their constituencies.

Even if Dahl's strict argument (that observing intensities is impossible) does not hold, it is reasonable to assume it difficult for candidates to know the intensities of every voter on every issue. There is no physical instrument that can measure intensity with exact precision. Candidates are *uncertain* about voter intensity.

However, once we admit that candidates are uncertain about intensity, a larger problem confronts candidates. Members of a less-intense majority know that candidates might set policy with an intense minority if they believe the majority does not care enough about the issue. Although the majority does not care as much about the outcome as the minority, they still prefer their position over the alternative. And, they know that the candidates will not cross the majority if the candidates believe the majority cares intensely.

The majority, therefore, has an incentive to obfuscate when the candidates are uncertain about voter intensity. The majority wants the candidates to *believe* they care intensely about the policy even if they care only modestly. The candidates, also realizing the majority's incentive to obfuscate, appreciate that they cannot simply ask voters to report their intensities.

3.2 MIXING INGREDIENTS INTO A THEORY

What are the political consequences of intensity in a setting of electoral competition with the six ingredients presented above? The main dynamic in this setting is the interplay between candidates wanting to propose policy to win votes, high-intensity voters who want candidates to know they are high-intensity while low-intensity voters are not, and low-intensity voters who, all else equal, would prefer candidates to incorrectly believe they are high-intensity. Candidates use whatever information they have about which voters are high- and low-intensity to set policy. High-intensity voters choose whether or not to take costly actions to communicate to candidates their intensity, and low-intensity voters choose whether or not to take costly actions in anticipation of the actions taken by high-intensity voters.

Costly actions need not be incredibly costly and, as I discuss in Chapter 4, action motivated by expressive rather than instrumental goals could also communicate issue intensity to candidates. I discuss the free-rider problem in large electorates in Chapter 5.

When would voters voluntarily choose to incur certain costs that do not lead to certain benefits? In this setting, high-intensity voters might choose to incur costs to communicate to candidates that they care intensely about the issue.

Setting aside other dynamics, imagine there are two voters who differ over whether the government should regulate emissions of carbon dioxide from power plants. Voter 1 has a family member who works at a power plant and so values the government not regulating at $100. Voter 2 believes carbon dioxide emissions damage the environment and so values regulation at $50. These valuations mean that Voter 1 would be indifferent between paying $100 and having no regulation and paying nothing and having regulation. Voter 2 would be indifferent between paying $50 and having regulation and paying nothing and not having regulation.

Voter 1 would be willing to pay $1, $2, $3, ..., $51, $52, $53, ..., even $99 to keep the government from regulating carbon dioxide emissions. Voter 1, of course, would not pay $101 to gain $100 in benefit. Voter 2, on the other hand, would be willing to pay $1, $2, $3, ..., $49 for regulation, but would not be willing to pay more than $50.

Because candidates do not know the intensity of each voter, costly actions allow high-intensity voters to demonstrate that they care intensely. High-intensity voters incur a magnitude of cost that a low-intensity voter would not. Voter 1 would be willing to pay from $50 to $99 whereas Voter 2 would not. So, for example, if Voter 1 makes a political contribution of $51, the candidates know that Voter 1 cares intensely about emission regulations.[5]

---

[5] I assume here the contribution has no additional influence on policy. If contributions have additional (non-electoral) influence, this might increase the potential for frustrated majorities (Baron, 1994).

Meanwhile, Voter 2 is unwilling to make a contribution of \$51. Because Voter 2 chooses not to incur the cost, Voter 2 reveals to the candidates that their preference is less intense than that of Voter 1.[6]

This setting is called a "signaling game" in game theory because actors who know they differ from others on some important dimension must signal this difference to help attain their goals. Here, costly political actions and expressions separate high-intensity voters from low-intensity voters. Candidates already know which voters support which position but with costly actions learn the balance of high-intensity supporters and opponents. With this knowledge, candidates then set policy to win as many votes as they can.

3.2.1 Theories of Politics with Costly Signaling

I am not the first to observe that costly political actions may benefit those who take them as technologies of communication rather than as instrumental contributions to the target of the action. Lohmann (1993) argues that costly actions communicate to public officials and other citizens about level of opposition to the government. Pre-election communication occurs in Meirowitz (2005) through responses to public opinion polls and in Shotts (2006) through votes at a first-stage election. These models differ from the theory I present here in having private information about voter ideal points (Meirowitz, 2005; Shotts, 2006) or about the common level of discontent in an autocratic setting (Lohmann, 1993) rather than intensity of preference. More similar to my argument is Gause (2022), who argues that voters attend protests to communicate issue salience.[7]

3.3 INTENSITY FOR POLICY OR INTENSITY FOR IDENTITY?

Although I interpret intensity theory in the context of citizens caring intensely about issues of public policy, nothing in the theory or model

---

[6] Voter 2, anticipating a high-intensity voter will make a contribution of \$51, makes a contribution of \$0 knowing they gain nothing contributing more than zero.

[7] More common in political science are models where *politicians* possess knowledge that the voter does not (e.g., Canes-Wrone, Herron, and Shotts, 2001; Ashworth and Bueno de Mesquita, 2014; Fox and Van Weelden, 2015; Patty, 2016; Schnakenberg and Turner, 2019). See Gordon and Hafer (2005) for a model where corporations hold the private information.

requires that voters care intensely about public policy. Voters might care more or less intensely that a social or political identity is reflected in the rhetoric, platforms, or symbols of the candidates running for office. Readers interested in a setting where voters care about identity or rhetoric might consider substituting their preferred voter motive for "policy" as they read, e.g., consider *identity intensity*. The theory can be read as response to the call by Achen and Bartels (2016, ch. 11) and others for more theory about political identities.

The model could have similar explanatory power if political choices follow from expressive motives, although I focus on voters taking political action in pursuit of representation on the issues they care most about. If, alternatively, the voters who care intensely choose to take political actions and make vote choice to gain expressive benefits on issues about which they care intensely, candidates would similarly want to observe these actions and expressions to infer how vote totals respond to policies proposed. Taking political action with the goal of instrumental influence on policy is not the only route through which action can communicate intensity.

* * *

For the remainder of this chapter, I present an introduction to the model that I use to explore the operation of intensity theory. My hope is that this introduction provides an intuition for the mathematical model that undergirds the results presented in Chapters 4 and 5. These results depend upon models with algebra more complicated than that here, drawing on the theory of Bayesian games of incomplete information and presented in Appendices A and B.

3.4 HOW ELECTIONS INFLUENCE CANDIDATES

Voters influence what candidates say and do through the electoral connection. Candidates make policy choices in anticipation of how voters will respond at the next election. I imagine each individual voter makes a choice between competing candidates by considering what each candidate proposes to do in office, how much the voter cares about what the candidates propose, and how much the voter cares about other factors of the election such as incumbency or economic and foreign policy context.

In the model, candidate platforms can encompass a wide variety of actions to take in office. In general, these actions relate to some government activity over which the candidate who wins the election has influence. While an obvious case is a specific public policy issue, it could also be something more abstract. It might be the candidate's general orientation toward government intervention in the economy or the rhetoric that the elected politician will employ when in office. A voter who cares intensely about a social identity might value the symbols an elected representative displays in public, while a voter who cares intensely about economic policy might value the economic policy proposals to be acted upon by an elected representative.

I will use the word "policy" to capture any of the activities over which an elected representative has influence. I include expression of symbols or rhetoric in this definition. Policy, as formalized in the model, must have two features. First, policy must be something that the voter cares about either intensely or to a modest degree. I set aside policies for which some voters care not at all because the interesting case is how candidates navigate voters who care about a policy to varying degrees.

Second, candidates must have some control over the manifestation of policy if elected to office. Government law-making, orientation toward government intervention, or symbolic actions and expressions each have these two features.

The other factors that influence the voter could be any of a variety of contextual influences on vote choice separate from "policy" as defined above. This might include the reputation of political parties, symbolic actions or political choices previously made by the incumbent government, the state of foreign or economic affairs, or the voter's idiosyncratic preferences for individual candidate characteristics such as business experience, political history, or background. Importantly, these other factors do not meet the second condition of policy in the paragraph above because candidates are unable to change these factors when elected to office.

The magnitude and direction of the influence of other factors on vote choice is uncertain prior to the election. As is usually the case in competitive democratic settings, neither the candidates nor voters are certain which candidate will win. While there may be a general belief that one candidate is favored, no one is able to predict the result with certainty.

A voter with intense preferences on policy weighs candidate positions on policy more heavily in their vote choice than does a voter with less intense preferences. The voter with less intense preferences weighs other factors more heavily than the intense voter. Intensity influences vote choice by increasing the weight of the policy consideration relative to the influence of the other factors.

3.4.1 A Model of Intensity and Electoral Choice

To clarify the operation of intensity, I present a basic mathematical model of intensity and electoral choice. Consider an electorate of voters who must decide for which candidate to vote, Candidate A or Candidate B. Each candidate proposes a position, s_A and s_B, on a single policy issue s. Policy proposals take one of two values, zero or one. For example, if Candidate A proposes policy at one, $s_A = 1$. If candidate B proposes policy at zero, $s_B = 0$.

Voters each have a preference over policy s and, on average, favor candidates who propose the policy they prefer. Voters also each have a magnitude of intensity for their preferred policy. I represent each voter's intensity for policy with the Greek letter β. Voters who care more about policy have a higher value β. Voters who care less about policy have a lower value β.

We can represent how the voter evaluates policy – their utility function – with the equation

$$v_i(s, \beta_i) = \begin{cases} \beta_i s & \text{if voter i prefers } s = 1 \\ \beta_i(1 - s) & \text{if voter i prefers } s = 0, \end{cases} \tag{3.1}$$

where s is the policy, the function $v(\cdot)$ returns a number that indicates how much the voter benefits with policy proposal s given their intensity β_i, and the variable i indicates that each voter i might have a different preferred policy s and different intensity β_i. Voters who prefer $s = 1$ get β_i when $s = 1$ per the first line, while voters who prefer $s = 0$ get β_i when $s = 0$ per the second line ($\beta_i(1 - s) = \beta_i$ when $s = 0$). For simplicity, I assume that if policy is implemented opposite the voter's preference, they receive benefit of zero.

Let us define the parameter δ_i to represent the voter's net preference for Candidate B from the other factors. If δ_i is positive, these other factors favor Candidate B. If δ_i is negative, the other factors favor A. Each voter has their own value δ_i representing individual experiences and idiosyncratic tastes. I assume these factors are not fully known to (or perhaps cognized by) the voter until the day of the election and so δ_i cannot be communicated to candidates in advance.

Each voter's choice involves a comparison of the policy platforms of the two candidates and the other factors of the election. On election day, a voter who prefers policy $s = 1$ chooses Candidate A over Candidate B when

$$\beta_i s_A > \beta_i s_B + \delta_i. \tag{3.2}$$

When Candidate A proposes the policy favored by a voter who wants policy at one, $s_A = 1$, the voter receives a benefit β_i if A is elected. Likewise, when Candidate B proposes the policy favored by the voter, $s_B = 1$, the voter receives a benefit β_i if B is elected. If indifferent, they choose between the candidates with equal probability 0.5.

A voter who prefers $s = 0$ makes a similar comparison represented by the inequality

$$\beta_i(1 - s_A) > \beta_i(1 - s_B) + \delta_i$$

so that they get β_i when a candidate proposes $s = 0$. For simplicity of exposition, I'll continue with an $s = 1$ voter but note the decision is symmetric for voters who favor $s = 0$.

The comparison represented by Eq. (3.2) highlights how intensity maps into vote choice. Imagine that Candidate A proposes $s_A = 1$ and Candidate B proposes $s_B = 0$. The voter gets a benefit of β_i if A is elected and a benefit of δ_i if B is elected. Their vote, therefore, depends on whether β_i is greater than or less than δ_i, if how much they care about policy issue s outweighs the other factors on their choice δ_i.

I have assumed that the other factors δ_i are uncertain for both voters and candidates up until election day. In the mathematical models of this book, I represent unknown features of the world with a probability distribution.[8] The probability distribution for δ characterizes the beliefs voters and candidates hold about how likely idiosyncratic factors are to favor Candidate A or B and with what magnitude.

Imagine that each δ_i is independently drawn from a uniform distribution with a minimum of -10 and a maximum of 10. In a uniform probability distribution, every value between the minimum and maximum is equally likely. Here, all values from -10 to 10 are equally likely so that, on average, δ_i is zero and neither candidate believes they are more likely than not to benefit from the other factors. For some voters the other factors will favor Candidate A (δ_i less than zero), for other voters Candidate B (δ_i greater than zero).

The importance of intensity for vote choice depends upon the magnitude of intensity relative to the other factors. Candidate policy positions

---

[8] A probability distribution is a function that maps each value that a random variable might take to the probability that value is returned on each realization of that variable. For example, the probability distribution for a fair coin maps each value the coin might take (heads or tails) to the probability of each value on each flip (0.5 for heads and 0.5 for tails).

are a greater influence on the vote choice for a voter who feels intensely on the issue (higher β_i) than for a voter who feels less intensely (lower β_i).

Consider a voter who feels intensely that policy should be set at one with a β_i of 5 and, as above, $s_A = 1$ and $s_B = 0$. The probability that this voter chooses A is the probability that $\beta_i > \delta_i \Rightarrow 5 > \delta_i$. We can use the characteristics of a uniform probability distribution to compute this probability. For a random variable that follows the uniform probability distribution with minimum -10 and maximum 10, 75 percent of its probability mass is below 5 and 25 percent above. Therefore, this voter has a 75 percent chance of voting for A and a 25 percent chance of voting for B when $s_A = 1$ and $s_B = 0$.

In contrast, consider a voter who feels less intensely with a β_i of 1. This voter still values policy at their preferred $s = 1$, but less so than the previous voter. This voter chooses A when $\beta_i > \delta_i \Rightarrow 1 > \delta_i$. On a -10 to 10 uniform distribution, 55 percent of probability mass is below 1. This voter's probability of voting A over B is 55 percent when $s_A = 1$ and $s_B = 0$.

This difference, 75 percent versus 55 percent, is why intensity influences candidate platforms. Although Candidate A has proposed the policy preferred by both of these voters and Candidate B has proposed against their preference, one voter chooses A three out of four times while the other chooses A a bit more than half of the time. Policy is more likely to determine the choice of the more intense voter than the choice of the less intense voter.

3.4.2 Candidate Perspective

Having described the decision process of the voter, let us now consider the candidates A and B. For the model, I assume candidates care only about winning votes. This is not because I believe politicians care only about maximizing vote total. Rather, other scholarship has often assumed that candidates care about things other than winning elections and that these other things are the cause of frustrated majorities.[9]

For example, we might imagine that candidates for office only go to the trouble of running for office *because* they know that their personal

---

[9] I follow the standard practice in mathematical models of elections in assuming candidates seek to maximize vote share. This goal does not always generate the same candidate strategies as the goal maximizing probability of election (Patty, 2002). In some cases, both goals lead to the same strategy, such as in the example I present on page 62.

policy preferences are in the minority, and entering the election pulls policy toward what they want (see Besley and Coate, 1997). Alternatively, we might imagine politicians receive bribes from special interests in exchange for policy favors and that politicians value bribes over winning votes. Either of these mechanisms could generate frustrated majorities.

But in these settings, frustrated majorities occur because the theory assumes an imperfect electoral connection. Extra-electoral influences frustrate majorities rather than electoral competition itself.

My assumption that politicians care only about winning as many votes as they can serves a specific analytical purpose. It allows us to see if issue intensity can produce frustrated majorities exclusively through politicians' desire to win election. Other explanations of non-majoritarian outcomes sometimes assume politicians care about things beyond election, for example if the politician cares personally about policy or if the politician desires campaign contributions. Because I show you that frustrated majorities occur even when politicians care only about winning the votes of voters, I believe it demonstrates that intensity is a fundamental feature of democratic politics.

What policies should A and B propose if they seek only votes? Clearly, in the single voter example above they should each propose $s = 1$ whether or not $\beta_i = 5$ because that is what the deciding elector prefers. No matter what value of δ_i is realized on election day, neither candidate can do better than siding with the single voter.

An election with voters on only one side of the issue is not interesting, so let us increase the size of the electorate to three voters who disagree about policy. For electoral competition to be compelling, imagine that two electors, Voter 1 and Voter 2, prefer that $s = 1$ and another, Voter 3, prefers that $s = 0$. Policy $s = 1$ is the majority position, $s = 0$ that of the minority.

When policy is the only consideration for voters and there are no other influences on the choice (i.e., $\delta_i = 0$ with certainty), each candidate should side with the majority and propose $s = 1$. When $\delta_i = 0$ for all i, the voter decision governed by the inequality in Eq. (3.2) leads deterministically to voters choosing the candidate proposing their preferred policy (or flipping a fair coin when candidates propose the same policy). Because in this three-voter electorate two voters prefer $s = 1$ and there are no other factors of vote choice, the candidates can do no better than proposing $s_A = s_B = 1$ regardless of how intensely Voter 3 cares about the policy. This, of course, is the median voter result of Downs (1957) and Black (1958).

However, when vote choice moves from being determined exclusively by policy to being determined partially by policy and partially by unpredictable other factors, the median voter result no longer holds (Davis and Hinich, 1968; Calvert, 1985). In such settings, variation in intensity is an important consideration for vote-seeking candidates.

Intensity can lead candidates to propose policy with an intense minority over a less-intense majority. To see how this might happen, imagine that Candidate B proposes policy with the majority $s_B = 1$ and Candidate A must decide what to propose. Candidate A wants to maximize their vote total, which means considering the choice probabilities of each of the three voters under each of two scenarios. First, if they propose policy with the majority $s_A = 1$, second if they propose policy with the minority $s_A = 0$.

When the majority is as intense or more intense than the minority, vote-seeking candidates should propose with the majority because there is no trade-off between siding with a majority or siding with the intense set of voters because the intense set of voters in this case is in the majority. Let's consider instead the interesting case where minority Voter 3 has intense policy preferences $\beta_3 = 5$, majority Voters 1 and 2 have less intense preferences $\beta_1 = \beta_2 = 1$, and the other influences on each voter's decision are drawn independently from a uniform distribution that ranges from -10 to 10.

With these assumptions, the three voters vote A when

$$1 * s_A > 1 * s_B + \delta_1 \qquad \text{(Voter 1)},$$
$$1 * s_A > 1 * s_B + \delta_2 \qquad \text{(Voter 2)},$$
$$5 * (1 - s_A) > 5 * (1 - s_B) + \delta_3 \qquad \text{(Voter 3)}.$$

With Candidate B proposing $s_B = 1$, the choices are

$$1 * s_A > 1 + \delta_1 \qquad \text{(Voter 1)},$$
$$1 * s_A > 1 + \delta_2 \qquad \text{(Voter 2)},$$
$$5 * (1 - s_A) > 0 + \delta_3 \qquad \text{(Voter 3)}.$$

Given the range of the uniform probability distribution over δ, if Candidate A sides with the majority, proposing $s_A = 1$, A's expected vote from each voter is

$$1 > 1 + \delta_1 \rightarrow E(0 > \delta_1) \rightarrow 0.5,$$
$$1 > 1 + \delta_2 \rightarrow E(0 > \delta_2) \rightarrow 0.5,$$
$$0 > 0 + \delta_3 \rightarrow E(0 > \delta_3) \rightarrow 0.5,$$

where $E(\cdot)$ represents the expected value operator. When A sides with the majority, each candidate expects to receive 1.5 votes. This is because the probability that zero is greater than a random variable drawn from a uniform distribution that ranges from -10 to 10 is one half. On average, a voter's δ_i is less than zero half the time, greater than zero half the time.

Alternatively, if Candidate A sides with the minority and proposes $s_A = 0$, A's expected vote from each voter is

$$0 > 1 + \delta_1 \rightarrow E(-1 > \delta_1) \rightarrow 0.45,$$
$$0 > 1 + \delta_2 \rightarrow E(-1 > \delta_2) \rightarrow 0.45,$$
$$5 > 0 + \delta_3 \rightarrow E(5 > \delta_2) \rightarrow 0.75,$$

which is an expected vote total of 1.65 votes. Candidate A has a lower probability of capturing the votes of Voters 1 and 2 when proposing policy with Voter 3, but a higher probability of capturing the vote of Voter 3 that, in expectation, is greater than the loss in probability for 1 and 2.[10]

With an intense minority $\beta_3 = 5$, Candidate A chooses to propose policy with the minority even though Candidate A knows they are more likely to receive majority votes if they propose $s_A = 1$. This choice follows from the relative importance of other factors. Other factors are less likely to sway the vote of an intense voter than sway the vote of a less intense voter against a candidate who proposes their preferred policy.

Of course, the above exercise assumed Candidate B sided with the majority. In reality, Candidate B faces considerations symmetric to those of Candidate A. The game-theoretic mathematical models must account for strategic electoral competition, where both candidates and voters consider how other actors will respond to intensity and policy preference. I take up that task in the next chapter.

The exercise in this section establishes that variation in intensity of preference can lead candidates to propose policy with a minority even when candidates aim to win a majority of votes.

---

[10] In this case, siding with the minority maximizes both vote total and probability of winning the election. If Candidate A proposes $s_A = 0$ and Candidate B $s_B = 1$, A has a 57 percent chance of winning two or three votes: winning all three voters $((0.45) * (0.45) * (0.75))$ or winning both majority voters and losing the minority voter $((0.45) * (0.45) * (1 - 0.75))$ or winning only one majority and the one minority voter $((0.45) * (1 - 0.45) * (0.75) + (1 - 0.45) * (0.45) * (0.75))$.

3.5 TURNOUT AND PARTY IDENTIFICATION

I have assumed that turnout is universal in this example. In most representative democracies, however, many eligible voters do not participate in each election. One reasonable belief is that turnout is actually related to issue intensity, with those who care more intensely more likely to vote than those who care less (manifesting in an "enthusiasm gap," e.g., Hill, 2014).

The dynamics of candidate incentives would not change if turnout were related to intensity and the policies proposed, though the mathematical model would need to be modified. Candidates respond to changes in their expected electoral fortunes. They set policy with the group that yields a higher expected vote conditional on what they believe their opponent will do.

Under universal turnout, policy influences vote totals through the greater responsiveness in vote choice of high-intensity voters and so candidates favor setting policy with intense voters, all else equal. If, alternatively, turnout of supporters or opponents were to respond to policy because of the intensity of these voters, the composition of the electorate would depend on policy. Different composition of the electorate can change vote totals (Hill, 2017a) and, so, setting policy with intense voters would again be of benefit to vote-seeking candidates. Because vote totals in such a setting depend on turnout, the incentives for candidates are substantively similar in settings where turnout rather than (or in addition to) choice responds to policy.

How electoral fortunes respond to policy platforms motivates candidate choice of policy. The mechanism connecting platform to electoral fortunes could be through the votes of certain-to-turnout high-intensity voters, the turnout choice of high-intensity voters, or some combination of the two. In each case, electoral fortunes are more responsive to policy for high-intensity than low-intensity voters, and candidates sometimes choose to frustrate majorities to win votes from intense minorities.

3.5.1 Party Identification and the Mathematical Model

Party identification does not explicitly enter the model as an influence on vote choice. This is purposeful because party identification is sometimes offered as an explanation for limits on policy responsiveness by candidates. The story goes that identifying with a political party influences vote choice more than do voter policy preferences, allowing candidates to diverge from faithful representation and frustrate majorities.

My goal, instead, is to set aside other potential causes of frustrated majorities, foreground the idea of issue intensity in electoral competition, and evaluate how intensity influences the incentives of candidates and voters. This is why the model centers on policy preference and intensity. I account for other inputs to vote choice with the idiosyncratic error term δ_i.

Readers who think party identification should take a more central place in the model might consider the following. They might assume that δ_i represents attachment to party. The magnitude of δ_i could be large relative to the magnitude of β_i, indicating a larger influence of party identification on choice than of policy preference. A larger δ means that vote choice is more responsive to the idiosyncratic factors and less responsive to policy.

I show in analysis of the mathematical model, however, that even if the magnitude of the other influences on vote choice (such as social identifications) are large relative to policy preferences, this does not change the incentives for candidates as they decide what policies to propose. As long as some voters might have their choice influenced by policy position – even if a small number of voters or if partisan identity is generically a large influence – candidates seeking votes attend to policy preferences and platform construction.

In fact, one of the requirements for frustrated majorities in the mathematical model is that policy preference cannot be so important to the voter that policy determines vote choice. There must be non-zero probability that some voters will choose a candidate who proposes the policy they do not prefer. Other factors of vote choice, such as party identification, are a condition for frustrated majorities even when voters have well-formed policy preferences.

3.6 UNCERTAINTY ABOUT INTENSITY

To this point, we have seen that when candidates know the minority supports its policy position more intensely than the majority supports the opposite position, candidates can expect to be better off siding with the minority. This result, however, assumes the candidates *know* the intensity of the voters.

Other scholars who have considered intensity have noted the difficulty of observing intensities of others (see, e.g., Dahl, 1956, and other references in Chapter 2). To complement the arguments of these other scholars, I also want to point out a strategic reason that intensity is difficult to observe. Voters who are lower-intensity but who nonetheless value policy would like candidates to *believe* that they hold their preferences with intensity. That is, if voters know candidates are more likely to set policy with voters the candidates believe to be high-intensity, low-intensity voters have an incentive to obfuscate. This incentive to obfuscate, by itself, makes it unlikely that candidates are certain about voter intensities.

To modify the model to allow for candidate uncertainty about intensity, we have to change the way candidates calculate their expected vote totals as a function of policy proposal. Instead of knowing with certainty the intensities of the three voters, β_1, β_2, and β_3, candidates must use what information they have to make a best guess at the intensity of each voter. Define the candidates' guesses as $\hat{\beta}_1, \hat{\beta}_2$, and $\hat{\beta}_3$, with the $\hat{}$ indicating a best guess. For simplicity, I assume candidates have access to the same information so that their best guesses are equivalent.

With their best guess of the intensity of each voter, candidate beliefs about the probability that each voter selects Candidate A are

$$\Pr(\hat{\beta}_1 * s_A > \hat{\beta}_1 * s_B + \delta_1) \quad \text{(Voter 1)},$$
$$\Pr(\hat{\beta}_2 * s_A > \hat{\beta}_2 * s_B + \delta_2) \quad \text{(Voter 2)},$$
$$\Pr(\hat{\beta}_3 * (1 - s_A) > \hat{\beta}_3 * (1 - s_B) + \delta_3) \quad \text{(Voter 3)},$$

where $\Pr(\cdot)$ returns the probability that the inequality argument holds.

We are now in a setting where what the candidates *believe* about the intensities of each voter determine whether they set policy with the minority or the majority. If $\hat{\beta}_1 = 1$, $\hat{\beta}_2 = 1$, and $\hat{\beta}_3 = 5$, the candidates propose policy with the minority, just as they did in the previous section when they knew intensity with certainty.

Note, however, that if $\hat{\beta}_1 = 5$, $\hat{\beta}_2 = 5$, and $\hat{\beta}_3 = 5$, the candidates propose policy with the majority. Thus, even if the two majority voters are low-intensity $\beta_1 = \beta_2 = 1$, they *want the candidates to believe* that they are high-intensity. If they can deceive the candidates to think they are high-intensity, they induce candidates to propose the policy that they want. At the least, if candidates ask voters to report how much they care, voters might be tempted to exaggerate.

This is where costly political action enters the strategic interaction. A low-intensity voter who benefits from policy at $\beta_i = 1$ would not pay a cost of 2 to gain policy because their net benefit would be -1. A high-intensity voter who benefits from policy at $\beta_i = 5$, however, would pay a cost of 2 to gain policy because their net benefit would be 3.

In other words, costs greater than the benefit to low-intensity voters would only be paid by high-intensity voters. The actual magnitude of the necessary costs for high-intensity voters to pay depends on the magnitude of high- and low-intensity, prior beliefs about intensity, and the size of the minority, as I document in the next chapter. However, the intuition is as I describe here. When a candidate observes a voter taking costly actions of expected net negative benefits for a low-intensity voter, the candidate infers they must be observing a high-intensity voter.

This dynamic also suggests an avenue through which politics changes policy. Change in beliefs about the relative intensity of minority and majority can induce candidates to change their policy proposals. Thus, policy proposal can be set with the majority at one election but with the minority at another due to changes in beliefs about intensity, even if the size of the majority and minority remain the same. The mathematical model allows me to quantify when these dynamics would lead to change in policy and, in contrast, when changes in beliefs would not lead to change in policy.

I suggest costs incurred are likely to be costly political actions. Why *political* actions? To communicate intensity to candidates, voters must take actions of clear individual cost that are observed by the candidates for office so that candidates can match costs to individual voters. Political actions like protesting, boycotting, volunteering, making campaign contributions, or attending public rallies serve exactly this role. Expressions such as the display of yard signs, stating that a free and fair election was fraudulent, or stating negative stereotypes about political others might also serve this role. Politicians or staff can observe each action or expression and know the action or expression has certain costs without certain benefits.

High-intensity voters take costly political action to communicate to candidates how much they care about policy. They incur costs of a magnitude higher than the value low-intensity voters ascribe to policy. Because low-intensity voters would not choose to incur such a magnitude of costly political action, politicians know that voters who choose that magnitude must have intense preferences.

Candidates create their best-guess beliefs $\hat{\beta}_1$, $\hat{\beta}_2$, and $\hat{\beta}_3$ after observing the costly actions and expressions chosen by each voter. They use these beliefs to determine what policy maximizes their expected vote share.

Thus, costly political action can lead candidates to propose policy with an intense minority over a less-intense majority when, absent the action, they would not have frustrated the majority.

* * *

In this chapter, I have sketched out the six ingredients I use to construct a theory of elections with intensity as a central factor of vote choice and policy competition. I then introduced application of these ingredients to a model of electoral competition. This model generates two key results. First, there are settings where candidates maximize votes by proposing policy with an intense minority and frustrating majorities. Second, high-intensity voters sometimes choose costly political action in pursuit of political goals to communicate to candidates that they care intensely.

These results explain why even majoritarian republics sometimes do not implement policy known to be preferred by electoral majorities and why voters choose to take political actions with certain costs and uncertain benefits in pursuit of political interests.

In the next chapter, I present the key results from a game-theoretic model that provides logical and strategic weight to the results presented in this chapter. Game theory allows me to derive what strategies and choices each actor would pursue given the strategies, beliefs, and incentives of the other actors. What policies would a candidate propose given beliefs about what other candidates might propose and beliefs about the voters? How many costly political actions and expressions should voters incur, given what they believe about how other voters will act and how candidates will respond to those actions? Do voters in the minority make different choices about political action than voters in the majority? The game-theoretic model allows formal descriptions of how intensity influences representation, elections, and political action and how an intense minority can attain representation and frustrate majorities in a setting of strategic electoral competition.

4

Theory and Model Results

Issue Intensity, Costly Action, and Minority Representation

Planned Parenthood of Greater Texas on August 4, 2020 acknowledged their intention to open a clinic in the city of Lubbock. The clinic would provide reproductive health services including abortion. In response, advocacy group Right to Life East Texas and Texas State Senator Charles Perry held meetings in Lubbock advocating a city ordinance that would require $2,000 civil penalties for any individual who assists in the procurement of an abortion and would declare Lubbock a "Sanctuary City for the Unborn." Beginning with Waskom in 2019, other cities in Texas had already enacted similar ordinances, but none had reproductive health clinics within their borders.

In accordance with the Lubbock City Charter, a citizen initiating committee filed a proposed ordnance with the City Secretary. The Secretary validated the filing, triggering a 60-day window for the organizers to gather at least 3,651 signatures of Lubbock residents. Lubbock's population was about 260,000 in 2020. Three weeks later, the committee filed a petition with the city with 5,780 signatures (City of Lubbock, n.d., Agenda Item 9398, November 2, 2020).

The City Council consulted attorneys on the legality of the proposed ordinance. The attorneys concluded that the ordinance violated state and federal law, which the City Council announced publicly on October 14.

On October 26, the City Secretary verified the petition signatures and ruled the petition valid. This ruling required the City Council to consider and vote on the petition (City of Lubbock, n.d., Agenda Item 9398, November 2, 2020).

At its November 17, 2020 meeting, the City Council reported receiving 498 email comments on the proposed ordinance prior to the 12:00 pm deadline, 473 in opposition and 22 in favor. At the meeting itself, however, 80 spoke in favor of the ordinance with 7 in opposition. The public comment period extended past 11:00 pm with five and one-half hours of comments. Supporters spoke with passion and intensity about the need to ban abortion within the city (City of Lubbock, n.d., November 17, 2020 minutes and video recording).

After the citizen comment period, each Council member spoke about their position on the issue. Council members offered support for the idea but said the ordinance would be unenforceable and only lead the city to incur extensive legal expenses in a lost cause. Some noted that they swore an oath to uphold the state and federal constitutions and felt voting for something they believed illegal violated that oath. The Council voted down the ordinance 7-0 (City of Lubbock, n.d., November 17, 2020 minutes and video recording).

Pursuant to the Charter rules on initiated petitions, after the Council voted down the ordinance the citizen committee requested a special election that would put the question to the voters. In a May 1, 2021 special election with only the sanctuary city item on the ballot, 24 percent of registered voters turned out and the ordinance passed with 62.5 percent in favor.

***

In this chapter, I present results from a mathematical formalization of intensity theory.[1] I apply tools from game theory to analyze the dynamics of electoral competition when voters vary in how much they care about policy and when candidates do not know which voters care more and less intensely. I show that candidates for office choose policy platforms as a function of the size and intensity of opposing policy coalitions. Candidates sometimes set policy with an intense minority even though they know that a less-intense majority wants the opposite policy. But they also sometimes choose not to frustrate majorities even with an intense minority, as appears to have been the case surrounding the sanctuary city ordinance in Lubbock.

Why the mathematical formalization? Game theory disciplines analysis of the actions and outcomes of voters and candidates such that the conclusions I draw follow from reasoned choices by actors each pursuing

---

[1] Parts of this chapter are sourced from Hill (2022a), originally published by the University of Chicago Press and reprinted with permission.

their goals. We can be confident that the theory is logically consistent when using the mathematical model and that the results do not depend on actors making choices that contradict their interests or beliefs.

I present the mathematical analysis in Appendix A. Here, in Chapter 4, I summarize the setup and key results from that analysis with a minimum of mathematical notation. Readers can, I hope, feel more confident in the conclusions I draw knowing that they rest upon a formal mathematical analysis. I encourage interested readers to liberally consult the full presentation in Appendix A.

I present two results from the model that show how intensity theory can help us understand frustrated majorities. Each of these results is a game-theoretic *equilibrium*. An equilibrium describes a set of strategies and beliefs of candidates and voters such that no voter or candidate can do better by behaving differently given the actions and beliefs of the other voters and candidates. In two distinct equilibria I summarize in this chapter, high-intensity voters choose political action and expression of certain cost. Voters choose to take these actions and expressions despite the costs because candidates learn about voter intensity from the actions taken and expressions made. Candidates use what they learn about intensity to decide what policy platform to propose.

In each equilibrium, candidates propose policy with a high-intensity minority when candidates believe that minority cares enough about the policy relative to the majority. In a minority-only equilibrium (Section 4.4), only voters in the minority who also care intensely engage in costly political action, while voters in the majority always abstain from action. In a second equilibrium (Section 4.5), both minority and majority voters who care intensely take costly action to communicate to candidates (a separating equilibrium).

4.1 WHEN AND WHY CANDIDATES FRUSTRATE MAJORITIES

I start by showing when and why candidates choose to frustrate a majority by siding with a known minority of the electorate. To make the choice facing candidates as clear as possible, the first model considers a setting where candidates know both the policy position and the intensity of all voters. Because the election result is uncertain due to the idiosyncratic considerations of each voter, candidates sometimes side with an intense minority over a less intense majority because they can be more certain of winning the votes of the intense minority.

Because candidates know voter intensity and issue positions with certainty in this first model, we can be confident that siding with the minority is not due to candidate uncertainty about intensity or positions. I later remove the assumption that candidates know each voter's intensity to show that candidates still sometimes choose to side with the minority and to show how uncertainty about intensity leads voters who care intensely to incur costly political action.

See Section A.1 for the full analysis.

4.1.1 Model of Electoral Competition

I represent electoral competition with a mathematical model that builds from the presentation in Chapter 3. There are two candidates, A and B, and an electorate of three voters. Candidates seek to maximize votes at an election.

Voters care about a binary policy question, something like, "Should the city build a new library?" Two voters are on one side of the issue, say opposing the new library, while the third voter is on the other side, supporting the new library.

To focus on the consequences of differences in intensity, I assume the candidates A and B and all three voters know what each voter wants. That is, the majority and minority positions are clear to everyone. Note that this simplification does not mean I believe voters and candidates always know the policy positions of all voters. Instead, this allows me to show that candidates sometimes choose to side with the minority even though they are certain a majority of voters prefer a different policy.

In addition to their policy preference, voters vary in the intensity with which they care about the issue. One voter might believe the library should be built but might care more about other issues so that, when asked to vote in an election, whether the candidate advocates building the library is much less important to the voter than other issues. Another voter, however, might own the house across the street from the potential library site and, so, care deeply about the library issue. When asked to vote in an election, the choice of this voter might primarily depend upon the candidate positions on the library.

In this version of the model, candidates and voters each take one action. First, each candidate proposes a policy platform to the voters. In our library example, both candidates might propose to build the library, both candidates might propose to not build, or one candidate might propose building while the other does not. Candidates propose platforms prior to the election and all voters learn these proposals. This assumption allows me to rule out candidates siding with the minority because some or all voters do not know candidate platforms.

Second, the election is held and each voter decides which candidate to support based upon the policy platforms proposed plus idiosyncratic factors of the election. Other factors encompass a range of other inputs to vote choice from candidate traits to the weather on election day.

For voters who care intensely, candidate position on the library is more likely to dominate other factors in their choice. For less-intense voters, in contrast, other factors are more likely to dominate their choice than candidate position on the library. Both types of voter prefer a candidate who advocates their policy to one that does not, but for some voters the other factors might override candidate positions on the library issue.

4.1.2 Candidate Policy Proposals

Candidates know that each voter makes their choice as a function of policy platforms, the voter's policy preference and issue intensity, and the other factors. How should candidates who want to win votes decide what policy to propose?

The mathematical model shows that office-seeking candidates should side with the majority in most situations. When one or both of the majority voters cares about the issue as much as does the minority voter, candidates should side with the majority. If none of the voters care intensely about the issue, candidates should side with the majority.

If, however, the voter in the minority cares intensely about the issue while the voters of the majority care less intensely, candidates should sometimes side with the majority but sometimes with the minority. Candidates choose to side with the minority when the minority's vote choice is sufficiently more responsive to policy than is the majority's because they care sufficiently more intensely about the issue. We have already seen an example of candidates making this choice in Section 3.4. If the candidates expect the majority's vote is more influenced by other factors while the minority's vote is more influenced by policy, the candidates might prefer to frustrate the majority and side with the minority to be more certain about winning their vote.

When the balance of minority size and minority intensity falls in a specific range, candidates cater to the intense minority to minimize the chances of losing their votes. In these settings, being more certain about the votes of the minority is worth the risk of losing some votes from the majority. This risk is worthwhile because even when candidates propose policy with the minority, they can still sometimes win the votes of a less-intense majority.

Of course, just because the minority is intense does not mean they secure the policy they want. Sometimes the minority is either too small or does not care sufficiently more than the majority for candidates to take their side. This might be what happened in Lubbock, where the City Council did not believe siding with the intense minority would gain enough votes from the minority to offset the risk of losing votes from an opposing majority.

The mathematical model tells us exactly when candidates expect to win more votes siding with the minority (Lemma A.1). The best electoral strategy, for both candidates, is to side with the minority if, and only if, the intensity of the minority is greater than the sum of the intensities of the majority. In the case of a three-voter electorate, if the minority voter cares more than twice as much about the issue as the majority voters, the candidates expect to win more votes siding with the minority than they do siding with the majority.[2]

This result (Lemma A.1) is sufficiently important that I present an accessible version of it here in Lemma 4.1:

Lemma 4.1 (When to frustrate the majority). For both candidates, the best electoral strategy is to propose the policy preferred by the minority if, and only if, the intensity of the minority is greater than the sum of the intensities of the majority.

Proof See Appendix Section A.2. □

Lemmas 4.1 and A.1 are of central importance to the politics of issue intensity and representation. They show that candidates pursuing only votes – i.e., no personal preferences for policy or quid pro quo corruption – sometimes side with an intense minority over a less intense majority. Even when they know with certainty the size of the majority and the intensity of all voters, candidates still sometimes choose to frustrate majorities to win votes in elections.[3]

---

[2] Comparing the intensities of different voters at first glance seems to be an interpersonal comparison of utility, a problematic exercise. However, what the candidates really compare is the response of vote choice to policy. The vote choice maps individual voter preference orderings to a common choice scale.

[3] For interested readers, I provide numerical examples of Lemma A.1 in Appendix Section A.3.

As in other mathematical models of candidate competition (mean or median voter), in my simple model both candidates converge on the same policy position in equilibrium. As with other models, this convergence is due to a simplified electoral setting. Complicating the setting with additional inputs of real world politics can cause candidates to propose divergent platforms. Candidates sometimes propose different platforms, for example, when they have personal policy preferences (Calvert, 1985; Besley and Coate, 1997), when they have divergent beliefs about what the electorate wants (Dixit and Londregan, 1996), or when competition occurs across multiple policy dimensions without an obvious center to the distribution of preferences (McKelvey, 1976).

Adding any of these complications to induce incentives for divergence would not change the underlying electoral incentive for candidates with respect to intensity. All else equal, candidates who want to win votes will more often favor voters whose votes are most responsive to their policy platform. When voters most responsive are in the minority, candidates sometimes choose to side with the responsive minority and to frustrate the majority in pursuit of votes.

4.2 WHEN CANDIDATES DO NOT KNOW VOTER ISSUE INTENSITY

To this point, we have determined that candidates will side with a known minority if that minority cares sufficiently more than the majority about policy. What happens, though, if candidates are uncertain about the intensity of each voter? With uncertainty about intensity, would candidates be better off to just side with the majority? Or does uncertainty about intensity generate new and interesting dynamics of electoral competition and policy? In this section, I add to the mathematical model the second feature of intensity theory, that intensity of preference is difficult to observe.

4.2.1 When Intensity Unknown, Candidate Beliefs about Intensity Determine Policy

How do the candidates approach their policy platform choice when they are uncertain – for whatever reason – about the intensity of each voter? Candidates who care to win votes make use of whatever information they have in making a policy platform. I show in Lemma A.3 that candidates do best in pursuit of their goals by applying the same policy rule used were they to know voter intensity with certainty (the rule of Lemmas 4.1 and A.1). When uncertain about intensity, candidates' best electoral strategy is to use their best guess of each voter's intensity and proceed as if accurate.

If candidates *believe* that the minority voter's intensity is greater than the sum of the intensities of the majority voters, they frustrate the majority and propose policy with the minority. If candidates *believe* that the minority voter's intensity is less than the sum of the intensities of the majority, they propose policy with the majority.

4.2.2 Because Candidate Beliefs about Intensity Determine Policy, Even Voters Who Care Modestly Want Candidates to Believe They Care Intensely

Because candidates select policy based upon their beliefs about the intensity of each voter, voters who care about an issue even to a modest degree prefer that candidates *believe* that they care intensely. I show in Lemma A.4 that both majority and minority voters prefer that candidates believe they care intensely even if they care only modestly. Because voters who care modestly still prefer candidates who propose policy with their preference to candidates who propose policy against their preference, and because candidates are weakly more likely to propose policy with voters who care intensely than with voters who care modestly, each individual voter prefers that candidates believe they care intensely when they only care modestly.

This result shows that voters who care modestly might want to obfuscate when asked how much they care about policy. It also shows that candidates cannot necessarily learn how much voters care through an instrument used to measure intensity that is subject to obfuscation.

4.2.3 Candidates Uncertain about Intensity

Because candidates propose policy based upon their beliefs about the intensities of each voter (Section 4.2.1) and because voters who care modestly prefer, all else equal, candidates deceived into thinking they actually care intensely (Section 4.2.2), when candidates do not know intensity, voters who care intensely want to convince candidates that they really do care intensely and that those who care modestly really do not care intensely. In this section, I extend the model to incorporate actions available for high-intensity voters to convince candidates how much they care and, equivalently, how much less others care.

To model the consequences of unobserved intensity, I modify the mathematical model so that each voter's intensity is known only to the voter themself (see Appendix Section A.4). Each voter knows how much they personally care about the issue but does not know how much others care. Neither candidate knows how much any voter cares.

For simplicity, in the model both candidates and all voters share a common prior belief that any individual voter cares intensely. Assuming that all actors hold the same prior belief does not reflect my belief about real world politics. Instead, this assumption allows me to show that frustrated majorities and costly political action do not require that candidates or voters act under different beliefs about the political world.

I also modify the mathematical model to allow voters to choose to take costly political actions in the tradition of game-theoretic models of costly signaling (e.g., Jervis, 1970; Spence, 1973). These costly actions have two important features. First, candidates observe the costly actions taken by voters so that the candidates know the costs incurred by each voter. Second, actions have certain immediate costs but uncertain future benefits. That is, voters are sure that taking the action will cost them time or money, but are not sure whether or not that action will lead to the future benefits they hope it might cause.

Because of these two features, costly political actions and expressions can be used by intense voters to communicate how much they care about policy. Similar to the example in Section 3.2, only voters who care intensely would be willing to incur costs greater than the value low-intensity voters ascribe to policy. Those who incur costs of a sufficiently large magnitude can only be voters who care intensely. Thus, candidates who observe some voters incurring such costs know that (at least) these voters must care intensely about the issue.

4.3 EQUILIBRIUM RESULTS OF THE MATHEMATICAL MODEL

Analysis of the mathematical model with intensity unknown leads to two key results. Each of these results is an *equilibrium*. An equilibrium describes a set of strategies and beliefs of candidates and voters such that no voter or candidate can do better by behaving differently given the actions and beliefs of the other voters and candidates. Voter strategies describe the actions voters would take depending on whether they were in the majority or minority and whether they cared more or less intensely. Candidate strategies describe the platforms candidates would propose given their beliefs about how much each voter cares about policy.

Candidate beliefs describe the inferences candidates draw about the intensity of each voter after observing which voters take what magnitude of costly political action and expression.

I describe two equilibria of political interest. Because they are equilibria of the mathematical model, we can feel confident they depend only upon the electoral competition between candidates and the costly actions and intensities of voters. This is not to say other factors might not also generate frustrated majorities. But we can say that when voters pursue policy representation and candidates pursue only votes from voters, and when they both know with certainty the size of the majority and minority, it is sometimes in the best interest of all actors for some voters to incur costly political actions of uncertain benefit and for candidates to sometimes side with a minority against a known majority.

The first result presents an equilibrium where only minority voters choose to take costly political action and only when they care intensely. In the first equilibrium, majority voters always abstain from action and minority voters who care only modestly abstain from action. In this equilibrium, candidates propose policy with the minority only when the minority takes action.[4]

The second result presents an equilibrium where both minority and majority voters, when they care intensely, choose to take costly political action. Minority and majority voters who care only modestly abstain from action. In this equilibrium, candidates propose policy with the minority when the minority takes action and the majority abstains, propose policy with the majority if the majority takes action, and propose policy with the majority if no voter takes costly action.

4.4 MINORITY VOTERS WHO CARE INTENSELY TAKE COSTLY ACTION

The first analysis presents an equilibrium where a high-intensity minority communicates preferences through costly political action, while both low- and high-intensity majority voters abstain from action (see Proposition A.1 in Appendix Section A.5). In this equilibrium, candidates propose policy with the minority when the minority chooses costly action and

---

4 Both equilibria are technically continua of equilibria. I present them in the singular to distinguish each individual result from the set of two. One could also apply an equilibrium refinement to characterize two unique equilibria, as in Hill (2022a).

TABLE 4.1. *Policy proposal by minority political action in first equilibrium*

		Majority No action
Minority	Costly action	Policy with minority (Frustrated majority)
	No action	Policy with majority

Note: Majority always abstains from taking action.

propose policy with the majority when the minority abstains from action. When the low-intensity minority voter chooses costly political actions and expressions, this communicates to candidates that he or she cares intensely about the policy. When candidates believe the minority cares intensely and the majority does not, vote-seeking candidates choose to frustrate the majority. I summarize this equilibrium in Table 4.1.

The intuition for the first equilibrium is that the minority can only gain policy representation by convincing the candidates that they care intensely. They choose to convince the candidates by taking costly political action when the benefits to obtaining representation times the probability that the action leads candidates to side with the minority outweigh the certain costs of taking action.

Only when the candidates believe that the majority is not too likely to be high-intensity does a minority-only equilibrium hold. If the candidates were to believe that the majority almost certainly cares intensely about the policy, even if the minority were to take costly action to convince candidates they care intensely the candidates would still side with the majority; they believe the majority is almost certain to care intensely. Only if the candidates believe there is a good enough chance the majority does not care intensely would they choose to side with the minority.

Three results from Proposition A.1 are important for our understanding of politics. First, in this equilibrium only voters who both care intensely and are on the minority side of the issue choose to engage in costly political action. Voters in the majority benefit enough without action, on average, to make undesirable the costs of action. In such an equilibrium, society would observe costly political action taken only by intense members of policy minorities, while voters in the majority would abstain from political action. The politics of firearm regulation in the United States, discussed in Chapter 7, might be an example of this kind of equilibrium.

Second, this equilibrium is only supported when the prior belief that any individual voter cares intensely is relatively low. Candidate beliefs that voters care intensely absent observing costly political action must be lower than $1 - \sqrt{2}/2$ (Proposition A.1) – about 0.3. Candidates and voters must believe that intensity is relatively uncommon on the issue to support an equilibrium where only minority voters incur the costs of political action.

Third, the magnitude of costs required of the minority voter is relatively high. The costs must be large enough to keep a high-intensity majority voter from choosing to take action. The high-intensity majority voter in this equilibrium decides they would rather take the risk that the minority takes action and they lose out on policy – which is a probability less than 0.3 – than incur certain costs of action in exchange for certain representation. Majority voters know that because the probability this minority cares intensely is somewhat low, there is a reasonable probability they will get majority policy without taking action. Because of this, the equilibrium requires greater costs incurred by the intense minority voter than in the second equilibrium below.

The minority-only equilibrium highlights a need to clarify the meaning of "frustrated." Because the majority would be worse off, in expectation, by engaging in costly action at this magnitude to obtain their policy preference, if policy ends up against their preference they should not be "frustrated" in the sense of angry or upset. They abstained from action knowing there was some possibility they would not get what they want. Rather, the majority has been frustrated – prevented – from gaining representation because of the costly actions of the minority. The majority would not act differently if they were confronted with the same choice again.

4.5 MAJORITY VOTERS SOMETIMES TAKE COSTLY ACTION TO PREVENT MINORITY POLICY

In the first equilibrium, only voters in the minority choose to take costly political action. Members of the majority – even if they care intensely about the issue – always abstain from action. The mathematical model identifies a second equilibrium, however, where majority voters join the minority in choosing costly action when they care intensely about the issue (see Appendix Section A.6).

Unlike voters in the minority, voters in the majority sometimes get what they want even if they abstain. This makes them less interested than voters in the minority to engage in costly action, all else equal. In the second

TABLE 4.2. *Policy proposals by combination of majority and minority political action in equilibrium*

| | | Majority | |
		Costly action	No action
Minority	Costly action	Policy with majority	Policy with minority (Frustrated majority)
	No action	Policy with majority	Policy with majority

equilibrium, however, voters in the majority who do care intensely choose to incur costly action to secure their policy preference.

In this second equilibrium, each voter chooses to incur costly political action when high-intensity and to abstain when low-intensity. Costly action, when taken either by voters in the minority or voters in the majority, communicates to candidates which voters care intensely. After observing which voters take action, candidates propose policy platforms. They frustrate the majority and propose policy with the minority if, and only if, voters in the majority abstain and voters in the minority take action. I present the mathematical result in Proposition A.2 and summarize in Table 4.2.

There are two differences between the political settings of the first and the second equilibrium that lead to the majority choosing to take action in the second. First is the prior belief a voter cares intensely. In order for voters in the majority to choose to take costly action, the second equilibrium requires that the prior belief that any voter cares intensely be middling. The candidates should be neither nearly certain that no one cares intensely – a prior belief that intensity is rare – nor nearly certain that everyone cares intensely – a prior belief that intensity is common.

When the prior belief is middling, the combination of intensities where the majority does not get what it wants is more likely to occur: the minority cares intensely and the majority does not. Because the candidates believe this combination more likely when the prior belief is middling, voters in the majority, when they care intensely, decide to take action to make sure they get the policy they want.

Second, the magnitude of costly action taken by high-intensity voters is lower in the second equilibrium than in the first. A lower magnitude of costly action makes it more worthwhile for intense majority voters to incur costs even though there is some chance they could secure policy were they to abstain from action.

The second equilibrium holds three results important to the under-standing of politics. First, in this equilibrium, voters who care intensely on both sides of the issue choose to take action to communicate to candidates. In such a setting, we would observe voters of both the majority and the minority sometimes taking action to inform candidates how much they care about the issue. This means that, in some settings, even voters who know they are in the majority on the issue know they might not secure the policy that they want unless they engage with politics. One setting that might be consistent with this equilibrium is the politics of abortion in the United States, where both sides of the issue include many activists taking costly political action (e.g., Luker, 1985).

Second, the equilibrium is supported under a much wider range of prior beliefs about the rate voters care intensely on the issue. The first equilibrium holds only when candidates believe intensity is rather uncommon. The second equilibrium holds at a range of beliefs in between very uncommon and very common. Further, the mathematical results shows that this range is increasing in the magnitude of intensity. The more the policy influences the vote choice for those who care intensely, the more likely the second equilibrium holds.

Third, the costliness of the action required for voters who care intensely to convince candidates of their intensity is strictly less in the second equilibrium than in the first (see Appendix Section A.7). When we see more voters taking action, those voters who do take action incur lower costs than the minority voters who choose to take action in the first equilibrium. This provides an empirical prediction that the more voters that take action on an issue, the lower the costliness of those actions. The fewer voters that take action on an issue, the higher the costliness of those actions.

4.6 WHICH EQUILIBRIUM?

The mathematical model identifies two equilibria of political interest. In one, only an intense minority chooses to incur costly political action. In the other, both intense minorities and intense majorities choose to incur costs. What political conditions might lead us to one equilibrium instead of the other?

How settings of strategic interaction settle on one versus another equilibrium is the subject of extensive academic debate in economic theory. But some clues as to the political conditions that might be relevant to these two equilibria can be inferred from the results of the mathematical model.

First, the minority-only equilibrium requires a lower prior belief that voters care intensely about an issue. Suppose a new political issue enters the arena of electoral competition due to technological or economic change. If the issue only affects a small number of voters, then the common belief would be that relatively few voters care intensely about the issue. For example, imagine a new technology displaced an industry that employed only a small percentage of the population. This might lead to the first equilibrium because of the prior belief that few voters would care intensely about the technology.

If, on the other hand, the new issue immediately affected many voters across the population, then the prior belief could be that relatively more voters care intensely about the issue. Imagine a world war or an economic depression. This could lead to the second equilibrium because the prior belief about intensity is too large to support the first equilibrium.

Second, the first equilibrium requires that minority voters incur higher costs than does the second (Appendix Section A.7). If the first group of voters to take action on the new issue chose to incur a lower magnitude of costly political action, this magnitude might be consistent only with the second equilibrium. Imagine that the first action involves writing letters to members of Congress about the issue in contrast to more costly violent insurrection or large campaign contributions.

The mathematical model does not allow me to say how a political setting evolves into one or the other equilibria. It also makes assumptions about common knowledge about the magnitude of intensity and the common beliefs about rates of intensity in the population. Future work might relax these assumptions or find empirical evidence to help us understand which equilibrium arises in settings with different political contexts.

4.7 EXPRESSIVE POLITICAL ACTION AND THE MATHEMATICAL MODEL

I have argued that voters choose to take costly political action when the immediate costs of action are outweighed by the potential – i.e., uncertain – benefits of taking action. This instrumentally rational interpretation of voter behavior differs from the standard interpretation of costly political action in political science. The standard interpretation is that voters gain expressive benefit – i.e., valuing the act itself rather than the consequences of the act – from engaging in politics. Readers might consider examples in popular textbooks such as Kernell et al. (2019, p. 573), Fiorina et al. (2011, p. 175), or Ansolabehere et al. (2018, p. 568). In this expressive telling, voters might feel it a duty to participate in politics, might enjoy engaging in politics as entertainment, or might feel social pressure to participate from family and friends. Expressive benefits generate political action through a different pathway than do instrumental considerations.

However, expressive political action might still communicate to candidates interested in understanding intensity. Because voters have limited time and limited resources, it is reasonable to assume they choose actions that provide the greatest expressive benefit. Presumably, the greatest expressive benefit follows from the issues about which they care most intensely. If they are taking action at personal cost, the action might very well correlate with intensity. Expressive motivations might generate a similar pattern of communication, learning, and influence on candidate platforms as do instrumental motivations.

4.8 SUMMARY OF MODEL RESULTS

This chapter has presented results from a mathematical formalization of intensity theory. The game-theoretic models yield two key results.

First, candidates for office who aim to maximize votes at an election sometimes side with an intense minority over a less-intense majority. Candidates set policy with that minority when the minority's votes are sufficiently more responsive to policy. When the minority's votes are sufficiently more responsive to policy, candidates expect to gain more votes by siding with the minority than by siding with the majority and so choose to frustrate the majority. In the next chapter, I use the mathematical model to characterize "sufficiently" as a function of the size of the minority.

> **Issue intensity and electoral competition lead candidates to frustrate majorities.**

This result explains why politicians choose to sometimes side with intense minorities, such as in 2013 when President Obama made the case for firearm regulations in the United States. Candidates expect to win more votes siding with intense opponents of regulations than they expect to lose among less-intense supporters of regulations whose votes are more determined by other factors. As I'll show in Chapter 5, even a small minority, if sufficiently intense, can frustrate a large majority.

Second, when candidates are uncertain about the intensity of voters, high-intensity voters sometimes choose costly political action to communicate their intensity. These voters have an incentive to incur certain costs with uncertain future benefits because doing so sometimes leads the candidates to side with the intense voters when they would not have otherwise.

When candidates do not know voter intensity, voters who care intensely about policy sometimes choose to take costly political action.

In a first equilibrium, only minority voters who care intensely choose to incur costly action in pursuit of policy benefits. In a second equilibrium, both minority and majority voters who care intensely choose action. The mathematical model has allowed me to characterize when voters choose to take action as a function of the magnitude of intensity of high-intensity voters, the magnitude of costly action taken, and candidate prior beliefs about intensity in the electorate.

The two equilibria of the mathematical model connect to President Obama's focus on candidate *beliefs* about intensity (page 47). When politicians do not know exactly who cares intensely about a policy, it is risky for them to side with a minority over a majority. But when members of that minority take costly actions – as do advocates of gun rights in Obama's telling – candidates are convinced they can expect to win more votes than they lose by siding with the minority.

The mathematical model results I have presented in this chapter support the qualitative presentation of intensity theory in earlier chapters. The model shows the theory is logically consistent with voters and candidates strategically pursuing their interests. Candidates frustrate majorities because of electoral competition, differences in issue intensity, and beliefs about intensity determined by differences in costly political action.

5

Model Extensions

Varying Size of the Minority, the Free-Rider Problem, and Social Welfare

Democratic laws generally tend to promote the welfare of the greatest possible number; for they emanate from the majority. (Chapter XIV)

If it be admitted that a man, possessing absolute power, may misuse that power by wronging his adversaries, why should a majority not be liable to the same reproach? (Chapter XV)

Alexis de Tocqueville (1835 [2013]), *Democracy in America*

In this chapter, I explore three extensions to the mathematical model presented in Chapter 4. As with Chapter 4, I leave mathematical details to an appendix (Appendix B) and present in the chapter the setup and key results.[1]

In Chapter 4, I considered a simplified electorate of three voters. Assuming an electorate of three voters fixes the ratio of majority to minority at two to one and, so, skeptical readers might wonder if results depend upon an electorate of exactly this balance.

In Section 5.1, I show that the results do not depend upon such a ratio. Instead, at any ratio of majority to minority size, candidates might side with an intense minority over a less-intense majority. Candidates do not side with any intense minority, only with those of a sufficient combination of size and intensity. Siding with the minority requires an increasing ratio of minority to majority intensity as the size of the minority decreases.

---

[1] Parts of this chapter are sourced from Hill (2022a), originally published by the University of Chicago Press. Reprinted with permission.

Second, I consider the free-rider problem. In a three-voter electorate, any individual voter can realistically believe they might be pivotal in determining the election outcome. They are, thus, each individually influential on the policy platforms of the candidates. I make a similar assumption in my analysis of the arbitrarily-sized electorate.

The free-rider problem, however, challenges inferences about how rational voters might behave when each voter is one of thousands or even millions (e.g., Olson, 1965). In large electorates, individual contribution to the election result is so small that the costs to an individual of voting in the election are unlikely to be offset by expected influence on the outcome. The benefits to political participation in general decline with the size of the electorate and, so, are less likely to outweigh the costs of participation (e.g., Downs, 1957). As such, the free-rider problem challenges the model results that voters would choose to incur costly political action as communication. It is important to note, however, that the free-rider problem does not challenge candidate incentives to frustrate majorities.

In Section 5.2, I discuss a modification to the mathematical model, following Lohmann (1993), where increasing the size of the electorate does not prevent some voters from choosing to incur costly political action. An alternative solution to the free-rider problem is to assume that political participation is expressive and that voters take action in politics only because they care intensely about issues rather than because they care intensely and they hope to use their action to communicate how much they care (see Section 4.7).

Third, I consider the social welfare implications of intensity theory. Two consequences of the results I presented in Chapter 4 are relevant to whether issue intensity and costly action are good for representative democracies. First, candidates sometimes choose to frustrate majorities. Majorities are strictly worse off with respect to policy representation relative to simple majority rule. Second, voters sometimes choose to incur costly political actions of certain cost and uncertain benefit. Sometimes these costs will not be outweighed by the benefits such that voters are worse off than had they been in a setting without costly action.

I describe the conditions where costly political action improves social welfare over a setting without the opportunity for communication of intensity. When the minority cares more deeply about policy than the majority, costly political action causes candidates to sometimes propose minority policy against the known preferences of the majority.

When intensity for policy is sufficiently strong, utilitarian social welfare is improved because expected benefits to the minority of sometimes gaining non-majoritarian policy are greater than expected losses to the sometimes frustrated majority.

5.1 VARYING THE SIZE OF THE MINORITY

A skeptical reader might wonder if the results of Chapter 4 depend on the simple three-voter election. What if the minority were extremely small? At the other extreme, would the candidates more often side with the minority if it were large, say, just less than half of the electorate?

In this section, I summarize results of extending the model to examine the effect of varying the size of the minority relative to the majority (see Appendix Section B.1 for the mathematical analysis). I find that, at any size of minority, candidates choose to side with the minority when the minority's preferences are sufficiently intense relative to the intensity of the majority.

The model again has two vote-seeking candidates but, instead of an electorate of three voters, the electorate is of arbitrary large size, removing the assumption of one minority voter and two majority voters. With the large-size electorate, I specify the size of the minority with the fraction p. The majority is size $1 - p$. When p is small, there are very few minority voters relative to the majority. As p approaches one half, the majority and minority are nearly the same size. As before, all voters and candidates know the size and policy view of minority and majority.

I allow each voter to have their own intensity. Some majority voters might care more intensely and others less intensely. Likewise, some minority voters might care more intensely and others less.

With an arbitrary number of voters, candidates want to know the average intensity of the majority and the average intensity of the minority. These averages tell candidates how they can expect their vote share to respond to policy proposals.

The mathematical model in Appendix Section B.1 shows that candidates side with the minority, as they did in the three-voter model, if, and only if, the minority is sufficiently more intense than the majority. In this case, "sufficiently more intense" depends upon the size of the minority. The math shows that candidates side with the minority if the ratio of the minority's intensity to the majority's intensity is greater than or equal to the ratio of the minority size to the majority size.

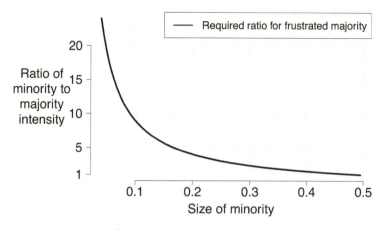

FIGURE 5.1 Intensity of minority must increase as size of minority decreases

The mathematical result is a bit complicated, but the intuition is straightforward. In order for the candidates to frustrate the majority when the minority is small, the minority's intensity must be much greater than that of the majority. Candidates wouldn't side with a small minority that only cares a little more than the majority. When the minority is almost as large as the majority, however, candidates would side with the large minority if they cared only a bit more than the majority.

To secure policy representation, and to frustrate majorities, the minority must be a large enough combination of size and intensity. The smaller the size, the greater the intensity, the larger the size, the lesser the intensity.

The mathematical results allow me to plot the relationship between minority size and average intensity necessary to frustrate majority policy, as shown in Figure 5.1. The x-axis measures the size of the minority from 1/25th of the electorate at the left to a bare minority of just less than one half of the electorate at the right. The y-axis measures the ratio of the average intensity of the minority to the average intensity of the majority. The solid line represents the minimum ratio of intensities to support frustrated majorities at each size of minority. At ratios lower than the height of this line above the corresponding size of the minority on the x-axis, the candidates do not propose policy with a high-intensity minority over a low-intensity majority. The minority must be sufficiently more intense – at or above the solid line – if candidates are to set policy that frustrates majorities.

The ratio of the minority's intensity to the majority's intensity must be greater than the ratio of the majority size to the minority size. For example, if the minority comprises 25 percent of the electorate, they must feel three times as intensely as the majority for the candidates to propose policy with the minority in equilibrium (the solid line is at the height of 3 on the y-axis above p = 0.25). The intuition is that the smaller the minority, the fewer votes they represent for candidates. The fewer votes they represent, the more certain candidates want to be that setting policy with the minority will not be counteracted by other factors that influence vote choice. Certainty of winning the minority's votes increases in the intensity of that minority.

In Appendix Section B.2, I use the extension of the mathematical model with a minority of arbitrary size and show that the two equilibria of Chapter 4 do not depend on a three-voter model. Instead, the dynamics that generate both equilibria hold with both small and large minorities, as long as the magnitude of intensity follows that presented in Figure 5.1.

* * *

The model with arbitrary minority size delivers the same result as a three-voter model. Candidates propose policy with the minority when intensity of the minority is sufficiently greater than that of the majority. Sufficiency depends on the size of the minority; a smaller minority requires greater intensity to secure policy representation. The two equilibria of Chapter 4 also hold with minorities of different sizes.

5.2 FREE-RIDER PROBLEM

Even when individuals share a collective goal, they do not necessarily join groups and exert effort in pursuit of that goal. Because a collective good is provided to all individuals regardless of the contribution each provides for its production, individuals have an incentive to avoid incurring costs of the collective effort. This is sometimes called a "free-rider" problem because individuals want to gain a free ride off the efforts of others.

Unless the group is small or the group provides other selective benefits that individuals desire, Olson (1965) argues that individuals will not rationally contribute their efforts to a large group. Olson (1965, p. 133) goes so far as to argue that costly action by individual members of large groups is only a "by-product" of groupings created for other purposes.

The free-rider problem is a challenge in large electorates and, therefore, the results of intensity theory on costly political action. Once an electorate becomes large, each individual voter's costly political action only communicates their own individual intensity. Because vote share responds infinitesimally to each individual voter, candidate response to the knowledge about individual intensity gained from the voter's choice of costly action is, likewise, infinitesimal. The potential benefits to these actions, therefore, might be highly unlikely to outweigh the certain costs, and an instrumentally rational voter would, therefore, be highly unlikely to incur the costs.

In the models above, costly political actions of minority voters are pivotal when the majority is low-intensity because there are three voters. In a large electorate, however, voters must consider abstaining from action, even if high-intensity, because the likely influence of their individual action on beliefs of the candidates, and, therefore, the policy platforms of the candidates, is minuscule. Even if we were comfortable assuming politicians had the acuity to observe the costly political actions chosen by every voter in a large electorate, the magnitude of cost taken by a high-intensity voter would be very small given their likelihood of being pivotal to platform choice.

5.2.1 The Lohmann Model

The model of Lohmann (1993) provides an explanation for costly political action in settings with large numbers of actors and also offers important connections to how I think about costly signaling about intensity. Her approach helps me suggest how intensity theory might extend beyond a three-voter electorate.

The Lohmann (1993) model is an early version of what is now considered a class of game-theoretic models called global games. Lohmann (1993) develops a signaling model of costly political action in a setting with a large number of citizens each deciding whether or not to take action. A useful working example is thinking about citizens in an autocratic state trying to decide whether or not to revolt against the autocrat. If the citizens dissatisfied with the regime knew there were many others who were similarly dissatisfied, they would be more likely to revolt. If, on the other hand, they knew few others shared their dissatisfaction, they would abstain from revolting because they would end up dead or in jail after participating in an unsuccessful revolt.

In her model, each citizen has a level of dissatisfaction based upon their experience under the regime. Some are relatively satisfied because they are favored by the autocrat. Others are relatively dissatisfied because they are repressed by the autocrat. No individual knows whether or not their individual satisfaction or dissatisfaction is typical, but they know the average level of dissatisfaction is somewhere in a range. Dissatisfaction cannot be too low because, if too low, the autocrat would not engage in repression. Dissatisfaction also cannot be too high because, if too high, the citizenry would be in revolt despite the autocrat's repression.

Because each citizen knows they share social and economic experiences with other citizens, they know their own dissatisfaction is related to (correlated with) the dissatisfaction of the rest of the population. This correlation means that their own dissatisfaction provides some information about the average level of dissatisfaction in the population. When a citizen is personally dissatisfied, they believe it more likely than not that the average dissatisfaction is high. On the other hand, when a citizen is personally satisfied, they believe it more likely than not that the average dissatisfaction is low.

In the Lohmann (1993) model, citizens with sufficient dissatisfaction choose to engage in costly political protests to communicate to the autocrat. The autocrat observes the number who choose to engage in protest and, if enough engage in protest, concludes that dissatisfaction is high enough that a revolt is likely if they do not take ameliorative action. If too few protest, the autocrat learns that dissatisfaction is low and so can continue to rule unreformed.

The key insight in the Lohmann (1993) model is that individual actions have extra power. Because, crucially, dissatisfaction is correlated across individuals, when one individual chooses to take action they are not only providing information about their own dissatisfaction but about the dissatisfaction of many others. This means an individual's costly action can be pivotal, not because their individual costly action overthrows the autocrat but rather because their individual costly action communicates important information to the autocrat about the rest of the citizenry.

It is not that the protestor chooses to light a torch because they believe the torch will be the one that burns down the palace. Rather, the protester choosing to light a torch tells the palace that many citizens are dissatisfied and that the king better do something.

A similar dynamic could be applied in the setting of intensity theory. Imagine that each individual voter has their own intensity but that intensities are correlated within policy preference type. That is, voters holding the minority view on the issue have similar intensities, on average, and voters holding the majority view on the issue have similar intensities, on average. These two averages can diverge.

As an example, consider the policy of regulating abortion. Part of the population believes government should increase regulations to decrease access to abortion, while another part believes government should decrease regulation. Candidates would like to know which side cares more intensely about government regulation of abortion. If only voters who care strongly about abortion policy – on both sides of the issue – choose to incur costly political action, candidates for office can observe how many voters of each type engage in action. They can then use these counts to form beliefs about the average intensity of those who want to regulate versus deregulate access to abortion. Because each individual activist stands in place for other voters with correlated intensities, the actions of the activists can be pivotal to the candidates' beliefs about population-level intensities.

Candidates need to know three parameter values to determine policy best responses with an arbitrarily-sized electorate (Lemma B.1). Candidates must know the size of the minority, the average intensity of the minority, and the average intensity of the majority.

Members of the minority would like candidates to believe the average intensity of the minority is large to increase the chances that the candidates propose policy with the minority. Likewise, members of the majority would like candidates to believe the average intensity of the majority is large to increase the chances that the candidates propose policy with the majority.

When everyone believes that individual intensities are correlated within each policy type, each individual's knowledge of their own intensity is informative about the intensity of other members of their policy type. If I am a member of the minority and my private intensity is high, it is more likely that others in the minority care more rather than less intensely about the issue. If I am a member of the majority and my private intensity is modest, it is more likely that others in the majority care less rather than more intensely about the issue.

Applying the Lohmann (1993, Proposition 2) proof to this extension of my model indicates that there exist cutpoint values of intensity for each policy type. Voters with intensities greater than the cutpoint of their policy type choose to take costly political action. Those with intensities less than the cutpoint abstain. Voters follow the cutpoint rule because intensities above the cutpoint are large enough to suggest that the average intensity of their policy type is sufficiently large to be worth communicating to the candidates.

Voters who choose to take action, therefore, have intensity above the cutpoint, and voters who abstain have intensity below the cutpoint. Candidates, knowing of this action rule, infer from the count of voters taking action how many have intensities above and below the cutpoint, and thus the average intensity of voters with that policy view.

Candidates use the number of majority voters taking action and the number of minority voters taking action to draw inferences about the average intensity of the majority and minority. If the number of voters taking action generates beliefs consistent with the requirements of Lemma B.1, candidates propose policy with the sufficiently intense minority over the insufficiently intense majority. If not, candidates propose policy with the majority.

Importantly, even with a large electorate, intense members of the majority and the minority choose to take costly action in equilibrium. Sometimes these intense voters take action even though their policy type is insufficiently intense. They do not know before taking action that their intensity is too unusual to induce representation. They still incur costs in equilibrium, however, because they expect to benefit on average from following the cutpoint strategy.

* * *

This extension of the model leads to three important conclusions.

First, some voters choose to take costly action while others do not. This is true even among voters with the same policy view and with correlated intensities. Taking action depends on whether the voter's intensity is above or below a threshold value. This threshold value depends upon the size of the minority on the issue and prior beliefs about the incidence of intensity.

Second, some voters take costly action even though it does not generate policy success. The activists do not know the intensity of other voters but, because their intensity is sufficiently high, they know they expect to be on average better off taking costly action even though it might not lead to their desired outcome. In other words, many voters incur costs in pursuit of "lost causes" because, while they care intensely about the issue, the remainder of voters who share their views are insufficiently intense to secure desired policy.

Third, despite free-rider problems, policy is sometimes proposed with an intense minority over a less-intense majority. The cutpoint decision rule for taking action means that voters with intensity above the cutpoint have a non-zero probability of being pivotal in determining candidate beliefs.

When voters follow this decision rule, candidates learn the intensities of minority and majority. When the minority is sufficiently large and has sufficiently high average intensity, candidates choose to frustrate the majority following the same incentives as in the three-voter model.

5.3 COSTLY POLITICAL ACTION, FRUSTRATED MAJORITIES, AND UTILITARIAN WELFARE

In this section, I summarize analysis from the mathematical model that shows frustrated majorities and costly political action can increase social welfare. While the majority is strictly worse off than in a setting where policy is always set with the majority, when candidates sometimes side with an intense minority – but still sometimes side with an intense or less-intense majority – the expected gains to the minority are greater than the expected losses to the majority. This increase in welfare only occurs when those who care intensely about the policy issue care much more than those who care only modestly.

It is important to highlight that this welfare analysis takes a utilitarian perspective that readers might not agree with. The mathematical analysis should not be taken as definitive evidence that intense minorities and frustrated majorities are a normatively good thing. Different people have different values about how to trade off gains for some against losses for others. The utilitarian approach is only one way to value these trade-offs. Other approaches might not conclude minority representation as I describe it is, on balance, to the general good.

I present the full welfare analysis in Appendix Section B.4. As in all of the mathematical models, voter benefit from policy depends upon their policy preference and their intensity for policy. I define the voter's total welfare as their benefit to policy less any costs incurred from political action. If they incur action and obtain the policy they want, their total welfare is benefit from policy minus costs to action. If they incur action and do not obtain the policy they want, their total welfare is zero minus the costs to action.

Social welfare is the sum of each voter's total welfare. Thus, social welfare depends on what policy the candidates propose, which voters care more and less intensely about the issue, and which voters choose to incur costly political action.

I compare the expected value of social welfare between two settings of policy choice. In both settings, electoral competition determines policy, as in the model presented above. In Setting 1, candidate strategies are independent of voter actions and voter strategies are independent of voter intensity. Candidates choose policy based only on ex ante beliefs about intensity among voters. Setting 2 analyzes welfare under the second equilibrium of Chapter 4 (Proposition A.2).

I show in Proposition B.1 that, in the three-voter electorate, social welfare is higher than majority rule when voters who care intensely value policy at least five times more than voters who value policy only modestly. If this ratio is at least five, social welfare is, on average, greater than under majority rule.

How can social welfare be higher when the majority is strictly worse off? The minority benefits if it can communicate intensity through costly action because under majority rule the minority never attains preferred policy. Expected welfare for the majority, however, is strictly lower in the equilibrium with costly action. The majority loses in the second setting through two channels. First, majority voters must sometimes take costly political action when high-intensity, costs they need not incur in the majority-rule setting. Second, candidates sometimes propose policy with the minority.

When those who care intensely care five times more about policy than those who care modestly, however, expected losses to the majority are outweighed by expected gains to the minority. The integer 5 here does not have inherent meaning. It is, instead, related to the size of the minority. The key point is that only when intense voters care much more about the issue than the less-intense is social welfare higher, on average, in a setting where voters communicate their intensity through costly political action.

5.4 WEALTH, RESOURCES, PARTICIPATION, AND WELFARE

One claim about political participation due to Schattschneider (1960) and others is that participation in politics is more common among those with higher socio-economic status. This is clearly the case for campaign donations, which require sufficient disposable wealth. Wealth and education also correlate with other forms of participation (Verba, Schlozman, and Brady, 1995; Leighley and Nagler, 2014).

Readers might be concerned that the welfare of the well-resourced is favored by this analysis because the model and welfare analysis do not differentiate the resources available to different voters. This concern, however, need not undermine the result. The communication value of costly action depends upon the net cost of action to the individual voter. If two voters incur different costs from the same action, then the two voters would have to choose different actions to incur the same magnitude of cost. A campaign contribution from a wealthy voter is likely to be less costly to that voter than a contribution of the same size from a voter living paycheck to paycheck.

The well-resourced have to take more costly political action – more contributions, more volunteering – to incur the same net cost as the less-resourced. In fact, this is the argument of Gause (2022): low-resource groups benefit from protests as costly communication more than high-resource groups due to higher relative costs.

* * *

I began the chapter showing that frustrated majorities do not depend upon an election with only three voters. Frustrated majorities can arise with minorities of varying size from very small to near majorities. The mathematical model shows that the smaller the minority, the more the minority must care about the issue to induce the candidates to frustrate the majority. There is no minority size, however, that theoretically precludes a frustrated majority. The ratios of intensity required for incredibly small minorities to motivate candidates to frustrate majorities, however, do seem unlikely to obtain in practice.

I then showed how free-rider problems in large electorates can be made consistent with incentives and strategic considerations facing voters and candidates in the model of Chapter 4. Applying a global-games model to the dynamics of intensity theory similar to that of Lohmann (1993) allows for an arbitrarily large increase in the number of voters without qualitative change to the incentives for intense voters to engage in costly political action.

I have also shown that frustrated majorities and costly political action can sometimes improve utilitarian social welfare over a setting of majority rule. This improvement does not hold at any intensity, only when intensity is notably strong.

EVIDENCE: EMPIRICAL PATTERNS
AND INTENSITY THEORY

6

Introduction to Empirical Evidence

In Part III of the book, I present empirical evidence in support of the value of intensity theory. These chapters do not "prove" the theory. Rather, they provide examples of how intensity theory is a reasonable approximation to the operation of electoral competition and frustrated majorities and provides a framework that improves our understanding of elections, representation, and political action.

One of the benefits of intensity theory is its many empirical implications. It explains when candidates choose to side with minorities over majorities. It explains when voters in the majority and minority choose to take costly action and how the prevalence of action corresponds with beliefs about the distribution of intensity in the population. It shows that when only voters in the minority choose to engage in political action, they choose to incur greater costs from that action than when voters in both the majority and the minority choose action.

The implications generate opportunities for quantitative political science to consider policy representation and political action and the relation of each to the distribution of voter preferences.

For example, if over time the size of the minority or the intensity of either majority or minority change with sufficient magnitude, politicians should change the policy they propose. If the American political landscape has increasingly oriented toward cultural or religious conflicts with intense minorities, intensity theory would lead us to expect majorities more often frustrated. If the structure of intensity across issues has shifted such that a smaller number of people feel intensely about multiple issues, we might expect that smaller groups of activists and ideologues would dominate political action and decision-making.

The theory provides general guidance on analyzing situations where majorities do not secure the policies they want. Instead of looking for extra-electoral causes of the frustrated majorities, intensity theory suggests we look first at the distribution of preferences and intensity among electoral constituencies. Is it reasonable to imagine there are enough voters who care enough about the issue to merit candidates risking some votes in the majority to feel more confident about the votes from an intense minority? I have already offered a few examples of such analysis in earlier chapters and provide more in-depth example case histories in Chapter 7.

With respect to political action, intensity theory suggests we ought to see the most costly actions taken in settings where only an intense minority takes action. In settings where more voters choose to incur costs, on the other hand, the magnitude of costly actions incurred should be smaller.

A second implication for costly action is that voters who care intensely and choose to take action in equilibrium target a specific magnitude of costs to incur. This magnitude of costs is Goldilocks, neither too high nor too low. They do not want to incur costly political action more than necessary to communicate their intensity to candidates. But they must incur enough costly political action to dissuade the less-intense voters from mimicry.

The equilibrium magnitude of cost has interesting implications. First, if one mode of costly action that intense voters had been using to incur costs and communicate intensity were closed, those intense voters would need to seek out an alternative avenue of political action to maintain the same level of costs. That is, if some exogenous change prevented intense voters from volunteering or making contributions, in order to continue to communicate to candidates how intensely they care about policy those voters would want a new mode of action in which to incur costs.

Second, if a new avenue of costly action that intense voters had not been before using to incur costs and communicate intensity were opened to them, those intense voters might not be interested in engaging in that action. They were already taking political action of a magnitude necessary to communicate their intensity. New opportunities for action would not be of great value to them. They might substitute the new action for old, but we should not observe great uptake of new opportunities for action without also observing decreasing action in other realms. Likewise, voters who were not previously taking action should not exhibit strong demand for new opportunities for action. They did not before care intensely enough to take action and so, absent change in their own intensity, they would ignore new opportunities for political participation.

There are additional implications of the theory that require moving beyond the simple version of the mathematical model. For example, in a world of multiple issues, activists might want to send issue-specific signals. Political actions that allow voters to indicate the issue for which they want to communicate intensity will be privileged over political actions that less clearly connect to a specific issue. Attending a fund-raiser hosted by the Sierra Club might be more valuable to communicate intensity about environmental issues than making a direct contribution to a candidate.

6.1 EMPIRICAL CHALLENGES

Although intensity theory has many empirical implications, at least three difficulties of measurement complicate empirical evaluation of the implications. First, intensity is difficult, if not impossible, to measure. Second, politicians probably do not care to admit when they purposefully side with intense minorities against majorities. More likely, politicians would prefer to demur or distract than admit to knowingly frustrating majorities.

Third, voters who care modestly but not intensely about issues have some incentive to obfuscate their intensity. All else equal, those who care modestly would prefer that candidates believed they care about the issue more than they actually do (Lemma A.4). This means that directly asking voters with a survey question how intensely they care about different issues might not lead to accurate responses, even if we set aside the first-order problem of finding an instrument to accurately elicit intensity.

The challenge of accurately measuring intensity makes it hard to evaluate how intensity relates to action, minority size, and representation with the traditional tools of social science. While the first instinct of many social scientists might be to field a survey that asks voters on what issues they feel intensely and then relate their responses on those questions to other outcomes, I want to be cautious given the theory's implication that voters who care modestly have incentive to obfuscate. This means that directly asking respondents how intensely they care about different issues might not be the best tool to evaluate the theory. Alternative approaches merit consideration. Tausanovitch (n.d.) offers an interesting possibility.

6.2 FOUR EMPIRICAL EVALUATIONS OF INTENSITY THEORY

I offer evidence in support of intensity theory through four chapters, two about issue intensity and frustrated majorities and two about issue intensity and costly political action. The first presents evidence on the relationship between intensity and politician policy choices. The second presents evidence on the relationship between intensity and vote choice. The third and fourth chapters show that the opening and closing, respectively, of opportunities for political action appear to be parsimoniously explained by intensity theory relative to other theories of political action.

Intensity theory argues that politicians frustrate majorities when a sufficiently intense minority faces a less-intense majority. In Chapter 7, I present two case histories in the settings of biotechnology and firearm regulation that suggest that politicians do, sometimes, willingly go against majority preferences to side with minority preferences. In each case, evidence suggests that the minority cared more intensely about the issue than the majority. The first case also appears to show that *changes* in the intensity of minority and majority induce changes in the policies of political officials. The abortion case in Lubbock, Texas presented in Chapter 4, in contrast, showed that an intense minority taking costly political action does not guarantee smaller groups of voters get what they want.

The first case in Chapter 7 is federal funding for stem cell research in the early 2000s. President George W. Bush set policy against what appears to have been majorities that supported allocating federal health research funds to projects using embryonic stem cells. Initially, the minority in opposition to new research appears to have been more intense than the majority. However, over time the size of the intense minority appears to have declined, and the intensity of the majority increased. As the relative size and intensity of the minority declined, first the legislature and then the executive reversed course on stem cell policy.

I then present the case of firearm regulation following the mass shooting at Sandy Hook Elementary School in 2012. While polls indicated that large majorities supported new legislation voted on in the Senate, in the end Congress did not revise firearm policy. I provide anecdotal and quantitative evidence that an intense minority opposed to reform took costly political action to communicate their intensity to politicians.

The second empirical chapter evaluates an important assumption of the theory, that vote choice responds to issues about which voters care intensely. Chapter 8 presents evidence that the issues voters most care about do explain their vote choices and offer explanatory power above and beyond standard predictors from political science such as party identification and demographics.

In a new experimental design, I ask subjects to provide their probabilistic guess about the vote choice of a respondent to the American National Election Studies, drawn at random. I sequentially provide the subject characteristics of the other, eliciting the subject's updated belief after each new piece of information. This design allows me to measure how well citizens believe each characteristic explains the other's vote choice. From this experiment, we learn that subjects believe issues of intensity explain voter decision-making.

Chapters 9 and 10 present evidence on issue intensity and costly political action. In Chapter 9, I show that voters in the city of Seattle, Washington responded to a new opportunity for low-cost political contributions with highly limited demand and without substitution for higher-cost monetary contributions. Seattle voters could use "Democracy Vouchers" to fund candidate campaigns without spending their own assets on the contribution. Less than five percent of the Seattle population, however, chose to use the vouchers in the first two elections with the option. The few residents who did use vouchers did not decrease their level of monetary contributions, on average. These patterns are consistent with intensity theory. New low-cost political action (such as vouchers) should not substitute for the equilibrium magnitude of costly actions (such as monetary contributions) necessary for high-intensity voters to communicate how much they care.

In Chapter 10, I estimate the behavioral response to the *removal* of a costly political action. When American states reform their institutions of nomination from closed partisan primary elections to open or non-partisan primaries, I find that monetary contributions to political candidates from individual citizens increase. I interpret this response as evidence that high-intensity voters must increase their costly actions in other realms when costly action in the realm of closed primary elections is removed from their portfolio of political participation. I also present evidence to support this mechanism in contrast to alternative mechanisms such as increased political competition in open primaries.

7

Politicians Side with Intense Minorities

Intensity theory argues that politicians sometimes benefit by siding with intense minorities over less-intense majorities. Candidates frustrate majorities when they believe that the minority is a sufficient combination of size and intensity relative to the size and intensity of the majority. Majorities are frustrated if candidates seeking to maximize votes expect to win more votes from the intense minority than they expect to lose from the majority when setting policy with the minority. Ambitious candidates, under this specific combination, benefit from aligning with the intense minority.

For two reasons, providing empirical demonstration that politicians choose to frustrate majorities is challenging. First, political science lacks instruments of measurement to gain a full accounting of intensity and policy preference in the electorate. We don't know exactly what voters want nor how they trade wants on one issue for wants on another. This challenge of measurement makes it difficult to provide the evidence we would like, showing that in settings where candidates should side with the minority per intensity theory they frustrate majorities, while in settings where candidates should side with the majority they side with the majority.

Second, if politicians indeed do sometimes choose to frustrate majorities, they probably prefer not to publicize this fact. All else equal, it seems imprudent for a politician to advertise that they choose to frustrate majorities. Although we can imagine settings where candidates might benefit by such advertising (Patty, 2016), I suspect that often candidates prefer to shroud choices to frustrate majorities in statements about principle or with claims that majorities actually support the position of the intense minority.

In this chapter, I present two case histories that suggest that politicians do, in some settings, willingly go against majority preferences to side with intense minority preferences.

First, I present the case of federal funding for stem cell research in the early 2000s. I find evidence that majorities supported allocating federal health research funds toward research using embryonic stem cells. President George W. Bush, however, chose to side with a minority of constituents who intensely opposed funding such research. Congress passed bills to increase the funding and scope of stem cell research in 2006 and 2007, both vetoed by Bush. However, in 2009, President Barack Obama reversed Bush's policy with an explicit appeal to the will of the majority while acknowledging the strongly held views of the minority.

The stem cell case appears to demonstrate that changes in the intensity of minority and majority induce changes in the policy proposals of ambitious political candidates. Over the course of the Bush presidency, the size of the intense minority appears to have declined, while the intensity of the majority increased. Such a change in the parameters of the mathematical model would lead to a change in the best policy response by candidates for office. When the minority's combination of size and intensity relative to the majority crosses threshold values (Section 5.1), candidates seeking votes ought to change their policy platform from siding with the minority to siding with the majority.

Intensity theory helps us understand the over-time dynamics of federal policy on stem cells.

As a second case history, I present the case of firearm regulation following the mass shooting at Sandy Hook Elementary School in 2012. In response to an incredible tragedy, polling indicated that large majorities – on some policies greater than 80 percent – of Americans supported new federal restrictions on access to firearms. New legislation was voted on in the Senate, but in the end shelved, apparently frustrating a large majority of voters. I provide anecdotal and quantitative evidence that an intense minority communicated their strong opposition to politicians.

Through these cases, I highlight common trends. Politicians appear to know that majorities prefer one policy. To justify opposition, however, politicians appeal to morals and principles. Whether or not these principles drive the choice, evidence suggests intense minorities. The outcome in each case suggests the empirical importance of intensity theory for political competition and policy representation.

7.1 FEDERAL FUNDING FOR STEM CELL RESEARCH

In 1998, new biomedical research became possible when scientists derived stem cells from human embryos (National Institutes of Health, 2020). Stem cells have a unique ability to renew themselves and so offer the potential for innovative medical treatments. The use of stem cells, however, raises serious ethical questions because the use of cells derived from human embryos requires the destruction of the embryo. Destroying embryos generates moral concern similar to terminating a pregnancy through abortion.

Early stem cell research was limited to stem cells derived from preimplantation embryos. Embryonic stem cells "have the ability to differentiate into all of the cells of the adult body" (National Institutes of Health, 2020). In 2006, scientists developed techniques to use adult stem cells for research. Adult stem cells may be of lesser moral concern than embryonic stem cells; however, they are constrained in potential uses because adult stem cells are specific to the organ or tissue from which they are derived. Stem cells of both types can be grown in culture dishes, preserving and replicating harvested stem cells for multiple uses.

Stem cells facilitate a variety of research. They support basic research on the biology of disease and the efficacy of chemotherapies. They might also be used for personalized medicine targeted at the cells of an individual patient. They might one day be used to grow transplantable tissues and organs.

7.1.1 Stem Cell Politics

Because of the cross-pressure of moral questions and scientific promise, stem cell policy (along with other biotechnology issues) generated political disagreement at the state and federal levels. Policy questions had to be resolved through politics. Would stem cell research be allowed and, if so, would state or federal funds be used to support research using stem cells? Would policy differ for adult versus embryonic cells? Because states and the federal government spent large sums on medical research, these questions required resolution.

Those who wanted to regulate or prohibit stem cell research argued that while the medical benefits could be great, there was no guarantee that research would generate such beneficial treatments. While the benefits were uncertain, destruction of embryos – and therefore moral concern – was certain. On August 9, 2001 President Bush said:

At its core, this issue forces us to confront fundamental questions about the beginnings of life and the ends of science. It lies at a difficult moral intersection, juxtaposing the need to protect life in all its phases with the prospect of saving and improving life in all its stages ... I'm a strong supporter of science and technology, and believe they have the potential for incredible good – to improve lives, to save life, to conquer disease. Research offers hope that millions of our loved ones may be cured of a disease and rid of their suffering. ... I also believe human life is a sacred gift from our Creator. I worry about a culture that devalues life, and believe as your President I have an important obligation to foster and encourage respect for life in America and throughout the world. And while we're all hopeful about the potential of this research, no one can be certain that the science will live up to the hope it has generated. (Bush, 2001)

Political proponents focused on the potential medical benefits. For example, the supporters of Proposition 71 (2004) in California argued, "Proposition 71 is about curing diseases and saving lives. Stem cells are unique cells that generate healthy new cells, tissues, and organs. Medical researchers believe stem cell research could lead to treatments and cures for many diseases and injuries, including: Cancer, heart disease, diabetes, Alzheimer's, Parkinson's, HIV/AIDS, multiple sclerosis, lung diseases, and spinal injuries" (California Secretary of State, 2004).

7.1.2 Puzzle: Dynamics of Federal Policy

The politics of stem cells demonstrate fascinating dynamics. The Bush administration focused on the morality of destroying stem cells and maintained strict regulations on research through his departure from office in 2009. Early in the 2000s, most Republicans supported the president of their party. But Republicans began to break ranks with Bush. The Republican-controlled Congress passed legislation in 2006 to expand federal funding for stem cell research, leading to the first presidential veto of Bush's presidency. Congress passed legislation again on a bipartisan vote in 2007, again vetoed by Bush. In 2009, Barack Obama reversed the Bush policy.

What explains these policy dynamics? Why did Republicans confront their co-partisan president on this issue, and what motivated President

Bush to maintain his policy against this opposition? Why did President Obama's 2009 policy appear to settle the issue? Were majorities frustrated but then satiated?

To evaluate the puzzle, I first walk through the policy dynamics and then turn to evidence about majority and minority preferences on the issue.

At the federal level, the politics of stem cells revolved around whether or not to use federal medical research funds to support projects using stem cell lines. Bush had campaigned against stem cell research in the 2000 presidential contest. As president, he directed on August 9, 2001 that federal funding would only be used for currently existing stem cell lines. Research on new lines would not be funded. This was his compromise between the needs of science and what he saw as his duty to protect human life.

The Bush policy held for three years until Congressional Republicans began to depart with Bush in 2004 and 2005. A bipartisan bill to expand federal funding passed the Republican-controlled House in 2005 and, in July, Republican Senate Majority Leader Bill Frist announced he would support the bill. The Senate passed the bill on July 18, 2006 followed by a Bush veto.

In a speech on July 19, 2006 on the veto, Bush said:

This legislation would overturn the balanced policy on embryonic stem cell research that my administration has followed for the past five years. This bill would also undermine the principle that Congress, itself, has followed for more than a decade, when it has prohibited federal funding for research that destroys human embryos. If this bill would have become law, American taxpayers would, for the first time in our history, be compelled to fund the deliberate destruction of human embryos. And I'm not going to allow it. (Bush, 2006)

With House approval on June 7, 2007, Congress again sent to the president legislation to ease restrictions on federal funding for stem cell research. The bill gained more than three dozen Republican votes in the House. Bush again vetoed the bill and maintained opposition to funding of new stem cell lines through the end of his presidency in 2009.

On March 9, 2009 the newly elected president, Barack Obama, reversed the Bush policy with Executive Order 13505. The order directed the National Institutes of Health to "support and conduct responsible, scientifically worthy human stem cell research" and specifically revoked Bush's August 2001 policy statement and Bush's Executive Order 13435.

In remarks about the executive order (Obama, 2009), Obama acknowledged the intense minority, "Many thoughtful and decent people are conflicted about, or strongly oppose, this research. I understand their concerns, and we must respect their point of view." He continued:

But after much discussion, debate and reflection, the proper course has become clear. The majority of Americans – from across the political spectrum, and of all backgrounds and beliefs – have come to a consensus that we should pursue this research. That the potential it offers is great, and with proper guidelines and strict oversight, the perils can be avoided.

The progression of Republican Party platforms (see American Presidency Project, 2020) reflects the dynamics of policy support on the issue of stem cells. The 2004 platform endorsed the Bush policy, "We strongly support the President's policy that prevents taxpayer dollars from being used to encourage the future destruction of human embryos. In addition, we applaud the President's call for a comprehensive ban on human cloning and on the creation of human embryos solely for experimentation."

The 2008 platform alluded to the policy, but with less clear endorsement of prohibition, "In that regard, we call for a major expansion of support for the stem-cell research that now shows amazing promise and offers the greatest hope for scores of diseases – with adult stem cells, umbilical cord blood, and cells reprogrammed into pluripotent stem cells – without the destruction of embryonic human life."

The 2012 and 2016 platforms returned to advocating a Bush-like policy, "We oppose federal funding of embryonic stem cell research." However, Republican President Donald Trump's 2017 executive order on stem cells did not return to the Bush policy.

7.2 INTENSITY THEORY AND THE CHANGING POLITICS OF STEM CELL RESEARCH

In this section, I present public opinion evidence that intensity theory provides a coherent account of the dynamics of federal stem cell policy. In the early 2000s, majorities supported federal funding but were opposed by intense minorities. The Bush policy frustrated these majorities and sided with an intense minority.

As the 2000s progressed, the size of the intense minority declined while the intensity of the majority increased. Survey evidence suggests that around 2004 the size of the intense majority surpassed the size of the intense minority. This is about the time Republicans in Congress began to break with the president on stem cell policy. By 2008 and 2009, the majority supporting federal funding had increased in size and intensity relative to the beginning of the decade. This is when Obama reversed the Bush policy and created the status quo that maintains through the writing of this book.

Election data suggest that Americans were closely divided on the stem cell issue with a small majority supportive of research. Voters in four states considered ballot initiatives on stem cells. State funding for stem cell research passed in California (Proposition 71, 2004) 59–41 percent and failed in New Jersey (Question Two, 2007) 53–47 percent. Missouri voters (Amendment 2, 2006) allowed stem cell research with certain regulations, 51–49 percent. Michigan voters (Proposal 2, 2008) authorized donation of embryos produced in fertility clinics that would otherwise be discarded, 53–47 percent.

Opinion surveys also suggest that majorities of Americans supported stem cell research, even in the first part of the Bush presidency. I plot a time series of moral judgment on stem cell research using data from Nisbet and Becker (2014, table 12) in Figure 7.1. The figure shows that slightly more than 50 percent of respondents indicated that stem cell research was morally acceptable in 2002 growing to 60 percent in 2013. Meanwhile, 39 percent responded that such research was morally wrong in 2002, declining to 32 percent in 2013. All polls during the Bush presidency had a majority indicating that stem cell research was morally acceptable against a minority objecting on moral grounds (see also their table 13).

Although Figure 7.1 suggests a majority felt the use of stem cells on balance was morally acceptable, Nisbet and Becker (2014, table 14) present survey evidence of an intense minority. Let us assume for this analysis that responding "strongly support" or "strongly oppose" indicates greater intensity on the issue than does responding "somewhat" support or oppose.

I plot the survey results from this table on the intensity of support for or opposition to stem cell research in Figure 7.2. In 2001, about 48 percent of Americans said they strongly or somewhat favored medical research using embryonic stem cells against 43 percent who strongly or somewhat opposed (proportion of respondents unsure is excluded from the figure). Those with strong opposition outnumbered those who strongly favored by 22 percent to 17 percent.

The survey evidence indicates, however, that over time intense opposition to medical research using stem cells declined and strong support increased. In the 2004 poll, the level strongly in favor surpassed the level

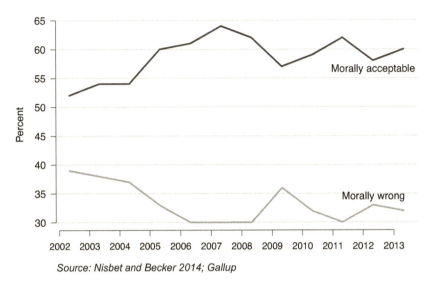

Source: Nisbet and Becker 2014; Gallup

FIGURE 7.1 Moral judgment on stem cell research

"Regardless of whether or not you think it should be legal, for each one, tell me whether you personally believe that in general it is morally acceptable or morally wrong. How about medical research using stem cells?" (Nisbet and Becker, 2014, table 12)

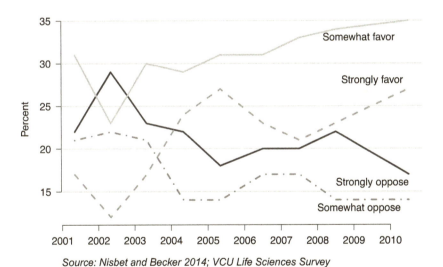

Source: Nisbet and Becker 2014; VCU Life Sciences Survey

FIGURE 7.2 Intensity of support for or opposition to stem cell research

"On the whole, how much do you favor or oppose medical research that uses stem cells from human embryos – do you strongly favor, somewhat favor, somewhat oppose, or strongly oppose this?" (Nisbet and Becker, 2014, table 14)

strongly opposed. Throughout the time period, somewhat favor grows while somewhat oppose and strongly oppose decline.

Figure 7.2 suggests that what was in 2001 and 2002 a less-intense plurality against an intense minority changed such that a growing and more-intense majority contrasted a shrinking and less-intense minority after 2006.

Consistent with a change in implications for electoral competition, in 2006 Democratic congressional candidates advocated for increased federal funding for stem cell research, believing it an issue that would work in their favor as they looked to retake control of Congress (Stolberg, 2006). Republicans also moved to support federal funding of stem cell research with the legislation of 2006 and 2007.

Why might congressional Democrats and some Republicans in 2006 move to reverse Bush's opposition? Why did President Obama revise the Bush policy by executive order? If we take the survey responses at face value, strong opposition was greater than strong support in 2001, 2002, and 2003, but strongly support captured more respondents than strongly oppose from 2004 onward. These numbers roughly correspond to the sequence of actions of Bush, Congress, and Obama.

* * *

The stem cell case history presents an example of a frustrated majority. Policy was set with the preferences of an intense minority. However, as the relative size and intensity of majority and minority changed over time, politicians began to advocate for the policy supported by the majority. A frustrated majority today is not necessarily a frustrated majority tomorrow.

7.3 FEDERAL REGULATION OF FIREARMS AFTER TRAGEDY

On December 14, 2012, in Newtown, Connecticut, 20-year old Adam Lanza shot and killed his mother Nancy with a .22 calibre rifle in the home they shared. He destroyed the hard drive on his personal computer then gathered a military-style AR-15 assault rifle, two pistols, and a shotgun. He drove the firearms in his mother's car to Sandy Hook Elementary School. Lanza broke into the school, shot, and killed 20 first graders and six adults before taking his own life.

Most of the victims were six or seven years old. The massacre reignited the on-again, off-again debate in the United States about the appropriate level of regulation of firearms along with the meaning of the Second

Amendment to the Constitution. Semi-automatic rifles and large-capacity magazines similar to those used by Lanza had been banned by Congress in 1994, but the ban had expired in 2004.

President Barack Obama stated he would use all the powers of his office to prevent mass shootings, and Congress considered a variety of policy proposals. Senator Diane Feinstein introduced the Assault Weapons Ban of 2013 to reinstate the lapsed ban, and Senators Joe Manchin of West Virginia and Pat Toomey of Pennsylvania created a bipartisan proposal that would require background checks for gun shows and internet sales and make selling to a prohibited buyer a felony punishable by five years in prison.

Despite initial momentum on the side of new regulations, Congress ended up declining to enact new law. On April 17, 2013, the Senate considered 29 amendments to the Safe Communities, Safe Schools Act of 2013.[1] The Manchin–Toomey Amendment 715 received 54 votes in support but failed because of the need for 60 votes to invoke cloture. Feinstein's Amendment 711 was defeated 60–40. Other amendments aimed at regulating firearms likewise failed to obtain the necessary 60 votes. Funding for mental health and addiction programs was approved 95-2 (Amendment 730).

Some state legislatures implemented new regulations with notable reforms in California, Colorado, Connecticut, Maryland, and New York. These states had already had stronger laws surrounding firearms.

7.3.1 The Politics of Guns

The political response to Sandy Hook followed the pattern of previous and subsequent American mass shootings. Following a tragedy, proponents of increased firearm regulations commit to new state and federal policy. Legislators ambivalent about new regulations state a willingness to consider new policy, and legislators opposed make no commitment. Although public opinion polls indicate large majorities of the public support more regulations, Congress moves slowly on considering the issue.[2] As the tragedy fades from the nation's attention, legislation stalls and ends up with insufficient support.

---

[1] See Congress.gov (2013).
[2] A Gallup poll taken April 22, 2013 asked whether the Senate should have passed the bill to expand background checks on firearm purchases, with 65 percent responding yes to 29 percent no (Gallup, 2020).

In a Pew Research Center poll in January 2013, 85 percent of respondents said they favored requiring background checks for private or gun shows sales, 67 percent said they favored a federal database to track gun sales, and 58 percent said they favored a ban on semi-automatic weapons (Pew Research Center, 2013). In Chapter 2, I plotted a time-series of public support for stricter regulations on firearms (Figure 2.1). The figure demonstrates evidence of frustrated majorities over many years.

Why does policy not follow the wants of the apparent majority? The Sandy Hook case history provides multiple clues that differences in intensity drive non-majoritarian outcomes on firearm policy.

First, political actors in 2013 indicated the importance of an intense minority on the vote outcomes in the Senate. Senator Toomey said, "The most important thing frankly is members of Congress need to hear from people, and the people who support these background checks need to be as vocal as those who don't" (Lengell, 2013).

After the Senate votes of April 17, President Obama (Obama, 2013) said:

[T]he gun lobby and its allies willfully lied about the bill ... those lies upset an intense minority of gun owners, and that in turn intimidated a lot of senators ... It came down to politics – the worry that that vocal minority of gun owners would come after them in future elections ... To all the people who supported this legislation ... you need to let your representatives in Congress know that you are disappointed, and that if they don't act this time, you will remember come election time ... And they make sure to stay focused on this one issue during election time. And that's the reason why you can have something that 90 percent of Americans support and you can't get it through the Senate or the House of Representatives.

Obama's (2013) statement could not come much closer to the argument of intensity theory. An "intense minority of gun owners" could "come after" their representatives at a future election. Why is the majority frustrated? Because the minority is more passionate, more organized, more vocal, and "focused on this one issue during election time." This intense minority might be single-issue voters.

7.3.2 Costly Political Action

The public statements of Senator Toomey and President Obama of their interpretations of the cause does not make it so. Is there evidence that opponents of firearms regulation actually took more costly political action to indicate their intensity? Respondents to the January 2013 Pew survey (Pew Research Center, 2013) expressed notable differences

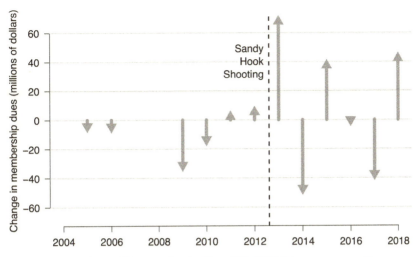

Source: Internal Revenue Service Form 990. 2007 data non-comparable.

FIGURE 7.3 Annual changes in National Rifle Association membership dues, 2005–2018

in costly political action by support for firearm regulations. Gun rights supporters were more than four times as likely to say they had contributed money to a political organization on the firearm issue (23–5 percent) and almost twice as likely to say they had contacted a public official about the gun issue (15–8 percent).

I have argued that respondents might misrepresent their intensity in opinion surveys, however, so I have collected non-survey evidence. I plot in Figure 7.3 annual change in membership dues reported by the National Rifle Association (NRA) on federal tax returns from 2005 to 2018. The x-axis is year of tax return, the y-axis is the change in membership dues from the previous year's return. The arrows above each year extend to the change in dues.[3]

The largest change in annual dues in the time-series occurs in 2013. The NRA's 2012 tax return reported membership due revenue of $108 million. Dues revenue was $176 million in 2013 (an increase of 63 percent) and $128 million in 2014. Even in 2018, reported dues were $170 million, not yet exceeding membership revenue in 2013.[4]

---

3 Data available from the Internal Revenue Service or compiled by ProPublica (ProPublica, n.d.).

4 The 2007 membership number is non-comparable as, in that year only, the NRA booked revenue from lifetime membership dues as annual revenue.

The year of largest increase, 2013, was the year where the Senate considered the bipartisan Manchin–Toomey compromise. Leading up to the vote, this compromise appeared to have sufficient support to pass, having overcome a procedural vote only days before. While I do not have access to the timing of the membership subscriptions, the trend of membership dues in Figure 7.3 is consistent with a surge in costly political action by opponents of increased regulations surrounding the 2013 Senate votes on new regulations. It is not a stretch to imagine that increased dues are correlated with other costly actions incurred by the intense minority. If these costly actions communicated intensity to politicians, it provides an explanation for the results in the Senate: frustrated majorities due to a sufficiently intense minority.

I cannot say whether a change to intensity or a change in beliefs about the extent of support for firearm regulations – i.e., a change in belief about the size of the majority – induced the increase in membership dues. It might even have been a change in belief about the intensity of the majority. But clearly some stimulus following Sandy Hook led those who cared strongly about gun rights to choose to increase dues sent to the NRA. And this costly political action might well have convinced some members of Congress that they should continue to side with the intense minority.

* * *

The dynamics of stem cell and firearm policy show how politicians sometimes side with an intense minority against the wants of a less-intense majority. When politicians believe the minority cares sufficiently more than the majority, they choose to side with that minority.

However, as the stem cell case suggests, frustrated majorities today are not necessarily frustrated majorities tomorrow. The case history shows that when the relative size and intensity of the majority and minority change, policy can also change. Since about 2004, more of the public has said they strongly support medical research using stem cells than has said they strongly oppose. Congress appears to have followed this lead beginning in 2005 and 2006. The 2009 reversal of the Bush prohibition continues as federal policy through the writing of this book.

The case history of firearms policy following Sandy Hook, however, suggests the importance of politician beliefs about the balance of intensity. My evidence suggests that costly political action might have been an important factor influencing those beliefs. What had appeared a promising bipartisan compromise by Senators Manchin and

Toomey – newspaper coverage prior to the vote suggested optimism about its passage – fell apart in a year when the NRA saw its largest ever increase in membership dues.

The apparent importance of costly action in the case history of Sandy Hook merits investigation in other settings. How common is it for voters who care intensely to incur costly political action to communicate that intensity to politicians? Does intensity theory explain different features of costly political action better than other theories of political participation?

8

Issues of Intensity Explain Vote Choice

Former member of Congress Steve Israel was a long-time proponent of federal legislation to regulate the sale and use of firearms with the goal of reducing gun violence. He became a public advocate on the issue after leaving Congress. In his view, the challenge facing legislation on firearms was not that a majority of Americans were opposed. To the contrary, large majorities reported support for new restrictions. Instead, the challenge was that voters varied in how intensely they felt about firearm regulations.

Many voters opposed to new regulation cared so much about the issue, Israel argued, that they ignored other issues in their vote choice. Israel believed many opponents of regulation were "single-issue voters." In contrast, although majorities cared about regulating firearms and lessening gun violence, they did not care so much as to ignore where candidates stood on other issues.

In a 2018 Op-Ed in *Newsday*, Israel explained his view.[1]

My former colleagues call it "voter intensity." The vast majority of people who support gun-safety measures cast votes on many issues, including gun violence, the economy, taxes, education, women's rights, the environment, etc. Or they don't bother voting. A good chunk of the vocal minority that opposes gun-safety measures cast votes on that single issue, with the NRA as their source of information about who is "pro-Second Amendment." For some, that bumper sticker really means: "I'm NRA, I Vote In Every Election, And Guns Are The Only Thing I Vote On."

---

[1] The National Rifle Association (NRA) referenced by Israel is an interest group prominently opposed to firearm regulation.

Our instinct is to blame Congress for this political calculation ... But it won't change until the political calculation does. And that won't change until voters do ...

When more members of Congress believe that voter intensity for gun safety is rising and automatic opposition is softening, things will get done. (Israel, 2018)

***

Intensity theory offers an explanation for frustrated majorities and variation in costly political action. In order for the theory to provide an explanation, however, voters must vary in how intensely they care about issues. Frustrated majorities only occur with a minority sufficiently more intense than a majority. Costly political action is equilibrium behavior only when voters and candidates expect that some voters care intensely and other voters care only modestly. If all voters care equally about an issue, there is no need for voters and candidates to communicate about intensity.

A key empirical question, then, is if voters indeed vary in their intensity over issues. While this may seem to be of obvious truth given casual observation of politics surrounding issues like abortion, firearms, tax policy, and immigration, empirical evidence in political science is ambiguous. Most scholars agree that voters do not have extensively informed policy preferences on all issues confronting the nation, but there is disagreement on how large a role issue preferences play in electoral behavior.

The goal of this chapter is to provide evidence that issue preferences influence vote choice similarly to their assumed operation in intensity theory. I will present some of the existing evidence on this matter, explain the debate, and then provide what I hope to be a novel empirical exploration. This exploration tries to deal with the difficult measurement challenges of determining the issue(s) that different voters care about most intensely. While other work aims to show that "issues matter" to vote choice, this chapter moves a step further with evidence that "issues most important to each voter matter more" to vote choice.

8.1 THE DEBATE ABOUT ISSUE VOTING

To rough approximation, scholars of elections might be classified as endorsing either issue-based or identity-based politics. While some suggest issue-based policy competition is the driving factor in electoral and party politics, others have argued that most voters care at most about a handful of policy issues – so-called "issue publics." Other political scientists and political psychologists push further against issue competition, arguing that issues are unimportant or even irrelevant to vote choice because political identities are the principle structure of political competition.

In my view, the reason these debates remain unresolved is because existing evidence is severely challenged by issues of measurement. Political scientists have used opinion surveys to try to arbitrate between issue-based and identity-based politics. Unfortunately while identities tend to be long-term, stable, socially constructed, and closely-held, issue positions depend on a variety of factors that are much more dynamic and individual. Status quo policies change, individual circumstances change, coordination and coalition issues change, and external features of the world change. Preferences may depend on information available to the individual (Hill and Huber, 2019) such that an issue preference captured at the time of the survey might not represent an issue preference subsequent to the individual learning more about the world or subsequent to participation in a political campaign (see, e.g., Zaller, 2003, on latent opinion). Further, many different issues confront polities at any given time, while scholars have only finite space when placing questions on surveys.

Many studies sweep aside the thorny issue of measurement and proceed to run regression models of vote choice on survey measures of political identities and policy positions. These horse-race designs regress vote choice on a host of survey measurements in a multiple regression and use coefficient estimates to evaluate which predictors are more and less important to vote choice. If issue-based variables explain more variance, the horse race suggests that issue-based politics are more important. If identity-based variables explain more variance, the horse race suggests identity-based politics more important.

In general, identity variables – especially party identification – explain more variation in vote choice than do issue variables. Many scholars interpret this to mean that identities are a "more important" factor in political choice than issues. However, others argue that measurement error or challenges to causal inference in horse-race models contradict conclusions that identities are the more important factor (e.g., Rivers, 1988; Ansolabehere, Rodden, and Snyder, 2008; Fowler, 2020).

8.2 TOWARD MEASURING ISSUES OF INTENSITY

Measurement challenges for issue politics are many. I focus here on two key challenges to measurement in the survey setting. The respondent answering the questions of the survey is different than the person designing the survey. Differences between these two individuals can lead the respondent to interpret questions differently than the designer had intended. The first measurement challenge is that the designer might or might not have anticipated the issues that are important to the respondent. If the designer failed to ask about the issue(s) about which the respondent feels most intensely, a horse-race method leads to incorrect conclusions. Thus, current horse-race studies that conclude issues do not matter might come to this conclusion because the survey questionnaire did not properly canvass all issues of importance to respondents. Let us call this challenge "enumeration error."

The second measurement challenge binds even if issues of importance are queried in the survey. Survey question design is a challenging process (e.g., Lohr, 2019), and survey questions measure the target quantities with varying levels of success. Survey questions vary in their *construct validity*. Current studies might yield misleading results because survey questions do not accurately measure intensity or preference. Let us call this second challenge "instrumentation error."

As an example of instrumentation error, while party identification is a strong predictor of vote choice, to the extent some respondents interpret the question asked as "which party are you likely to vote for?" instead of the psychological attachment imagined by the author of the survey question, the instrument fails to measure the construct. This example of construct validity, of course, would be a serious challenge to horse-race comparisons.

Enumeration error is often ignored despite being a central challenge to any horse-race comparison. Instrumentation error is widely recognized among survey methodologists but not always appreciated by applied political scientists. Either error can doom the validity of a horse-race comparison. If the survey either fails to ask or fails to measure the issue(s) about which the respondent most cares, and if indeed these important issues factor into vote choice, statistical comparisons would not properly account for the respondent's vote choice. Without evidence that the survey has asked the right questions and successfully elicited the right responses, interpreting evidence on relative explanatory power of different factors as evidence of relative importance may be misplaced.

8.3 AN ALTERNATIVE MEASURE OF ISSUES OF INTENSITY

In this chapter, I take an alternative approach to understanding how issue preferences map into vote choice. Given the argument of intensity theory,

I am particularly interested in how issues about which individuals care intensely influence vote choice. My measurement strategy to mitigate both enumeration and instrumentation error is to let respondents report in their own words the issue they most care about. When allowed to respond in their own words, they are not limited by a closed set of options from the designer (limiting enumeration error) and they provide a response in words that make sense to them (limiting instrumentation error).

Such an instrumentation has been fielded for many years, commonly referred to as the respondent's "most important problem" (MIP) following question text such as the American National Election Studies (2016a, ANES): "What do you think are the most important problems facing this country?" The ANES followed this question with: "Of those you've mentioned, what would you say is the single most important problem the country faces?" if the subject reported more than one problem.

Most important problem seems a reasonable approach to elicit an issue important to the subject while limiting enumeration error and lessening instrumentation error (though, see Rivers, 1988). Enumeration error is limited as respondents may report any issue without constraint. Instrumentation error is also limited in that the designer need not anticipate categories or classification of issues. For each respondent, we observe their own words about what is important to them in the realm of politics. While I do not claim this instrument entirely removes error, it is reasonable to suggest it more effectively mitigates enumeration and measurement error than standard closed-ended issue questions.

The challenge is how to then map this better-measured issue preference into vote choice. Because each individual uses their own words, each value is unique and one cannot simply add the words to horse-race regressions. Existing approaches include hand-coding responses into smaller categories or using a dimension-reducing natural language processing technique. While both approaches have merit, collapsing all responses into smaller categories would reintroduce enumeration error, and dimension reduction would reintroduce instrumentation error.

My approach is to leave the text reported by the respondent verbatim.[2] I then present an alternative method to the horse-race regression to understand how MIP issues map into vote choice. The strategy is to let normal citizens serve as cartographers for this mapping.

---

[2] Responses were recorded by interviewers, so there might be errors in transcription.

I fielded an experiment with online survey participants where each participant ("the participant") was matched to a randomly sampled respondent to the 2016 ANES ("the other").[3] The online survey platform Lucid delivered the sample. I present full details of the study sample in Appendix C.

I limited respondents to those who reported turning out and voting for one of the two major-party 2016 candidates, Donald Trump or Hillary Clinton. The task for each participant was to report their beliefs about the 2016 presidential vote choice of the ANES other. I use these beliefs to construct the mapping from most important problem into vote choice.

Beliefs were measured on a probability scale with the text "How likely do you believe it is that Person A voted for [Donald Trump/Hillary Clinton]? For example, 1 if you believe it is almost impossible, 99 if you believe it is almost certain, and 50 if you are totally unsure." I randomized whether they reported beliefs about vote for candidate Trump or Clinton. Participants were told the other reported voting for one of the two, so probability for one candidate is simply the complement of probability for the other.

I provided participants incentives to provide their best guess using the crossover scoring method (Karni, 2009; Hill, 2017b). The crossover scoring method elicits from subjects a probability p that a statement presented to them is true. For example, I asked subjects for a probability that the ANES other voted for candidate Clinton. The method provides an incentive for them to accurately report their probabilistic belief. On average their payoff is lower if they report a probability other than the probability that best describes their belief. It does so by essentially asking for what value p they would be indifferent between two possibilities. First, winning the incentive if the other voted for the candidate. Second, being entered in a lottery where the incentive is won at probability p. In the background, a computer algorithm implemented this procedure to either award the incentive or not for each elicited probability. Participants reported this belief using a slider on a web interface and were provided instructions about the incentive prior to the experiment.

Each participant reported five beliefs about each of four others (Persons A, B, C, and D). Their first belief was elicited after being told that

---

[3] Professor Taylor Carlson and I collaborated on this experiment, a different aspect of which we present in Carlson and Hill (2021). This chapter includes material sourced from Carlson and Hill (2021), published by Cambridge University Press and reprinted with permission.

the other had reported voting for either Democratic candidate Hillary Clinton or Republican candidate Donald Trump and had been validated to have voted using administrative records. After reporting this belief, they were then provided one trait of the other, drawn at random without replacement from the set {party identification, most important problem, race, gender, income, state of residence}. After being provided with this trait, they then reported a second belief. This second belief may have changed – though I did not require it to be changed – from the first belief after they learned about this new characteristic of the other. They then provided a third, fourth, and fifth belief after being sequentially provided with a second, third, and fourth characteristic of the other.

The experiment reveals how participant beliefs change in response to each new piece of information. This study allows me to understand how these non-scholar participants valued the text ANES respondents gave in response to the MIP question. Because I know how the ANES respondent actually reported voting in 2016, I observe the probability the participant gave to the vote choice, and so I can measure accuracy of participant beliefs. I compare improvement in accuracy when participants are provided with MIP compared to improvement in accuracy when provided with other characteristics. If issues of intensity are an important factor of vote choice, learning MIP should lead to material increases in accuracy of beliefs about vote choice.

Because of randomization, I also observe the delivery of MIP as the first characteristic of the other as well as a later-delivered characteristic. This is useful to see how informative MIP is compared to how much it serves as a proxy for other characteristics. I present analysis on these questions below.

With two assumptions, this design allows me to estimate if the issues voters care most about are a key input to vote choice. First, I assume that *on average* participants in my study have an understanding of how other Americans make voting decisions and how they trade off different group-based and issue-based considerations. Such an understanding could follow from two features of the electorate. Citizens might either have a reasonable understanding of others (e.g., Carlson and Hill, 2021), or citizens might have a reasonable understanding of their own vote choice that they apply when considering others. Averaging individual self-knowledge across a population-representative sample yields an estimate of population knowledge.

Second, I assume responses to the MIP question capture an issue voters care about with intensity. Perusing the responses makes clear most

TABLE 8.1. *Random sample of most important problem open-ended responses*

1.	There are worse problems than those, but people rioting needs immediate attention
2.	Trump as president
3.	Federal Debt
4.	Unity
5.	The economy
6.	The fear of people who are different from yourself.
7.	Las armas de fuego
8.	NOT INCLUDING ALL PEOPLE
9.	Mental Illness and caring for the kids
10.	Economy. Jobs. Too many going overseas.
11.	Racism.
12.	lack of infrastructure spending
13.	SHORT TERM-HEALTHCARE, LONG TERM - CLIMATE CHANGE
14.	Homelands security
15.	pharmaceutical companies

Note: From 2016 American National Election Studies responses to "What do you think are the most important problems facing this country? If you think there are more than one, please briefly tell me one problem now." From post-election survey.

ANES respondents were thinking about issues facing the nation that were important to them. I present a random sample of fifteen text responses in Table 8.1.

8.4 RESULTS: ISSUES OF INTENSITY AND VOTE CHOICE

In each of twenty rounds, participants reported their belief that the other voted for Clinton or Trump. Others and order of characteristics were assigned at random. The quantity of interest is how beliefs move in response to observing the MIP text of the other relative to how beliefs move in response to the other characteristics of the experiment. With random assignment, averaging across observations yields the average increase in accuracy for each characteristic.

Figure 8.1 presents distributions of change in belief for each characteristic. Change in belief is the difference between the elicited probability after seeing the characteristic and the elicited probability immediately previous to seeing that characteristic. Beliefs are elicited on a zero to 100 scale, so change in beliefs can vary from −100 to +100. Each group of bars on the x-axis represents a range of change in beliefs. For example, the first group on the left represents all changes in belief from −100 to −50.

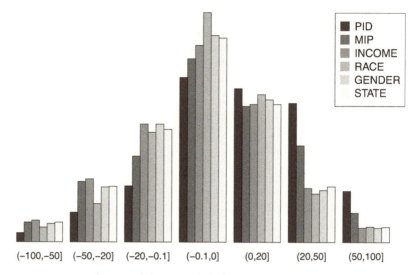

FIGURE 8.1 Distribution of change in beliefs in response to each characteristic

Note: Bar heights represent the proportion of changes in belief for that characteristic corresponding to the range indicated on the x-axis.

Bar heights represent the proportion of changes for that characteristic in that range of changes of belief.

The modal response is a change in beliefs of zero (indicated by the highest set of bars in the middle) but the heights in the positive range of the x-axis to the right are higher than bar heights to the left, demonstrating that, usually, subjects learned from the information toward the actual vote choice of the other. On average, in response to new information about the other, beliefs about their vote choice moved toward truth (values on x-axis greater than zero). That said, it was not uncommon for beliefs to move away from the true vote of the other.

Importantly for our inquiry about the importance of issues of intensity for vote choice, the bar heights for MIP are notably higher in the positive learning part of the figure relative to the traits of income, race, gender, or state. Bar heights in the +20 to +50 and +50 to +100 ranges are higher than bar heights for other characteristics in those ranges with the exception of party identification.

It is important to appreciate that Figure 8.1 represents average learning across all values of each characteristic. Carlson and Hill (2021, figure 3) show that specific values of characteristics are much more informative than average, finding that race black, ethnicity Hispanic, MIP, and geography Washington, DC approach the informative value of party identification values.

* * *

The initial evidence from Figure 8.1 shows that the participants in the experiment – our cartographers for mapping issue intensity to vote choice – learned about the 2016 vote choice of others from the text reported as the most important problem facing the nation. Issues of intensity helped participants understand how others chose to vote, suggesting such issues are important inputs to voter decision-making. Of course, so too are the responses to party identification questions.

8.5 STATISTICAL MODEL FOR COMPOUND TREATMENT

One challenge to the conclusions from Figure 8.1 that intensity drives vote choice is that in many cases the MIP phrase is a compound treatment. When a voter says their most important problem is "lack of infrastructure spending," our cartographers learn two things. First, the other's most important problem, but second, in many cases *where they stand* on that issue. This is not the case for all phrases (e.g., "economy"), but for some MIP phrases changes in the cartographer's beliefs about the vote choice of the other follows from two new pieces of information. Because we want to see that it is intensity driving vote choice, we have a problem of confounding.

I do not have a full solution to this problem, but here I present one approach. Suppose party identification informs subjects of the issue preferences of the other – see, for example, evidence in Orr and Huber (2020). That implies that subjects who have learned the party identification of the other possess beliefs about the policy preferences of the other. Observing MIP *after* party identification would be less informative about issue preferences, on average, than observing MIP *before* party identification.

This suggests a statistical procedure to evaluate the importance of intensity itself. Because the experiment delivered characteristics of the other in random order, in some cases subjects viewed MIP before party identification, while in other cases party identification was seen before MIP. If the informative value of MIP is mostly in its ability to inform about issue preferences, then subjects who observe party identification before MIP should learn much less from observing MIP than subjects who do not observe party identification before MIP. If, on the other hand, MIP provides information about the issue about which the other most cares, then subjects who observe party identification before MIP should not learn much less from observing MIP than subjects who do not observe party identification before MIP.

To gain a quantitative estimate of the relevance of MIP to vote choice relative to the information available in other characteristics, I use a statistical regression model. The regression specification is a rough approximation to a structural model of Bayesian learning (see Hill, 2017b, for a fully structural version). A participant following Bayes' rule to learn about the other would use each new characteristic to update prior beliefs to posterior beliefs. The regression specification in Eq. (8.1) approximates that model with

$$y_{ijt} = \beta y_{ijt-1} + \boldsymbol{\gamma} X + \varepsilon_{ijt}, \tag{8.1}$$

where y is the probability given by participant i for other j in elicitation t, β is a lag coefficient on the prior belief at $t - 1$, X is a design matrix indicating which characteristic was presented to participant i for other j in elicitation t, $\boldsymbol{\gamma}$ is a vector of coefficients representing the average learning for each characteristic mapped from X to y, and ε is an idiosyncratic disturbance. The coefficients decompose participant beliefs at each elicitation as a function of prior beliefs (β), information value of characteristic delivered (γ), and unexplained error (ε).

8.5.1 Results: Issues of Intensity Explain Vote Choice

I present estimation results of the regression model from Eq. (8.1) in Table 8.2. The dependent variable is the subject's elicited probability scored in the direction of the actual vote choice reported by the other. The first column presents the main result. Across 52,011 elicitations, expected posterior beliefs after delivery of each piece of information are a combination of a fraction of prior belief (0.7) plus movement toward truth between 15 and 28 points. The amount subjects move toward truth depends upon the characteristic delivered. On average, party identification causes the largest increase in accuracy of beliefs (28 points). But a clear second-most-informative characteristic is the other's report of MIP (20 points). Race is the third-most-informative with average learning of 17.6 points, and the remaining three characteristics average around 16.

Taking the coefficient estimates from column one at face value suggests indeed that MIP is an important explanation of vote choice and, if MIP measures an issue about which respondents care intensely, issue intensity is an important feature of electoral competition.

TABLE 8.2. *Average effect of voter characteristic on accuracy of beliefs about vote choice of others*

	Basic	After PID	After MIP	After Race
Prior	0.70*	0.76*	0.71*	0.71*
	(0.00)	(0.01)	(0.01)	(0.01)
Party identification	28.82*	–	27.44*	28.20*
	(0.31)		(0.56)	(0.58)
Most important problem	20.34*	15.70*	–	19.38*
	(0.32)	(0.59)		(0.59)
Race	17.59*	14.75*	17.65*	–
	(0.32)	(0.58)	(0.57)	
Gender	16.13*	13.14*	15.41*	16.54*
	(0.32)	(0.59)	(0.57)	(0.59)
Income	15.46*	12.18*	15.27*	16.16*
	(0.32)	(0.58)	(0.57)	(0.60)
State	16.33*	13.12*	16.54*	16.19*
	(0.32)	(0.58)	(0.57)	(0.60)
N	52,011	12,827	13,274	12,918
RMSE	23.42	21.55	22.52	23.30
R^2	0.87	0.91	0.89	0.88
adj R^2	0.87	0.91	0.89	0.88

*$p \leq 0.05$.
Note: Ordinary least squares regression estimates with standard errors in parentheses. Dependent variable is beliefs in round after exposure to information of class in rows. PID = party identification.

In columns two, three, and four of Table 8.2, I evaluate the informativeness of each characteristic in elicitations after the subject had been delivered each of the three most informative characteristics estimated in column one. Column two estimates the information for characteristics after the subject has observed the party identification of the other, column three after observing MIP, and column four after observing race.

Coefficients in column two are smaller than those in column one, meaning that average movement toward truth with these characteristics is smaller if the subject has already been delivered the party identification of the other. Attenuation in column two is notably greater than attenuation in columns three and four, where characteristics appear to be similarly informative to subjects after they have learned about MIP or race of the other.

Nonetheless, even having been delivered party identification, MIP continues to generate movement in beliefs toward the reported vote choice of the other. Conditional on knowledge of party identification, participants found MIP to be a relevant factor in beliefs about how others vote. Likewise, column four shows that MIP remains informative after the participant has learned the other's race.

These results show there is information in the MIP response beyond information in party identification and other characteristics. This suggests that learning about intensity per se informed our cartographers. Participants believe issues of intensity to be an important feature of vote choice.

* * *

The cartographers in this experiment have helped map the importance of issues of intensity to vote choice. Cartographer beliefs about the relationship between the text response of others about the most important problem facing the nation and the 2016 candidate vote of others helps us understand how issues factor into vote choice. It appears that the issues voters most cared about in 2016 were an important factor in their presidential vote choice.

9

Opening Avenues of Costly Action

Institutional Change to Costs of Campaign Contributions

In this chapter, I consider the consequences for costly political action where an institutional change opens a less costly avenue of political action. The setting is the program of *Democracy Vouchers* implemented in 2017 by the city of Seattle, Washington. The program issued vouchers to all residents in Seattle. Residents could send vouchers to any eligible candidate running for a city office, who could then exchange vouchers received for publicly funded campaign contributions. The program did not prevent direct contributions but provided an alternative route for voters to offer pecuniary support.

I first describe the implementation and institution of Democracy Vouchers. I then show that the institution of Democracy Vouchers has different empirical implications for three existing theories of political action than for intensity theory. I present the three theories and then present a research design and data to evaluate the different implications. Statistical analysis suggests that intensity theory more effectively explains the patterns of Democracy Vouchers than do existing theories.

I want to note at the beginning that my view of the empirical analysis is not that it rules one and only one theory applicable to political contributions. The social world is complicated and filled with voters of many different motives. Surely each theory helps explain the actions of some voters and some settings. My hope is that this empirical analysis shows that intensity theory adds to our existing understanding of political action and increases our ability to explain empirical patterns.

9.1 RESEARCH SETTING: DEMOCRACY VOUCHERS

In November 2015 voters in Seattle, Washington passed the Honest Elections Seattle Initiative (I-122), which implemented a set of campaign finance reforms for city elections. One reform was the creation of *Democracy Vouchers*. Funded by an increase in property taxes of about $8.00 per resident per year and sunsetting after ten years, in each municipal election every resident in the city is eligible to allocate up to $100 in Democracy Vouchers to candidates who agree to limits on their non-voucher fund raising and expenditures and who agree to participate in candidate debates.[1] Candidates may exchange vouchers received with the City for cash that can be used as would direct contributions.

Vouchers were first used in the 2017 municipal elections. Each eligible resident (age 18+, U.S. citizen, foreign national or lawful permanent resident, and a Seattle resident) could use up to four $25 vouchers to allocate to eligible candidates. Residents who were registered to vote automatically received vouchers by mail. Those eligible but not registered could follow an application process.

In 2017, the Seattle Ethics and Elections Commission (SEEC) mailed four vouchers each to 546,258 residents, processed 80,000 vouchers returned, and disbursed $1.04 million in funds to eligible candidates.[2]

In the 2019 municipal elections, the SEEC mailed vouchers to about 476,000 residents. Just more than 38,000 residents allocated 147,128 vouchers worth $2.5 million to 35 eligible candidates.[3]

Importantly, I-122 did not change the ability of Seattle municipal candidates to collect (non-voucher) contributions from out-of-city contributors. These out-of-city contributors can serve as a comparison group to help evaluate the impact of vouchers on political action.

9.2 EXISTING THEORIES OF POLITICAL CONTRIBUTIONS

I now describe three existing theories of political contributions. I present a simplified taxonomy that serves as a rough summary of the political science of campaign contributions but necessarily leaves important nuance aside.

---

[1] Seattle Municipal Code section 2.04, https://library.municode.com/wa/seattle/codes/municipal_code.

[2] See www.seattle.gov/Documents/Departments/EthicsElections/DemocracyVoucher/2017_Biennial_Report.pdf.

[3] See www.seattle.gov/Documents/Departments/EthicsElections/DemocracyVoucher/2019_Biennial_Report.pdf.

Expressive theory One theoretical approach suggests that campaign contributions follow from contributors' intrinsic desire to express support for certain candidates or causes (e.g., Brown, Hedges, and Powell, 1980; Brown, Powell, and Wilcox, 1995; Francia et al., 2003; Bonica, 2013; Hill and Huber, 2017). Under these theories, contributors do not strategically allocate contributions because they believe contributions are instrumental to changing election results. Instead, contributors donate to gain personal satisfaction from political expression.

Candidate support theory A second theoretical approach suggests that contributors act in pursuit of instrumental interests. They donate to candidates in contests they anticipate to be close or to candidates with whom they'd like to have special access if the individual is elected (e.g., Barber, Canes-Wrone, and Thrower, 2017). Under this theory, contributors send money to candidates and causes following calculation of the expected costs and benefits to that action.

Resource theory A third theoretical approach suggests that variation in resources explains variation in political actions, including contributions (e.g., Brady, Verba, and Schlozman, 1995; Sinclair, 2012). Some voters lack time, skills, and money and so do not have the resources to take political action. Voters also reside in different social networks. Some networks are more connected to politics such that voters in those networks are more likely to be asked to give. Other social networks are less connected to politics so that individuals in those networks are less likely asked to contribute. An individual's time, skills, wealth, and networks comprise their level of political resources, which generates the basis of political participation such as contributions.

I have presented rough versions of these three theories such that they are not fully disjointed. Both expressive theory and candidate support theory suggest contributors give to candidates and causes that they support. Nothing in resource theory implies contributors give to candidates or causes that they oppose. The likelihood of contributions increases in personal wealth and in the political connections in social networks, both defining features of resources but also important precursors to making instrumental or expressive contributions.

9.3 DIFFERENTIAL IMPLICATIONS OF INTENSITY AND EXISTING THEORY

I consider three theoretical implications of the introduction of Democracy Vouchers that differentiate intensity theory from the existing theories of political contributions. First, overall demand for vouchers, second, correlation at the individual-level between monetary contributions and the use of vouchers, and third, changes in contribution behavior from elections without vouchers to elections with vouchers.

The goal of identifying differing empirical implications of the different theories is to then take those implications to the data and see if empirical observation suggests greater relevance of one theory than others.

9.3.1 Demand for Vouchers

Resource theory, expressive theory, and candidate support theory all suggest that the adoption of vouchers should be relatively widespread. Under resource theory, voters with high resources are embedded in networks where politics are discussed and contributions solicited. Vouchers are a new item to be solicited in social networks. Vouchers are also of benefit to low-resource voters who might be dissuaded from monetary contributions due to limited wealth. Finally, vouchers automatically mailed to all registered voters might lessen the importance of the political networks in which individual contributions are generated.

With respect to expressive theory, vouchers offer a new expressive opportunity. Residents who return vouchers have their names publicly recorded. If the public record or the act of sending the voucher offer expressive benefits to interested voters, vouchers should be widely adopted.

Finally, under candidate support theory, vouchers offer a low-cost way to directly support candidates in pursuit of instrumental goals. Voters motivated to offer instrumental support to candidates they support should use vouchers in pursuit of those goals.

Intensity theory, on the other hand, suggests limited demand for vouchers. High-intensity voters could already incur the costly action of monetary contributions without the need for vouchers. Adding less-costly vouchers to the portfolio of available actions would not change their need to incur the greater costs of monetary contributions to separate themselves from low-intensity voters. Further, even though vouchers might appear to be most useful for low-income residents, the communication value of vouchers depends upon the individual costliness to the resident. A monetary contribution – even of lower magnitude than for higher-income voters – more clearly communicates cost for a low-income voter than does a voucher.

9.3.2 Relationship between Voucher Use
and Monetary Contributions

Among voters making monetary contributions before the implementation of vouchers, expressive theory and candidate support theory suggest that the use of vouchers should increase as the individual voter's monetary contributions increase. If contributions provide expressive benefit, a higher level of contributions implies higher demand for expression. Because vouchers are publicly reported, voucher use should increase with demand for expression, i.e., increase with the level of monetary contributions.

For contributors motivated to support candidates, the benefits of Democracy Vouchers to candidate or cause are likely greater than the cost to the voucher contributor. If larger contributions from an individual indicate greater motive to support candidates, voucher use should increase with level of contributions. This is especially true for those already making contributions who have already paid the search costs of identifying candidates to support.

The predicted relationship of vouchers to contributions under resource theory is ambiguous. If the level of pre-voucher contributions indicates political skills, wealth, and networks, then those previously making contributions should be more able to successfully understand and use vouchers. Resource theory, however, also suggests that those with limited resources do not participate because the costs of participation are greater than the resources at their disposal. To the extent vouchers are a less-costly form of participation, resource theory might suggest voucher uptake at high rates among those with low resources.

Two of the existing theories suggest voucher use should increase with the level of contributions, and resource theory offers ambiguous predictions. Intensity theory offers empirical predictions that diverge from the other theories about the relationship between contributions and vouchers. Prior to vouchers, low-dollar and non-contributors incur that low level of costly action because they do not care intensely enough to incur the costs of political contribution. Demand for vouchers should be low for those who previously made few or no political contributions because they do not care enough about policy to engage in political action.

Under intensity theory, those making large contributions prior to the introduction of vouchers, on the other hand, incur the costs of contributions to communicate that they care intensely. Providing high-intensity voters with the lower-cost option of vouchers does not provide much additional opportunity to incur the costs necessary to communicate intensity. Using vouchers does not indicate intense preferences as clearly as monetary contributions.

Intensity theory's implications for those making a middling level of contributors prior to vouchers is ambiguous. Voters who contribute a modest amount in dollars communicate that they care enough to incur some costs but not as great a cost as high-dollar contributors. Because vouchers incur modest costs to use, such modest contributors might indeed choose to use vouchers. The value of communication for a voucher, however, might be less clear than the communication value of cash. Candidates know exactly what $25 in cash represents and, although they know that the cost to the donor of sending a $25 voucher is less than $25, they might not know how much less costly. Contributors might, therefore, stick with the more clear monetary contributions to directly incur an equilibrium magnitude of cost.

Thus, intensity theory suggests either a flat relationship with previous contributions, if middling contributors decide to stick with cash contributions, or an inverse-'U' relationship, with non-contributors continuing to abstain from costly action, large-contributors continuing to need the high-cost actions to signal their intensity, and middling-contributors choosing to use vouchers to signal middling intensity. The inverse-U is not predicted by other theories. Only resource theory implies a flat relationship, and even then that prediction is tentative rather than clear.

9.3.3 Vouchers Do Not Much Change Contributor Actions

A third empirical implication from applying the theories to the institution of vouchers less clearly differentiates intensity theory. Imagine that contributors have a fixed budget of monetary contributions to make in each election. This might be due to a personal budget constraint or due to a fixed number of candidates and contribution limits. Under intensity theory, the contribution budget is the magnitude of costly action incurred in pursuit of the equilibrium magnitude of costs to communicate intensity.

Intensity theory suggests, then, that adding a new, low-cost political action should have little consequence to the other political actions taken by high-intensity voters. High-intensity voters make monetary contributions of a certain amount to communicate their issue intensity to politicians. Vouchers do not substitute for the informational value of

TABLE 9.1. *Summary of differential empirical implications with Democracy Vouchers*

Implication	Existing theories	Intensity theory
Demand	Widespread demand for vouchers.	Limited demand for vouchers.
Correlation	Positive relationship between voucher use and level of contributions (expressive and instrumental). Ambiguous or flat relationship (resources).	Flat or inverse-'U' relationship.
Change	Potential substitution or complement of monetary contributions with vouchers.	Little change in monetary contribution patterns with vouchers.

monetary contributions. Thus, the introduction of vouchers is unlikely to cause large changes in patterns of contributions.

Existing theories, however, do not so clearly suggest little change in contribution behavior. Vouchers might change the political actions taken by voters because they provide new resources for participation, provide a new opportunity for expression, or provide straightforward opportunity for candidate support. When the motive of voters is something other than incurring a specific level of individual costs, new opportunities to influence politics are more likely to be undertaken. Vouchers might serve as substitutes for or complements to existing contribution patterns.

* * *

Table 9.1 summarizes the three differential empirical implications for political contributions, comparing existing theories with intensity theory in the context of Democracy Vouchers. These different implications lead to opportunity for quantitative analysis to evaluate the value of each theory. It is important to note that one challenge is that intensity theory predicts limited or zero changes, and it is difficult to "prove a null."

9.4 DEMOCRACY VOUCHERS, RESEARCH OPPORTUNITY, AND DESIGN

Democracy Vouchers provide a natural experiment to evaluate the etiology of costly political action among individual citizens. Prior to vouchers, residents in Seattle offered support to candidates through actions such as volunteering and direct monetary contributions. Vouchers opened a new route of support without prohibiting other actions.

I assume that Democracy Vouchers are *less costly* than direct contributions or volunteering. While vouchers are a "public act" such that the names of residents allocating vouchers are a matter of public record, so too are campaign contributions. Vouchers require citizens to determine which local candidate(s) to support. This search for candidates requires time and effort for each individual, but so too do campaign contributions. How do citizens respond to a new but less costly opportunity to support candidates for office?

9.4.1 Data and Measurement

To measure individual campaign contributions, I use the lists of campaign contributions for each election cycle available from the SEEC (Seattle Ethics and Elections Commission data, 2020). I purge the list of corporate contributors by a manual read of contributor names. Candidates received more than $5 million in contributions in 2019, $4 million in 2017, $3.8 million in 2015, $3.3 million in 2013, and $1.8 million in 2011.

As required by I-122, Democracy Voucher records are available from the SEEC (Seattle Democracy Voucher Program data 2020). The database includes records for all vouchers returned to the SEEC by mail or online and indicates whether the voucher was successfully redeemed or was invalid. More than ten percent of returned vouchers were invalid because they were allocated to candidates who did not meet the eligibility requirements or because the vouchers were incorrectly filled out by the resident.

I also use population counts to measure per capita rates of participation in contributions and vouchers. Population data are estimates from the United States Census American Community Survey. I present summary statistics in Appendix Table D.1.

9.5 RESULTS: VOUCHERS AND POLITICAL CONTRIBUTIONS

9.5.1 Demand for Vouchers

I begin by evaluating the differential implication on demand for Democracy Vouchers. Existing theories suggest widespread demand for new vouchers, while intensity theory suggests limited demand.

In Figure 9.1, I present two bar charts that demonstrate limited demand for vouchers. The top chart presents the proportion of Seattle residents aged 18+ who made a monetary contribution for each election year under study (darker bars) and the proportion who returned one or more Democracy Vouchers (whether or not successfully redeemed) in 2017 and 2019 (lighter bars).

The top frame shows that contributions are made by one to two percent of the Seattle population with an increase in proportion contributing across time. In 2017 and 2019, larger proportions of residents used Democracy Vouchers than made contributions with more than two times as many residents returning vouchers than making contributions in 2019.

The rate of voucher return, however, is still a small proportion of the total population, about 2.5 percent in 2017 and 4.5 percent in 2019. While contributions might seem a reasonable benchmark, note that vouchers were mailed directly to individual residents from city officials. There was no such solicitation for contributions.

The lower frame in Figure 9.1 breaks apart contribution and voucher rates by 2015 household income in the resident's ZIP code.[4] Here, each group of bars represent four sets of ZIP codes categorized by median household income less than $55,000, $55,000 to $65,000, $65,000 to $85,000, or more than $85,000.

The lower frame shows that rate of contributions in each election is roughly increasing in median household income. Contributors are about twice as likely to reside in the highest income ZIP codes than in the lowest income ZIP codes. This pattern is consistent with wealth constraints limiting the rate of contributions from lower income voters.

Vouchers in both 2017 and 2019 (groups of bars three from the right and farthest right), however, exhibit the same pattern of increasing political action with income. In fact, the relationship between income and participation appears steeper for vouchers than for contributions. This suggests that it may not be a wealth constraint that limits engagement of lower income voters in costly political action.

Demand for vouchers does not appear widespread, with less than 5 percent of residents returning vouchers in 2019 and 2.5 percent in 2017. Further, vouchers do not appear to have appealed to a group of residents who wanted to contribute but lacked the monetary resources to do so. Despite being mailed four $25 vouchers to contribute as they

---

4 Because Seattle incomes grew substantially from 2011 to 2019 due to an employment boom, I use 2015 income to keep ZIP codes in constant groups for comparison.

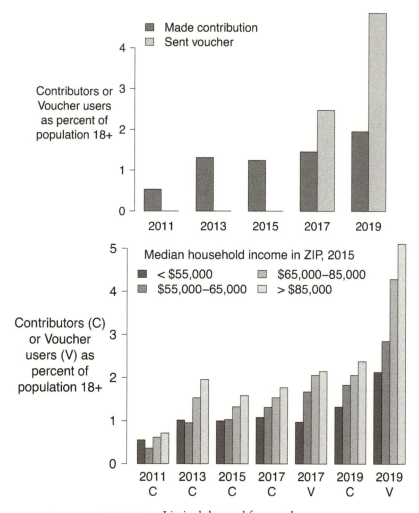

FIGURE 9.1 Limited demand for vouchers

Note: Bar heights correspond to counts of contributors or residents who returned at least one voucher divided by the population aged 18+. Median household income in 2018 inflation-adjusted dollars.

wished, most residents declined to do so. Overall, Figure 9.1 suggests limited demand for Democracy Vouchers from Seattle residents.

9.5.2 Relationship between Voucher Use and Monetary Contributions

Figure 9.1 presented the relationship between Democracy Voucher use and resources as measured by ZIP code median household income.

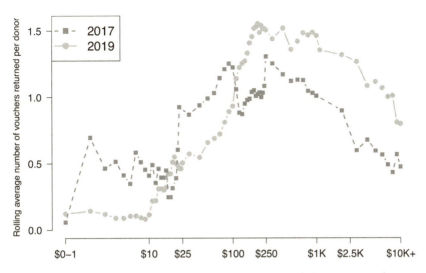

FIGURE 9.2 Largest and smallest contributors are less likely to use vouchers

Note: Each point is the number of vouchers returned divided by the number of contributors at that value of (rounded) monetary contribution total. Points are smoothed with a 10-bin trailing average. Version without smoothing in Appendix Figure D.1.

In Figure 9.2, I compare voucher use to magnitude of contributions at the individual level. This figure addresses the second differential implication of existing theories and intensity theory.

Contribution records from Seattle in 2017 and 2019 note the voucher identification number for each contributor (Seattle Ethics and Elections Commission data 2020). I merge voucher records (Seattle Democracy Voucher Program data 2020) to contribution records on that identifier. I then append to the merged data records of vouchers returned that do not match to a contributor. I assume these records represent residents who returned vouchers but did not make a monetary contribution.

Each point in Figure 9.2 represents a group of Seattle residents who made total political contributions of a given dollar amount in that election cycle (2019 circles, 2017 squares). I first top-code individual contributions per election at $10,000. The x-axis is an amount (or small range of amounts) of contributions. The height of the y-axis corresponds to the number of vouchers returned per contributor at that magnitude of contributions.

For example, the leftmost circle represents the set of Seattle residents who gave $0 or $1 in 2019. On average, one voucher was returned for every ten such residents, indicated by the height of the point at about 0.1.

Because many of the contribution amounts have a small number of residents, the trend is smoothed using a 10-bin trailing average. I present a version of the figure with the raw data in Appendix Figure D.1.

Intensity theory implies that if contributions serve as costly actions to communicate intensity, individuals making few or many contributions obtain little benefit from incurring the small costs of returning Democracy Vouchers. The relationship between contributions and voucher use in Figure 9.2 roughly follows this pattern. Voucher use starts at a low level for those making zero or small contributions, increases in contributions up to about $250, and then declines. Voucher use is lowest for those making contributions of less than $25.

Those making zero or a small amount of contributions and those making large contributions are less likely to return Democracy Vouchers. This is inconsistent with the empirical implication of existing theories and provides an example of how intensity theory gives new insight to the politics of participation.

9.5.3 Vouchers Do Not Much Change Contributor Actions

Finally, Figure 9.3 evaluates the third differential implication that Democracy Vouchers do not much change contributor actions. Addressing this question requires counterfactual reasoning. We cannot simply compare contribution patterns in years with vouchers to years without vouchers because each election cycle is different. Different offices on the ballot, different mixes of candidates, and different contexts lead to variation in contributions across elections not attributable to vouchers.

To get closer to the comparison of interest, we'd like to see how the same contributors respond in the same election to having versus not having the ability to use vouchers. As an approximation to this experiment, I compare the contribution behavior of Seattle residents to the contribution behavior of non-residents. Because Seattle policies affect not only residents of the city but also those who commute to work in the city or who have business in the city but do not reside there, city politics generates many contributions from individuals whose residence is not within the city limits.

Non-residents continued to make contributions in 2017 and 2019 without having access to vouchers. Residents, in contrast, were able to add vouchers to their portfolio of contributions. If we are willing to assume that vouchers did not substantively change the goals or strategies of non-residents, we can compare how non-resident contributions changed to how resident contributions changed to evaluate the effect of vouchers on resident contributions – a difference-in-differences design.

Identifying the same contributor across time using contribution records is extremely difficult. There is no unique individual identifier to match across elections. Rather, contributions are only recorded when they are made (i.e., non-contributors are not identified). The SEEC records contributions by name of contributor. However, names are not standardized and so even if the same individual makes two contributions, the name may not be equivalently recorded.

To make the comparison within the limitations of the recording of contributions, I use a partial aggregation approach. The approach sums contributions to the surname-resident-period. For elections held before and after the institution of vouchers and separately for contributors with ZIP code in and out of Seattle city limits, I sum contributions recorded to each surname.[5] Thus, if "Jane and James Polk" living in Seattle made a contribution in 2015 and "J Polk" made a contribution in 2017, the two would be matched together when aggregating contributions to the surname "Polk."

I present in Figure 9.3 change in contribution behavior from the pre-voucher elections of 2011, 2013, and 2015 to the post-voucher elections of 2017 and 2019 by surname. I present these changes separately for Seattle residents (top frame) and non-residents (bottom frame). Each line connects the sum of contributions for a surname prior to vouchers (top line) to after implementation of vouchers (bottom line). Lines that slope rightward indicate increasing contributions with vouchers. Lines that slope leftward indicate decreasing contributions with vouchers.

Thick lines with solid circles connect mean contributions in quintiles of pre-voucher contribution to help summarize the patterns. For example, the solid circle farthest left on the top line is the average sum of contributions among the 20 percent of surnames with the smallest sums of contributions in elections prior to vouchers. The line connects this average sum to the average sum of those same surnames in elections with vouchers. The next solid circle is for the second 20 percent of surname contributions, then third, fourth, and finally top 20 percent.

Figure 9.3 provides little evidence that the introduction of vouchers influenced contribution patterns. For both residents and non-residents, lines slope both left and right without a clear trend. For both residents and

---

5 I again top-code individual contributor totals per election to $10,000.

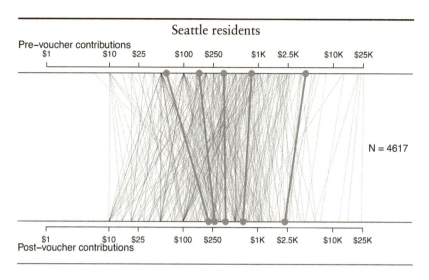

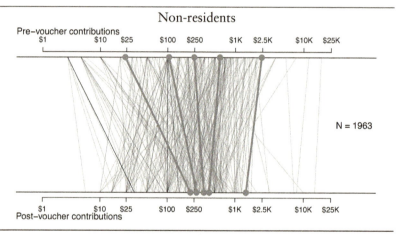

FIGURE 9.3 Little change in patterns of monetary contributions with option of vouchers

Note: Lines connect sum of contributions from pre-voucher elections 2011, 2013, and 2015 (top axis) to sum of contributions from post-voucher elections 2017 and 2019 (bottom axis) for each contributor surname with at least $1 in contributions in both periods. Light lines random sample from full set. Each thick line represents a pre-voucher quintile of surname contributions. These lines connect pre-voucher to post-voucher mean contributions for that quintile. Top frame is Seattle residents, bottom non-residents.

non-residents, patterns aggregated to the quintile show small reversion to mean with similar reversions in the two frames. Smaller contributors prior to vouchers on average increase contributions with vouchers and larger contributors on average decrease contributions.

More importantly, the changes in contribution patterns of residents in the top frame, who gain vouchers, are nearly identical to changes in contribution patterns of non-residents in the bottom frame. In slope, magnitude, and spread, we see little evidence of differential changes in contribution patterns. In sum, there is little evidence that Democracy Vouchers changed the actions of individual contributors.

9.6 CONCLUSION AND CONNECTIONS

This chapter has presented evidence that intensity theory helps us understand how voters respond to new opportunities for political action. There are four key findings. First, Seattle residents exhibit only limited demand for Democracy Vouchers. Second, the use of vouchers appears to increase with income rather than inspire the greatest action from those with wealth constraints. Third, the relationship between the use of vouchers and monetary contributions is an inverse-'U', with the greatest voucher use among those making monetary contributions around $250. Fourth, the implementation of vouchers does not appear to have changed the distribution or pattern of contributions.

The overall empirical pattern is that opening a new avenue of less costly political action does not substitute for the costly actions of those previously taking action. This new institution provided new resources for participation, automatically sending vouchers by mail to every registered voter – at mailing costs to taxpayers of the city of more than $300,000 – yet had almost no effect on patterns of monetary contributions.

In my view, these empirical results suggest the value of intensity theory to our understanding of electoral politics and representation. The theory offers a different explanation for voter choices over political actions that adds to existing theories of behavior. Voter motivation to communicate issue intensity could be a key driver of the choice by some to participate in politics and others to abstain from participation.

Closing Avenues of Costly Action

Reform to Primary Elections

Intensity theory proposes that high-intensity voters incur costly actions to communicate issue intensity to public officials. In equilibrium, three factors determine the magnitude of costs intense voters choose to incur: expectations about the proportion of the electorate that is high-intensity, the size of the majority, and the strength of preference of high-intensity voters relative to the strength of preference of low-intensity voters. High-intensity voters choose a set of actions and expressions of sufficient personal cost to communicate their intensity.

The theory does not speak to which of many costly actions high-intensity voters might incur; to maintain parsimony, I assume simply that voters incur some magnitude of costs. However, one implication of the theory is that if the political system changes such that it limits a costly action that was previously available to voters, to incur the same magnitude of cost as before high-intensity voters would need to find and incur new costly actions.

In this chapter, I consider the consequences for costly political action where an institutional change closes one avenue of costly political action previously taken by high-intensity voters. I show that when the rules of primary elections become less stringent, individual campaign contributions increase. That is, when the costly action "participating in closed party primaries" is removed by institutional reform, a different costly action, individual campaign contributions, increases in magnitude. I present statistical analysis to estimate a causal link between reform to primary elections and individual campaign contributions.[1] I show in the Appendix that the mechanism of the increased contributions does not appear to be either increased competitiveness or an increase in the number of candidates running for office.

I assume that participation in closed primary elections serves as a costly action to communicate to general election candidates. I do not claim that communicating intensity is the only motive for participation. What I do claim is that if some citizens participate in closed primaries at least partly to communicate that they care more about policy than others, if reform ends closed primaries, those citizens must find some other pathway to incur costs in pursuit of communication.

10.1 RESEARCH SETTING: DIRECT PRIMARY ELECTIONS

Political parties have used different institutions to nominate candidates for office throughout American history. The direct primary election was a Progressive Era reform aimed at reducing the power of parties by allowing more of the electorate to participate in candidate nominations (Merriam and Overacker 1928; though see Ware 2002). The direct primary election allows voters who are not formal members of the party organization to determine which candidates appear on the general election ballot. Previously, party conventions, caucuses, or private meetings nominated candidates to represent the party on the general election ballot.

The direct primary remains today an important American political institution. Depending on the state, a combination of party organization rules and state legislature statutes determine nomination procedures for each state-party. These rules describe how and when the election is held (if concurrent with other elections, if by plurality or majority rule with runoff), what limits are placed on which voters may participate (if the voter must be registered with the party and, if so, if they may register day of election or must do so earlier), and whether voters may vote for candidates of different parties in different offices on the ballot or must limit themselves to candidates of only one party for all offices.

Because of different state rules and legislative settings, reformers have recently succeeded in modifying primary rules in some states to ease access to the primary ballot. To make it easier for more voters to participate

---

[1] This chapter includes material sourced from Hill (2022b), published by Cambridge University Press and reprinted with permission.

in nominations, reforms have relaxed or eliminated party registration requirements and have loosened ballot restrictions. Reforms began in the early 1990s and have continued through the 2020s. One goal of primary reform is to increase representativeness of nominees by decreasing the relative influence of ideologues and partisans. A large body of research in political science aims to estimate the consequences and success of these reforms (e.g., Gerber and Morton, 1998; Hirano et al., 2010; Bullock and Clinton, 2011; McGhee et al., 2014; Hill, 2015; Kousser, 2015; McGhee and Shor, 2017; Kousser, Phillips, and Shor, 2018).

The basic idea of this chapter is to see if reforms to primary institutions that decrease the costs to participating lead to increases in costly actions taken by voters in other settings.

10.1.1 Assumption That Closed Primaries Costly

The central assumption to using this setting to evaluate consequences of closing one avenue of costly action is that voting in closed primary elections is costly to the individual voters who participate. My assertion that participation in these elections is costly is supported both by considered observation of the institution and by litigation on the direct primary in front of the United States Supreme Court.

Reasoning about the institution of a closed primary itself, participating is more costly than either staying home or participating at a general election. In a closed primary, the voter must register with a political party days or weeks prior to the election. This registration requires foresight and forecloses late decisions. Even after registering, the voter must incur the voting costs of participation in lower-salience primary elections and is limited to voting only for candidates from that single party. While these costs are not incredible, they are clearly non-zero.

Cognitive demands on voters can also be lower in general elections and in some open primary elections when candidates have different party labels. These party labels can serve as heuristics for voters to make choices when they do not know much about the candidates on the ballot. A closed party primary, on the other hand, by definition includes only candidates of the same party and so making an informed choice in closed primaries often requires greater investment on the part of voters.

In addition to this simple reasoning, litigation suggests that many actors believe closed primaries to be costly. Political parties themselves have filed lawsuits to prevent reforms that open access to their primary elections. In 1979, the attorney general of the state of Wisconsin sued the National Democratic Party after the Party had ruled that Wisconsin's open primary violated national party selection rules. The Party had decided not to seat Wisconsin delegates nominated from an open primary at the convention. The case was appealed to the Supreme Court in *Democratic Party* v. *Wisconsin* (Democratic Party v. Wisconsin ex rel. La Follette, 450 U.S. 107, 1981).

The evidence before the Court and opinion of the Court follow from the presumption that closed primaries are costly. The 1980 National Democratic Party selection rules stated that "the delegate selection process in primaries or caucuses shall be restricted to Democratic voters only who publicly declare their party preference and have that preference publicly recorded." Requiring voters to both publicly declare and have publicly recorded an affiliation indicates that the national party wanted to limit participation in nomination to those willing to incur some costs to do so.

The national party argued that open access to primary elections would prevent the election from screening out voters whose affiliation was "slight, tenuous, or fleeting." This statement is exactly the idea of intensity theory, that the costs of participating in a closed primary separated voters whose interests were slight, tenuous, or fleeting from those motivated by greater intensity.

In *California Democratic Party et al.* v. *Jones* (California Democratic Party et al. v. Jones, 530 U.S. 567, 2000), the Supreme Court struck down the blanket primary following litigation initiated by political party organizations in California. The Court ruled that the blanket primary violated the parties' First Amendment rights to free association by preventing them from limiting participation to associated members. The author of the opinion, Justice Scalia, while skeptical that costs to participating in closed primaries are very high, nonetheless affirms there are costs,

even when it is made quite easy for a voter to change his party affiliation the day of the primary, and thus, in some sense, to 'cross over,' at least he must formally become a member of the party; and once he does so, he is limited to voting for candidates of that party ... The voter who feels himself disenfranchised should simply join the party. That may put him to a hard choice ...

Scalia suggests that registering with a party can be a "hard" – i.e., costly – choice. The opinion also agrees that publicly declaring a party affiliation is costly, although it concludes costs are not high enough to be a compelling interest of the State.

10.2 DIFFERENCE-IN-DIFFERENCES DESIGN

I estimate how reform to closed primaries influences the magnitude of individual political contributions at the level of the state-party primary. To estimate the effect, I implement a difference-in-differences (DID) statistical model. The DID design measures the effect of an intervention by comparing how the outcome of interest for units (here, state-parties) subject to that intervention changes relative to the outcome of interest for other units not subject to the intervention. The comparison units include both that same unit from earlier or later time periods when not subject to the intervention and other units not subject to the intervention. In this case, my design measures the change in magnitude of individual campaign contributions for state-parties whose rules of primary elections are made less stringent.

I use a two-way fixed effects statistical model. The model measures the effect of within-state-party changes in primary institutions across elections, holding constant all time-invariant features of the state and state-party. These time-invariant features include state-specific factors such a party balance, party organization, geography, average policy views, and legislative institutions. Effects are identified when a state-party changes its institution.

The statistical model is

$$y_{ijt} = \alpha_{ij} + \gamma_t + \beta x_{ijt} + \varepsilon_{ijt}, \qquad (10.1)$$

where y is the outcome of interest in state i for party j in election cycle t, α is a state-party fixed effect, γ is an election cycle fixed effect, β is the coefficient of interest on x measuring a less-costly or non-partisan primary election institution, and ε is a random disturbance. The unit of observation is the state-party-year.

Variation in rules (x_{ijt}) comes from varying success by reformers across states and times in relaxing restrictions on participation in primary elections. This variation provides empirical leverage to evaluate if closing off one avenue of costly communication leads to increased effort in other realms. Because reforms switch on and off in response to various state-specific factors such as court rulings and citizen initiatives, state-parties are treated to primary reform in different states at different times.

Because states (and sometimes parties within states) influence or choose their own rules of primary elections, one concern with this identification strategy is that institutional change is endogenous to features of the electoral environment. Table 10.1 presents the legal and statutory changes that generate identification. The cause of institutional reform varies across

TABLE 10.1. *Changes in primary institutions*

State	Year	Party	Switch	Cause
AK	1996	Rep	Became non-partisan	State supreme court approves statewide blanket primary
UT	1996	Dem	Left less costly	State legislature moved primaries to closed (HB 359)
UT	1996	Rep	Left less costly	State legislature moved primaries to closed (HB 359)
CA	1998	Dem	Became non-partisan	Proposition moved primaries to blanket from closed (Prop 198)
CA	1998	Rep	Became non-partisan	Proposition moved primaries to blanket from closed (Prop 198)
AK	2002	Rep	Left non-partisan	Supreme Court strikes down blanket primary, Alaska moves to semi-closed
AK	2002	Dem	Left non-partisan	Supreme Court strikes down blanket primary, Alaska moves to semi-closed
CA	2002	Dem	Left non-partisan	Supreme Court strikes down blanket primary, California moves to semi-closed
CA	2002	Rep	Left non-partisan	Supreme Court strikes down blanket primary, California moves to semi-closed
WA	2004	Rep	Became less costly	Supreme Court declares state's blanket primary unconstitutional
WA	2004	Dem	Became less costly	Supreme Court declares state's blanket primary unconstitutional
LA	2008	Rep	Left non-partisan	State legislature moved primaries to closed (SB 18, Act 560)
LA	2008	Dem	Left non-partisan	State legislature moved primaries to closed (SB 18, Act 560)
WA	2008	Rep	Left less costly	Voter initiative approves top-two primary in 2004 (I 872); not implemented until 2008 following Supreme Court approval
WA	2008	Dem	Left less costly	Voter initiative approves top-two primary in 2004 (I 872); not implemented until 2008 following Supreme Court approval
CA	2010	Rep	Became non-partisan	Proposition moved primaries to non-partisan (State legislature-referred Prop 14)

(continued)

TABLE 10.1 *(continued)*

State	Year	Party	Switch	Cause
CA	2010	Dem	Became non-partisan	Proposition moved primaries to non-partisan (State legislature-referred Prop 14)
LA	2010	Dem	Became non-partisan	State legislature moved primaries to non-partisan blanket (HB 292)
LA	2010	Rep	Became non-partisan	State legislature moved primaries to non-partisan blanket (HB 292)

states and times from judicial rulings to legislative action to voter initiatives. That the etiology of reform varies across settings provides some comfort that there is no single omitted factor that always causes reform and would lead to a spurious estimate of the effect of reform.

To identify the causal effect of an intervention, DID designs require an assumption of parallel trends. The variation in etiology of reform in Table 10.1 is my strongest evidence in support of parallel trends. Because many of the factors, e.g., court rulings and citizen initiatives, generating change to primary rules are plausibly unrelated to trends in contributions across state-parties, the parallel trends assumption is more likely met. I provide some empirical evaluation of parallel trends in Appendix Section E.3.

10.2.1 Data and Measurement

To measure stringency of access to primary elections, I use the McGhee et al. (2014) compilation of state-party primary election rule changes from 1992 to 2008. I extend their time-series to 2014 through personal correspondence with the authors and with documentation of state election laws provided by the National Conference of State Legislatures.

Because I am interested in how actors respond to reforms that change the costs of participating, I categorize primary rules by considering how burdensome each rule is for individual voter participation. In my category "Costly," voters must formally register with a party in order to participate in that party's primary, often with some level of restriction on that registration. I assign Open and Open-to-unaffiliated primary systems to the category "Lower Cost," as any voter may participate in any party primary without restriction but must still choose a party ballot. I classify Top-Two and Blanket primaries "Non-partisan" because costs to participate are ambiguous relative to Open but likely less costly than the various versions of Closed (see Appendix Table E.1).

To measure individual campaign contributions, I use the Database on Ideology, Money in Politics, and Elections (DIME, Bonica 2013, 2019), which compiles contribution information from state and federal campaign filings. I use all contributions during an election cycle, both general and primary election classified. The DIME federal data includes contributions from individuals who made at least $200 in contributions or from individuals making contributions through intermediary bundlers such as ActBlue. It will miss some small-level federal contributors, though most states publicize even small contributions. For details on aggregation choices, see Appendix Section E.2.

10.3 RESULTS: PRIMARY REFORM INCREASES CAMPAIGN CONTRIBUTIONS

Recall that the question is if reforms that make primary elections less costly lead voters to incur costs in the alternative realm of action, political contributions. If so, we should see that less-costly primaries are associated with more individual campaign contributions.

In Table 10.2, I present results from estimating Eq. (10.1) on individual campaign contributions from 1992 to 2014. Dependent variables sum individual contributions to recipients of the two major parties in each cycle, with each observation a state-party-cycle. I also include logged versions of each count dependent variable given the different sizes of states. The natural log transformation allows interpretation of effects in percentage terms.[2]

The first column is total contributions, where the best estimate is that less-costly primaries increased contributions by about $16.4 million and non-partisan primaries by about $18 million to candidates of each party in each state with reform. The loglinear specification in column two indicates a 21 percent increase in contributions for less-costly primaries and a 9 percent increase for non-partisan. There is notable sampling variability in all four estimates.

The third and fourth columns consider effects of reform on counts of contributions and the fifth and sixth on counts of contributors.

---

[2] To calculate the percentage, apply the formula $100 * (e^b - 1)$ for a coefficient estimate b and Euler's number e.

TABLE 10.2. *Difference-in-difference effects of primary reform on individual campaign contributions*

	(1) Sum of contributions (1000s)	(2) Log sum contributions	(3) Count of contributions	(4) Log count contributions	(5) Count of contributors	(6) Log count contributors	(7) Percent contributions in primary
Less costly nominating institution	16,376** (3,935)	0.19** (0.06)	110,747 (70,809)	0.19 (0.14)	23,554** (8,745)	0.078 (0.11)	4.45* (2.08)
Non-partisan nominating institution	18,019** (6,607)	0.084 (0.11)	160,832 (119,489)	−0.057 (0.12)	19,804 (13,000)	−0.12 (0.10)	−1.37 (1.55)
Observations	1,200	1,200	1,200	1,200	1,200	1,200	1,200
R-squared	0.302	0.826	0.262	0.787	0.356	0.741	0.578
Number of Party-state	100	100	100	100	100	100	100
Party-state FEs	Yes	Yes	Yes	Yes	Yes	Yes	Yes
Election cycle FEs	Yes	Yes	Yes	Yes	Yes	Yes	Yes

**$p < 0.01$, *$p < 0.05$.
OLS coefficients with robust standard errors clustered on state-party in parentheses.
Money dependent variables in thousands of dollars.
Excluded category is institutions most costly for individual participation.
Note: OLS coefficients with robust standard errors clustered on the state-party.

Estimates have larger standard errors on coefficients so conclusions should be cautious. Point estimates suggest reform increases both the count of contributions reported and the count of unique contributors. The loglinear models (columns four and six) suggest -5 (non-partisan) and 21 (less-costly) percent increase in number contributions but -11 (non-partisan) and 8 (less-costly) percent increase in number contributors, all estimated with large uncertainty.

The seventh column addresses the destination of increased contributions. Results suggest reform increases percentage of contributions classified for the primary election (in open primaries) by around 4.5 points, but fewer primary contributions in non-partisan primaries relative to contributions in the general.

In sum, primary reforms increase campaign contributions in dollars and counts from individuals. Consistent with intensity theory, this evidence suggests that closing one avenue of costly action leads to increased costs incurred in another realm of political action.

10.3.1 Mechanism: Increased Contributions from Previous Primary Voters

A specific implication of intensity theory is that it is those high-intensity individuals who have lost an opportunity for costly action they were previously taking who must incur new costs in other realms of action or expression. The empirical implication in the setting of this chapter is that citizens who were previously participating in costly primary elections to communicate intensity would be more likely to increase campaign contributions following reform than those who were not previously voting in the costly primary.

This hypothesis rests on a set of assumptions and so the empirical analysis that follows should be regarded with some caution. For individuals to respond in this way, we must assume individuals who were high-intensity prior to reform continue to be high-intensity after reform (on average, at least). This may be violated if different issues are subject to electoral competition, if status quo policy changes, or if individual intensity is not stable across time. Note, however, that if any of these assumptions are violated, I would be less likely to find evidence consistent with this empirical implication.

A central challenge to this research design is merging individual voters between two different sets of administrative records each with millions of observations. Records of individual voter registration and turnout history are compiled by election officials in each state, while federal campaign contribution records are compiled by the Federal Election Commission.[3] Recording, compilation, and distribution practices vary across these settings, making the match of individual records challenging. Of particular note is that both voter registration and contribution records are hand-entered by print or computer and subject to transcription and data entry errors.

Difficulty in merging could seriously undermine analysis, as each record that fails to match to a correct record in the other data set makes it appear as if the registered voter made zero dollars in contributions or as if the contributor never turned out to vote.

To attempt to mitigate these challenges in individual matching, I propose a partial-aggregation procedure. The previous section analyzed records aggregated to the level of state-election. Here, I aggregate records to the state-election-surname. That is, instead of trying to match "J.K. Polk" from the registration file to "James Polk" in the contributors file, I aggregate all records in each data set for individuals whose surname is "Polk" and then match the summary of "Polk" turnout to the summary of "Polk" contributions. My presumption is that surname is the data field least-likely recorded with error.

With this partial-aggregation solution to the challenge of merging, I can then institute a DID research design similar to that above with the estimating equation

$$y_{ijt} = \alpha_{ij} + \eta' z_{ijt-1} + \beta x_{ijt} + \xi x_{ijt} z_{ijt-1} + \varepsilon_{ijt}, \qquad (10.2)$$

where y is the outcome of interest for surname-group i in state j in election cycle t, α is a surname-group-state fixed effect, z_{ijt} is a within-state category of previous primary participation among registrants in surname-group-state group i, η is a vector of fixed effects for election-participation category, β is the coefficient of interest on x measuring a less-costly or non-partisan primary election institution, ξ is an interaction coefficient measuring how y varies with reform and participation category, and ε is a random disturbance.

Estimates from Eq. (10.2) evaluate the empirical implication that individuals previously choosing costly political action respond to closing

---

[3] The DIME data set include some state contribution records, but these, too, are recorded by agencies separately from registration.

of that opportunity by increasing costly action in other realms. The coefficient ξ should be positive and of substantive importance when reform causes voters who were previously taking the greatest costly action in closed primaries to increase contributions more than previous non-primary voters.

10.3.2 Data

I do not possess records of registrants from all of the states and election years used in the previous analysis. I use the data I have available, which cover two states with primary election reform, California and Washington. I have been collecting voter file snapshots from California and Washington since 2006. These collections cover year of reform for these two reform states, which allows me to run a two-state interrupted time-series. The DIME compilation also covers contributions in these two states for this time period. I present details of the aggregation procedure in Appendix Section E.5.

In Table 10.3, I present interrupted time-series (ITS) statistical models of contributions on primary reform interacted with each of the previous primary turnout categories. Level of observation is the state-surname-election. An ITS analysis looks at change in an outcome variable with a change in policy. Difference in the average outcome before and after the switch provides an estimate of the effect of the policy on the outcome.

Because this data set includes only California and Washington for the subset of years 2006–2016, it covers only non-partisan reforms, and there is no less-costly reform category. The ITS has state-surname and election fixed effects, and I also include turnout category fixed effects. These fixed effects hold constant contribution patterns of each state-surname and turnout category as well as election-specific influences on contributions.

Coefficients of interest measure how contributions respond to primary reform by previous primary turnout, holding fixed average state-surname contributions, average primary turnout group contributions, and election-specific effects on contributions. All standard errors are clustered on the state-election.

The first column presents the relationship between the sum of contributions by state-surname and non-partisan primary reform interacted with category of previous primary turnout. The first coefficient estimates that among surnames with the lowest previous primary turnout, total

TABLE 10.3. *Interrupted-time-series by previous primary turnout*

	(1) Sum of contributions	(2) Log sum contributions	(3) Number contributions	(4) Log number contributions
Non-partisan*Bottom half previous primary turnout	122 (86.6)	0.29** (0.00)	1.70** (0.07)	0.12** (0.00)
Non-partisan*3rd quartile previous primary turnout	−658 (475.2)	0.45** (0.01)	13.2** (0.30)	0.33** (0.00)
Non-partisan*4th quartile previous primary turnout	342 (235.2)	0.40** (0.00)	2.87** (0.07)	0.21** (0.00)
Observations	11,120,076	11,118,830	11,120,076	11,120,076
R-squared	0.000	0.015	0.005	0.032
Number of Name-state	1,853,346	1,853,346	1,853,346	1,853,346
State-year FEs	Yes	Yes	Yes	Yes
Name-state FEs	Yes	Yes	Yes	Yes
Previous turnout group FEs	Yes	Yes	Yes	Yes

**$p < 0.01$, *$p < 0.05$.
OLS coefficients with robust standard errors clustered on state-election in parentheses.
Excluded category is closed partisan primaries. Limited to California and Washington.

contributions increased by an average of $122 after primary reform. In the second turnout category, the coefficient indicates total contributions decreased by $658 and in the third, highest-participating turnout category, increased by $342. Each of these point estimates is subject to large uncertainty such that the standard errors make uncertain whether any of the effects are greater than zero.

Coefficients in the remaining three columns are all estimated with greater certainty, allowing us to reject a null hypothesis of an effect less than zero. Column two presents the log-linear model, where the coefficients indicate that contributions increased following reform by 34 percent for surnames in the lowest half of previous primary participation, 57 percent for surnames in the third quartile, and 49 percent for surnames in the fourth quartile.[4] A similar pattern manifests for the number of contributions and log number in columns three and four.

Columns two, three, and four provide evidence for the mechanism of costly action to communicate intensity. In each case, registrants who had been previously participating in closed primaries at rates in the top half increased their contributions in response to reform at higher rates than those in the bottom half of previous turnout. Surnames with higher primary participation increased the dollar amount of contributions by 23 and 15 percentage points more than those in the lowest category, all else equal.

In sum, the partial-aggregate ITS analysis finds that individual political contributions increased more from those who were participating in closed primaries prior to reform.

10.4 ALTERNATIVE THEORETICAL EXPLANATIONS

In Chapter 9, I presented three existing theories of political contributions, expressive, candidate support, and resources. How might we explain the patterns I have uncovered here with those theories?

Under expressive theory, changes in contributions would, presumably, be related to changes in the ideologies or other features of candidates for office. However, the political science of primary elections estimates small, variable, and often zero effect of changes in primary institutions

---

[4] Log contributions include an additional dollar added to each count so that the log is defined. Surnames with negative sums of contributions are dropped because the log is undefined.

(e.g., Gerber and Morton, 1998; Hirano et al., 2010; Bullock and Clinton, 2011; McGhee et al., 2014; Hill, 2015; Kousser, 2015; McGhee and Shor, 2017; Kousser, Phillips, and Shor, 2018). Meanwhile, the estimates of Table 10.2 show increases in individual contributions of 9–21 percent. It is possible that large increases in contributions may follow small, variable, and often zero changes in the ideology of candidates.

I present evidence that primary reform did not change the political context of contributions in Appendix Section E.4. Using the same time-series of state-party primary institutional reforms, I show that, if anything, opening primaries *decreases* the number of primary candidates and *decreases* the competitiveness of primary elections. This suggests campaign contributions did not increase because primaries became more competitive or because different candidates chose to run.

The evidence in Appendix Section E.4 also seems inconsistent with candidate support theory. Under candidate support theory, increases in contributions should follow from increasing importance of contributions. However, I find no increase in competition following reform to primary elections.

Under resource theory, changes in contributions are related to changes in resources available or to presence in social networks. It seems unlikely that resources or networks changed concurrently with changes to institutions of nomination, particularly given all of the different sources of rules changes documented in Table 10.1. Even if there were concurrent changes, it would be surprising if it was of a magnitude to generate changes in contributions of 9–21 percent as estimated in Table 10.2.

I suggest that intensity theory provides a parsimonious and reasonable explanation for the patterns I document here. The distribution of costly political action taken by individuals in the electorate is an equilibrium. When institutional reforms modify the costliness of one action in that equilibrium, individuals respond by taking alternative actions to restore the equilibrium. When primary elections are reformed, individuals who had been using closed primary elections to communicate intensity increase contributions as substitute costly action.

* * *

To sum up, the response of voters to an institutional reform follows a pattern consistent with implications of intensity theory. The closing of one avenue of costly action leads to increased costs incurred in a second realm of costly political action. These patterns are hard to explain using existing theories of political science, while intensity theory provides a simple and reasonable explanation. This is not to say that the other theories are wrong, only that in this empirical setting behavioral choices appear consistent with motives to communicate through costly political action.

The results of this chapter, along with those of Chapter 9, have important implications for political reform. Actors who aim to change political institutions so as to change the operation and results of politics might want to conclude with some caution. Intensity theory explains why institutional reforms do not always do what advocates hope. To win votes, politicians want to know who cares intensely. To win policy, voters who care intensely want politicians to know how much they care. Both candidates and voters have strong incentives to find a way for this communication to occur. Changing the avenues for that communication does not change these incentives.

PART IV

CONCLUSIONS

I I

Conclusion

Implications for Representative Democracy and the Study of Politics

This book makes two central claims. First, that majoritarian elections can represent minority interests and frustrate majorities when an intense minority faces a less-intense majority. Second, that because intensity is hard to observe, some voters choose to incur costly political action to communicate to politicians how much they care. Intensity theory blends ideas from democratic theory and formal political economy with empirical evidence from behavioral political science to help us understand electoral competition, intensity of preference, costly action, and representation.

The theory explains *when* policy will frustrate rather than satiate majorities and explains *who* engages in costly political action and with *what magnitude* of cost. I have shown that when candidates are sufficiently uncertain about how policy platforms translate into vote totals, they propose policy with the minority if, and only if, they believe the minority cares sufficiently more about the issue than the majority (Chapters 3 and 4).

I have shown that when intensity is private information to each voter, voters might follow different strategies in pursuit of their interests (Chapter 4). Sometimes only minority voters who care intensely incur costly action. Sometimes both minority and majority voters who care intensely incur costly action. I concluded the theoretical analysis by showing that results hold for any size minority, suggested how the model might be made consistent with free-rider problems in large electorates, and provided analysis showing that costly political action can increase utilitarian social welfare when the minority is sufficiently more intense than the majority (Chapter 5).

I have provided four chapters of empirical evidence in support of the theory (summarized in Chapter 6). I first provided two case histories of frustrated majorities in the politics of biotechnology and firearms (Chapter 7). These case histories highlight the explanatory power of intensity theory for understanding when and why majorities are frustrated and provide evidence that policy change occurs with a change to the distribution of intensity among minority and majority in the electorate.

A crucial assumption of the theory is that vote choice responds more to issues voters care most about. I introduced a new method to account for factors of vote choice and have shown that the issues about which voters care most intensely explain vote choice above and beyond other factors such as party identification (Chapter 8).

The theory has important implications for how voters might respond to changes in opportunities for political participation. I show that intensity theory provides unique predictions for voter response to institutional reforms to campaign finance and primary elections and adds to current received wisdom in explaining empirical evidence on voter response to institutional reform (Chapters 9 and 10).

These two chapters, along with the argument of intensity theory, provide a theoretical framework to evaluate the likely consequences of political reforms. What happens when legislatures or citizens change the rules governing campaign finance, nominations, and other forms of costly political activity? Intensity theory and the evidence here suggest the consequences are not always what reformers anticipate.

The parsimony of intensity theory allows it to more easily travel across multiple settings at the expense of missing some nuances of political outcomes. The empirical chapters are exactly this, crossing multiple settings but perhaps not fully satisfying. Because I have argued that intensity is not only hard to observe but that low-intensity voters have an incentive to obfuscate attempts by politicians to measure intensity, it is difficult to directly observe the correlation between intensity and political action or the correlation between intensity and policy outcomes.

11.1 A RECIPE TO APPLY INTENSITY THEORY

Intensity theory can help scholars reason through the complexity of electoral competition and representation when voters vary in how much they care. To apply the argument to new situations, to summarize expected policy outcomes, and to describe likely incidence of political action, I present a recipe for application to new settings. The recipe proceeds through three steps:

(1) **Size of minority and majority.** For a given election and policy issue, what is the relative size of the group of voters who support and oppose each side of the policy? How much does the majority outnumber the minority?

(2) **Majority and minority intensity of preference, and costly action.** What is the average intensity of the minority and the majority? Relative intensity predicts how many voters engage in costly action and with what magnitude of costs. The distribution of costly action in the electorate predicts what uncertain candidates might believe about which voters care more and less intensely.

(3) **Dynamics of electoral competition.** Is the election result stochastic such that at least some voters might vote for a candidate even if that candidate opposes them on the policy? If stochastic, you may then apply the candidate decision rule (Lemma B.1): The minority gets policy representation if, and only if, the ratio of the minority's intensity to the majority's intensity is greater than the ratio of the majority size to the minority size. If the minority is either large and slightly more intense, or small and much more intense, candidates choose to propose policy with the minority against the majority (see Figure 5.1).

11.2 IMPLICATIONS FOR REPRESENTATION, ELECTORAL COMPETITION, AND POLITICAL ACTION

The first argument of intensity theory is that variation in issue intensity combined with electoral competition can sometimes cause policy proposed with a minority against the known interests of a majority.

I suggest four key implications for elections and representation if intensity theory is a fair approximation of electoral politics in large representative democracies. These implications provide new ideas about elections, representation, interest groups, coalition building, and public opinion.

The second argument of intensity theory is that costly political actions chosen by voters need not follow either from intrinsic psychological benefits nor from immediate instrumental incentive to change the election winner. Instead, actions serve as costly communication in pursuit of longer-term, uncertain, policy benefits. I suggest one implication from this second argument for our understanding of how voters interact with the electoral environment.

11.2.1 The Electoral Connection and Frustrated Majorities

Majorities can be frustrated through the electoral connection. Intensity theory shows that electoral competition in plurality elections does not necessarily lead to majoritarian outcomes, even with majoritarian institutions, vote-maximizing candidates, and the electoral connection. Candidates for office sometimes purposefully side with an intense minority and other times side with a majority. Intensity theory provides guidance on when elections deliver majoritarian and when non-majoritarian policy.

> **Non-majoritarian outcomes do not imply failure of the electoral connection.**

Because majoritarian outcomes are not a necessary consequence of the electoral connection, observation of *non-majoritarian* outcomes does not imply failure of the electoral connection. When we observe a "democratic deficit" with policy apparently against the wishes of electoral majorities, we need not conclude a failure of representation. We need not conclude that voters are insufficiently informed, that voters fail to use electoral actions in their own interests, or that voters make choices using non-issue considerations like psychological attachment to party.

Instead, policy favored by a minority of the electorate may maintain itself because that minority feels intensely enough about the issue relative to the majority to gain representation from ambitious vote-seeking candidates. The electoral connection might be functioning as theorized (by Mayhew, 1974, and others) even when delivering non-majoritarian outcomes.

11.2.2 Pressure Politics

Second, intensity theory helps square pressure politics with the electoral connection. Intensity theory suggests a mechanism through which interest groups and lobbyists might use pressure politics to influence policy. If interest groups represent intense minorities, the power of interest groups is proportional to the winnable votes they represent at elections.

Bombardini and Trebbi (2011) present empirical evidence consistent with this implication in the realm of large corporations (they study Walmart). This is also the argument of Congressman Israel (2018) regarding the National Rifle Association.

> **The power of interest groups is proportional to the winnable votes they represent at elections.**

While interest groups can offer resources such as information, expertise, legislative coordination, and campaign funds, if the electoral connection motivates candidates, the most powerful interest groups are those that represent groups of individuals that combine size and intensity. The AARP represents a large number of individual members (38 million members according to the 2019 annual report). Even though its members are not known for intensity, because of the count of voters AARP represents, its political power can be great.

This implication reinforces the difficulty for those aiming to use political reforms to mitigate the influence of special interests (see Chapters 9 and 10). Candidates attend to the relationship between policy platforms and votes. Limiting contributions or reining in political parties does not change the incentive for candidates to attend to intense minority interests. Special interests succeed because candidates seek votes in elections, not necessarily because of extra-electoral influence that can be reformed away.

Interest groups increase their effectiveness and impact on outcomes when they increase the intensity of their constituents, increase the magnitude of costly political action those constituents are willing to incur, or, of course, increase the size of their coalition. But interest groups also have an incentive to misrepresent the intensity of their members where possible or, perhaps, mislead their members to increase their intensity.

These latter two possibilities merit further exploration. Future research might investigate the political economy of interest groups. Once an interest is established, how do its employees and beneficiaries who profit from its resources (contractors, lobbyists, etc.) navigate serving the original mission versus maintaining and expanding their own material interests?

Intensity theory also suggests it crucial to understand how interest groups might encourage intensity of their members and aligned voters. How much can they influence and through what modes of communication? If they can influence, do they activate intensity selectively or in any instance the opportunity presents itself? With increasing opportunities for digital communication, there would seem to be excellent opportunities to explore the interaction between interest groups, members, aligned voters, and other political actors.

11.2.3 Political Parties and Coalitions

Third, intensity theory provides a different way to think about the construction of political coalitions. Candidates and parties might construct platforms where each policy appeals to an intense minority rather than platforms where each policy appeals to an electoral majority. If the elasticity of votes to policy is higher for the intense minorities, the best coalition could be a coalition of minorities.

> **Candidates and parties might construct platforms where each policy appeals to an intense minority rather than platforms where each policy appeals to an electoral majority.**

Coalitions of voters who care intensely about specific issues might also be a micro-foundation for the argument of the UCLA school of political parties (Cohen et al., 2008; Bawn et al., 2012; Masket, 2016). The UCLA school argues that parties are composed of groups of intense policy-demanders, but doesn't tell us who exactly these policy-demanders are nor why parties and candidates would listen if parties and candidates aspire to win elections. Intensity theory suggests parties and candidates listen because intense policy-demanders represent votes at elections. The argument in this book may help bring together the UCLA school with the political science of elections that focuses more squarely on voter behavior.

The theory might also speak more broadly to intra-party politics. How do political parties select candidates for president and other offices? Intensity theory suggests these candidates might build coalitions of intense minorities who will incur the costs needed to work within the political competition of nominations. This might help explain why many view party activists and elites as coalitions of extremists.

The implications for party coalitions and platforms suggests future empirical work. For scholars of party development, it would be interesting to quantify how often new issues positions adopted by parties side with electoral minorities. Likewise, when parties drop or play down a policy from their platform, is that policy the position of a minority or a majority in the electorate?

Do different parties construct different kinds of coalitions with some representing a coalition of intense minorities and others a coalition of majority positions? If so, what contextual factors and incentives lead parties to adopt one strategy versus the other?

11.2.4 Survey Research on Politics

Fourth, intensity theory offers a different interpretation of survey responses and suggests the need for new measures in opinion surveys. The theory suggests that survey researchers ought to apply special attention to measures of issue preferences. Asking respondents whether they support or oppose issues one by one without querying how they trade off different priorities might paint an incomplete picture of how voters make choices in elections. For recent efforts at more careful measures, see Tausanovitch (n.d.) and Hanretty, Lauderdale, and Vivyan (2020).

> **Opinion surveys that do not ask how voters trade off representation on one issue for representation on another might miss a key aspect of electoral democracy.**

Recent developments in formal democratic theory also suggest the importance of measuring the cardinality of voter preferences (Casella, 2005; Lalley and Weyl, 2018; Ingham, 2019; Patty and Penn, 2019). If existing measures of preferences from opinion surveys do not accurately capture intensity or cardinality, conclusions that government policy is incongruent with public opinion rest on untested assumptions about the distribution of intensity among supporters and opponents on each issue.

Intensity theory also implies that expressions in opinion surveys, if costly, might not be an unmediated reply to the question posed. Instead, survey responses might themselves be costly communication. To communicate intensity, survey respondents might give biased answers about matters of fact, claim negative affect about political others, show favoritism toward a political group in learning political information, or say they are fine with behavior inconsistent with democratic norms. Seemingly obtuse answers to survey questions might be efforts to communicate intensity rather than sincere reflections of attitudes and beliefs.

One path forward is to connect survey responses to costly political action either through the researcher inducing costs to the response (e.g., Bullock et al., 2015; Hill, 2017b; Berinsky, 2018) or by connecting survey responses to external evidence of costly action (e.g., Hill and Huber, 2017). Collecting observations on voters who engage in costly action through lists of political volunteers or lists of speakers at public meetings and subsequently interviewing those voters on their policy views could also be a promising research effort.

11.2.5 Dynamic and Participatory Voters

I suggest one key implication of intensity theory for political action. The use of costly communication provides a different perspective on how voters interact with politicians. In existing theories of elections, voters mostly *react* to politics. Citizens check the "degeneracy" of the elected (Federalist 57, 1788). Citizens make voting decisions *in reaction to* the candidates standing for office (Key, 1966; Barro, 1973), *in reaction to* the context of the election (Kramer, 1971; Fiorina, 1981), or *in reaction to* the content of campaign messaging (Huber and Arceneaux, 2007; Vavreck, 2009; Hill et al., 2013).

In broad stroke, the evaluative task of the voter in existing theories is the same. Voters ingest fixed information about candidates and output a vote choice. Elections are a mechanism of selecting the better – with definition of better differing by theory – candidate. Voters serve as a mathematical function, taking in candidates and context as arguments and outputting a vote choice as the response.

However, the empirical practice of political campaigns appears to include back-and-forth between voters and candidates. Candidates engage with voters at public meetings, town hall events, debates, and rallies. An implication of this book is that voters are more proactive and communicative than existing theories suggest. Voters who care intensely take action to communicate their intensity to candidates more than simply reacting to what candidates say.

> Voters communicate and participate in elections more
> than simply reacting to a fixed menu of choices.

Intensity theory conceives of voters as electoral *participants* with heterogeneous interests. Voters *communicate* to politicians about what they want. Politicians *listen* and *gather* information from voters. This give-and-take, back-and-forth communication exists within a system rife with informational challenges and incentive incompatibilities that complicate aggregation of voter wants. However, it is exactly these challenges of information and incentives that I argue generate common patterns of electoral competition, variation in political participation, and help determine the policy implemented by representatives in office.

This theory of voter choice contrasts with arguments made by Sniderman (2000) and Sniderman and Bullock (2004), who explicitly argue that voters should be conceived of as reacting to fixed menus of political choices. The fixed choice theory of elections argues that fixed choices provide workable heuristics for voters who are generally "minimally grounded on political principle, minimally informed by a knowledge of political affairs, minimally stable, and, above all, minimally coherent" (Sniderman, 2000, p. 67). Future work might think about how voter agency and social welfare differ in these two different conceptions of electoral competition. The theory of representation in Disch (2011) strikes me as one promising path to thinking about representative-voter dynamics.

These considerations also suggest pathways for research on campaigns and for candidate strategy. It would be interesting to look at candidates at the beginning of their political careers as they construct policy portfolios. How often do they advocate policies that side with minorities rather than majorities, and what positions do they emphasize in which venues? What information do they gather from voters early in the campaign, in what settings, and with what consequences for policy platforms and emphasis?

Much of campaign research focuses on the end-game of campaigns, the final get-out-the-vote drive and the advertising choices in the last few months. But intensity theory suggests that much of the campaign takes place before end-game activities. A fruitful path to improve our understanding of representation is research on why candidates select and emphasize some messages and positions over others and how these choices relate to intensity and support for the policies in the electorate.

* * *

Table 11.1 lists for reference the five implications for electoral competition, representation, and political participation.

TABLE 11.1. *Implications of intensity theory for elections, representation, and participation*

---

1. Non-majoritarian outcomes do not imply failure of the electoral connection.
2. The power of interest groups is proportional to the winnable votes they represent at elections.
3. Candidates and parties might construct platforms where each policy appeals to an intense minority rather than platforms where each policy appeals to an electoral majority.
4. Opinion surveys that do not ask how voters trade off representation on one issue for representation on another might miss a key aspect of electoral democracy.
5. Voters communicate and participate in elections more than simply reacting to a fixed menu of candidates.

11.3 DYNAMICS OF POLICY CHANGE

An important question left unanswered by this book is if and to what degree intensity varies over time. My argument focused on a single election with voter intensity and preference as fixed inputs to electoral competition. It seems likely, however, that to at least some degree preferences and intensities respond to changes in the status quo, changes in context, new information, or persuasive rhetoric. The case history in Chapter 7 on the politics of stem cell research, for example, suggested that policy evolved over time in response to changes in the preferences and intensities of the electorate.

According to the mathematical model, different intensities can induce differences in equilibrium policy. If the minority's preferences decrease in intensity, candidates might change policy proposal from siding with the minority and frustrating the majority to siding with the majority.

This suggests that change in the distribution of intensity might be related to political polarization or political rhetoric in American politics. If intensity of majority or minority changes, the model shows that candidates can move from proposing policy with a majority to proposing with a minority, or vice versa. Analysis of over-time dynamics in intensity might complement analysis of over-time dynamics of policy views to gain understanding of changes in candidate behavior and rhetoric.

That said, the dynamics of policy do not depend upon the actual intensities of voters. Policy depends upon *candidate beliefs* about intensity. Change to beliefs follow from changes in magnitude of action incurred by voters. This appears to be what occurred in the firearm regulation case history in Chapter 7. As Senator Toomey said, "The most important thing frankly is members of Congress need to hear from people, and the people who support these background checks need to be as vocal as those who don't" (Lengell, 2013).

These observations generate crucial empirical questions for political science surrounding the dynamics of policy change. Stability in policy connects to stability of preferences and intensities and the responsiveness of each to political factors. Changes in circumstances might induce changes in preferences or intensities. Persuasive rhetoric from those aiming to influence policy might induce changes in preferences or intensities. The stability of voter intensities over time seems to me to merit much more research.

A second influence on policy dynamics might be the rhetoric of political campaigns. Candidate rhetoric might be aimed at framing which issues are the subject of electoral competition. Campaigns and other policy-interested actors might use campaign messaging to influence voter beliefs about the policies at issue in the election, thereby influencing who takes action and how candidates respond with policy. This argument is anticipated by the seminal work of Professor Lynn Vavreck (2009).

11.4 MAJORITY RULE

I want to close the book by addressing the normative implications of my argument. As I have developed the argument, analyzed the evidence, and written the book, over and over I have observed that how we choose to judge a representative democracy depends on our normative beliefs about how collective choices should aggregate the varied interests of a diverse society. What is the proper "social choice function," as scholars of collective choice describe this process of aggregation?

The welfare analysis in Chapter 5 puts a mathematical formalization to a simple insight. If a minority cares sufficiently more about a policy than a majority, the utilitarian outcome is to implement policy with the minority (see Section B.3). From this perspective, observation of frustrated majorities does not necessarily indicate a problem with the system of representation (Ingham, 2019, makes a similar argument; see also

Mueller, 1999). Collective choice usually means that some members of the group do not get what they want. In the case of frustrated majorities, it is possible that the costs to the majority of losing out on policy that they care about less intensely are outweighed by the benefits to a more intense minority.

Of course, maximizing utilitarian social welfare is not necessarily the democratic objective. The Preamble to the American Constitution states as goals to "promote the general Welfare" but additionally to "establish Justice, insure domestic Tranquility," "and secure the Blessings of Liberty to ourselves and our Posterity." Considerations such as fairness, stability, opportunity, liberty, property rights, enrichment of the poorest, and adaptability could render the welfare conclusions I suggest misplaced. The operation of electoral democracy described by intensity theory might or might not strike you as just depending on the weights you apply to different considerations of what is in the common interest and how interests ought to be aggregated into a collective choice.

A further challenge to the welfare analysis is that the costs incurred by high-intensity voters might have negative consequences beyond their influence on policy. Campaign contributions might generate questions about corruption and legitimacy. Protests might devolve into violence. Obtuse expressions might lead to division, mistrust between voters, or questions about voter aptitude and motivation. Externalities from the costly political actions taken to communicate intensity might outweigh the utilitarian welfare gain from policy.

While my first goal for the theory is to help scholars and practicioners reason about patterns of electoral politics and representation in republics, the normative questions herein raised might be just as important. When is it just for minority goals to frustrate majorities? If we acknowledge that preferences can change over time, what magnitude of costs should a majority or minority bear in pursuit of utilitarian welfare at any single point in time? Do the externalities of costly communication outweigh the benefits to intense minorities of sometimes attaining policy representation?

I have argued that issue intensity is a central feature of electoral competition and representation that merits dedicated study. I hope that I have made some progress on the scientific explanation and political operation of Dahl's (1956) intensity problem. I look forward to future work in positive political science on the function of intensity in electoral competition and to further development of our normative understanding of issue intensity and frustrated majorities.

PART V

APPENDICES

Appendix A

Mathematical Model of Intensity and Electoral Competition

In this appendix, I analyze a mathematical formalization of intensity theory. The analysis serves as basis for the presentation in Chapter 4. I apply tools from game theory to analyze the dynamics of electoral competition when voters vary in how much they care about policy and when candidates do not know which voters care more and less intensely.[1]

I first present the logic of frustrated majorities with a three-voter model of electoral competition in a setting with probabilistic voting. I start with a model where candidates know both what voters want and how much they want it. I use this setting to show that candidates choose to side with minorities and frustrate majorities when the minority cares sufficiently more than the majority about the policy issue.

I then move to a setting where candidates do not know the intensities of voters. I show that candidates will use their best guess about voter intensities to decide what policy to propose and that voters who care only modestly would prefer candidates to believe they care more than they do.

Because candidates who are uncertain about voter intensity make policy decisions based upon beliefs about intensity, voters who care intensely sometimes engage in costly political action to communicate their intensity. I present two equilibria where voters incur certain costs for uncertain benefits in pursuit only of policy goals. Interested readers may consult additional analysis in Hill (2022a).

---

[1] Parts of this chapter are sourced from Hill (2022a), originally published by the University of Chicago Press and reprinted with permission.

A.I MATHEMATICAL MODEL WITH INTENSITY KNOWN

The first game-theoretic model considers a setting where candidates for office know both the policy position and the intensity of majority and minority voters. Because the election result is stochastic, candidates sometimes side with the minority in pursuit of maximizing votes.

A.I.I Model of Electoral Competition

I represent electoral competition through the following mathematical model, which builds from the presentation in Chapter 3. There are two candidates, A and B, and an electorate of three voters, Voters 1, 2, and 3. Candidates seek to maximize votes at an election.

Voters care about a binary policy s and are of type $\tau = 0$ (type-0) or $\tau = 1$ (type-1) preferring $s = 0$ or $s = 1$. Voter policy type is common knowledge for all voters and candidates. Assume, without loss of generality, that $\tau_i = 1$ for $i = \{1, 2\}$ and $\tau_3 = 0$, so $s = 0$ is the minority position.

In addition to ideal policy type, voters vary in the intensity with which they care about the issue, $\beta_i \in \{1, \bar{\beta}\}$, $\bar{\beta} > 2$, representing low- and high-intensity. If policy is set at the voter's preference (e.g., $s = 0$ for a type-0 voter), their benefit is the magnitude β_i, $\bar{\beta}$ if high-intensity or 1 if low-intensity. Payoff is zero when policy is set opposite their preference.

In this first version of the model, candidates and voters each take one action. The game begins with each candidate simultaneously proposing binding policy platforms s_A and $s_B \in \{0, 1\}$. Second, the election is held. Voters make a vote choice given τ_i, β_i, s_A, and s_B. Vote choice is a random variable, represented in the model with an additive election shock δ_i unique to each voter and revealed at the time of the election. For simplicity, I assume the δ_i drawn independently according to the uniform distribution with lower and upper bounds c and d common knowledge. Other distributions would not change the strategic incentives for candidates or voters.

I assume $c < -\bar{\beta}$ and $\bar{\beta} < d$, so that the vote choice of all voters is stochastic. This assumption states that there are no voters for whom the cumulative weight of other considerations never exceeds the weight that high-intensity voters place on the issue. This assumption is not necessary but simplifies presentation. I show in Section A.2.I that the results hold so long as $\bar{\beta} < c < -2$ and $2 < d < \bar{\beta}$. We might consider a setting with these parameter values of Section A.2.I a model of high-intensity single-issue voters.

A.2 CANDIDATE POLICY BEST RESPONSES

Candidates interact strategically in this first model. Lemma A.1 shows that the best strategy for both candidates is to propose $s = 0$ when $\beta_1 + \beta_2 \leq \beta_3$, else $s = 1$.

Lemma A.1 (Candidate best responses). When the support of election shock δ, (c, d), includes the values $-\bar{\beta}$ and $\bar{\beta}$, the best response to intensities $\beta = \{\beta_1, \beta_2, \beta_3\}$ for both candidates is to propose the policy preferred by minority Voter 3, $s^* = 0$, when $\beta_1 + \beta_2 \leq \beta_3$, otherwise to propose the policy preferred by majority Voters 1 and 2, $s^* = 1$.

Proof Begin by specifying expected votes for the two candidates. Voter utility from policy s is

$$v_i(s) = \tau_i \beta_i s + (1 - \tau_i)\beta_i(1 - s). \tag{A.1}$$

The probability voter i chooses A over B given election shock δ_i is

$$Pr(A) = Pr[\tau_i \beta_i s_A + (1 - \tau_i)\beta_i(1 - s_A)$$
$$> \tau_i \beta_i s_B + (1 - \tau_i)\beta_i(1 - s_B) + \delta_i],$$

$$Pr(A) = Pr[\beta_i s_A > \beta_i s_B + \delta_i] = Pr[\beta_i(s_A - s_B) > \delta_i], \ i \in \{1, 2\},$$

$$Pr(A) = Pr[\beta_i(1 - s_A) > \beta_i(1 - s_B) + \delta_i] = Pr[\beta_i(s_B - s_A) > \delta_i], \ i = 3.$$

Given the voters' weakly dominant strategy to vote for the candidate with greater expected utility and the uniform distribution on δ_i, the probability that each voter chooses Candidate A is

$$\pi_i^A = \frac{\beta_i(s_A - s_B) - c}{d - c}, \ i \in \{1, 2\}; \quad \pi_i^A = \frac{\beta_i(s_B - s_A) - c}{d - c}, \ i = 3,$$

per the cumulative distribution function for the uniform distribution with upper and lower bounds d and c (see Eq. (A.3)).

Because the δ_i are drawn independently and the expected value of a sum of independent random variables is the sum of expectations, Candidate A's expected vote count is the sum of the three voter probabilities:

$$V^A = \left(\underbrace{\frac{\beta_1(s_A - s_B) - c}{d - c}}_{\text{Voter 1}} + \underbrace{\frac{\beta_2(s_A - s_B) - c}{d - c}}_{\text{Voter 2}} + \underbrace{\frac{\beta_3(s_B - s_A) - c}{d - c}}_{\text{Voter 3}} \right),$$

$$= ([\beta_1 + \beta_2][s_A - s_B] + \beta_3[s_B - s_A])/(d - c) - 3c/(d - c), \tag{A.2}$$

with $V^B = 3 - V^A$.

Candidate A's best response to $s_B = 0$ is $s_A = 0$ when

$$V^A(0|s_B = 0) \geq V^A(1|s_B = 0),$$

$$0 - 3c/(d - c) \geq (\beta_1 + \beta_2 - \beta_3)/(d - c) - 3c/(d - c) \Rightarrow \beta_3 \geq \beta_1 + \beta_2.$$

Candidate A's best response to $s_B = 1$ is $s_A = 0$ when

$$V^A(0|s_B = 1) \geq V^A(1|s_B = 1),$$

$$(-\beta_1 - \beta_2 + \beta_3)/(d - c) - 3c/(d - c) \geq -3c/(d - c) \Rightarrow \beta_3 \geq \beta_1 + \beta_2.$$

Likewise, Candidate B's best response to $s_A = 0$ is $s_B = 0$ when

$$V^B(0|s_A = 0) \geq V^B(1|s_A = 0),$$

$$3 + 3c/(d - c) \geq 3 - (-\beta_1 - \beta_2 + \beta_3)/(d - c) + 3c/(d - c),$$

$$0 \geq (\beta_1 + \beta_2 - \beta_3)/(d - c) \Rightarrow \beta_3 \geq \beta_1 + \beta_2.$$

Candidate B's best response to $s_A = 1$ is $s_B = 0$ when

$$V^B(0|s_A = 1) \geq V^B(1|s_A = 1),$$

$$3 - (\beta_1 + \beta_2 - \beta_3)/(d - c) + 3c/(d - c) \geq 3 + 3c/(d - c),$$

$$(-\beta_1 - \beta_2 + \beta_3)/(d - c) \geq 0 \Rightarrow \beta_3 \geq \beta_1 + \beta_2.$$

Therefore, the best response for both candidates is to propose the policy preferred by minority Voter 3, $s_A^* = s_B^* = 0$ if, and only if, $\beta_1 + \beta_2 \leq \beta_3$. $\qquad \square$

Lemma A.1 describes when candidates maximize expected votes by proposing policy with the majority and when by proposing policy with the minority. The lemma states that the candidates are better off siding with the minority when the minority's intensity is larger than the sum of the intensities of majority voters.

A.2.1 Lemma A.2: Candidate Best Responses, $-\bar{\beta} < c$ and $d < \bar{\beta}$

I show here that the candidate best responses described by Lemma A.1 are also best responses when $-\bar{\beta} < c < -2$ and $2 < d < \bar{\beta}$.

The substantive meaning of moving $\bar{\beta}$ outside of the support of δ is that the votes of high-intensity types are deterministic rather than stochastic if the two candidates propose different policies, e.g., when $s_A = 1$ and $s_B = 0$. When $\bar{\beta}$ is larger, or $-\bar{\beta}$ smaller, than any value that might be drawn from the δ distribution, a high-intensity voter prefers a candidate who proposes their policy to one who does not with probability one. We should read this as a model of high-intensity single-issue voters.

Excluding the values $\bar{\beta}$ and $-\bar{\beta}$ from the support of election shock δ, $[c, d]$, leads to Lemma A.2.

> **Lemma A.2** (Candidate best responses, $-\bar{\beta} < c$ and $d < \bar{\beta}$).
> When the support of election shock δ, $[c, d]$, excludes the values $\bar{\beta}$ and $-\bar{\beta}$ and $c < -2$ and $2 < d$, the best response to intensities $\{\beta_1, \beta_2, \beta_3\}$ for both candidates is to propose the policy preferred by minority Voter 3, $s^* = 0$, when $\beta_1 + \beta_2 \leq \beta_3$, otherwise to propose the policy preferred by majority Voters 1 and 2, $s^* = 1$.

Proof Changing the values of c and d requires an expansion to the vote probabilities described in Lemma A.1 for cases when $-\beta_i < c$ or $d < \beta_i$. The cumulative uniform distribution with upper and lower bounds b and a to value x is

$$F(x) = \begin{cases} 0, & \text{for } x < a \\ \frac{x-a}{b-a}, & \text{for } a \leq x \leq b \\ 1, & \text{for } x > b. \end{cases} \tag{A.3}$$

Following Eq. (A.3), vote probabilities are

$$\Pr(A|\beta_i) = \begin{cases} 0, & \text{for } \beta_i(s_A - s_B) < c \\ \frac{\beta_i(s_A - s_B) - c}{d - c}, & \text{for } c \leq \beta_i(s_A - s_B) \leq d \\ 1, & \text{for } \beta_i(s_A - s_B) > d \end{cases} \tag{A.4}$$

for Voters 1 and 2, and

$$\Pr_3(A|\beta_i) = \begin{cases} 0, & \text{for } \beta_i(s_B - s_A) < c \\ \frac{\beta_i(s_B - s_A) - c}{d - c}, & \text{for } c \leq \beta_i(s_B - s_A) \leq d \\ 1, & \text{for } \beta_i(s_B - s_A) > d \end{cases} \tag{A.5}$$

for Voter 3.

Because the δ_i are drawn independently and the expected value of a sum of independent random variables is the sum of expectations, Candidate A's expected vote count is the sum of the three voters' independent probabilities. A's expected vote count is

$$V^A = \underbrace{\Pr(A|\beta_1)}_{\text{Voter 1}} + \underbrace{\Pr(A|\beta_2)}_{\text{Voter 2}} + \underbrace{\Pr_3(A|\beta_3)}_{\text{Voter 3}},$$

with $V^B = 3 - V^A$.

Consider the case where $\beta_1 + \beta_2 \leq \beta_3$, i.e., both majority votes are low-intensity and the minority voter high-intensity, $\beta_1 = \beta_2 = 1$ and $\beta_3 = \bar{\beta}$. Candidate A's best response to $s_B = 0$ is $s_A = 0$ when

$$V^A(0|s_B = 0) \geq V^A(1|s_B = 0),$$

$$\left[\frac{0-c}{d-c} + \frac{0-c}{d-c} + \frac{0-c}{d-c}\right] \geq \left[\frac{\beta_1(1-0)-c}{d-c} + \frac{\beta_2(1-0)-c}{d-c} + 0\right],$$

$$0 \geq 2 + c \Rightarrow -\bar{\beta} \leq c \leq -2,$$

which holds by definition. A's best response to $s_B = 0$ is $s_A = 0$.

Likewise, Candidate B's best response to $s_A = 0$ is $s_B = 0$ when

$$V^B(0|s_A = 0) \geq V^B(1|s_A = 0),$$

$$3 - \left[\frac{0-c}{d-c} + \frac{0-c}{d-c} + \frac{0-c}{d-c}\right] \geq 3 - \left[\frac{\beta_1(0-1)-c}{d-c} + \frac{\beta_2(0-1)-c}{d-c} + 1\right],$$

$$d \geq 2 \Rightarrow 2 \leq d \leq \bar{\beta},$$

which holds by definition. B's best response to $s_A = 0$ is $s_B = 0$.

Therefore, proposing policy with the minority $s_A^* = s_B^* = 0$ is a mutual best response when $\beta_1 + \beta_2 \leq \beta_3$ and $-\bar{\beta} < c < -2$ and $2 < d < \bar{\beta}$. □

Combining Lemma A.1 and Lemma A.2 provides the requirement for non-majoritarian policy that $c < -2$ and $d > 2$. Lemma A.1 shows that $s^* = 0$ if, and only if, $\beta_1 + \beta_2 \leq \beta_3$, which can only occur if $\bar{\beta} > 2$. As the Lemma assumes $c < -\bar{\beta}$ and $\bar{\beta} < d$, c must be less than -2 and d greater than 2. The proof to Lemma A.2 also shows that $c < -2$ and $d > 2$.

A.3 NUMERICAL EXAMPLES OF LEMMA A.1

To provide intuition to readers for Lemma A.1 as the remaining results of the model rest upon it, I consider here three numerical examples. To see the logic of candidate best responses, assume that there is no uncertainty about voter intensity and the interesting case of $\beta_1 + \beta_2 \leq \beta_3$, where the candidates propose policy with the minority in equilibrium holds. For each example, let $\beta_1 = \beta_2 = 1$, and $\beta_3 = \bar{\beta} = 5$. Then, vote probabilities for candidate A are

$$\Pr[\beta_1(s_A - s_B) > \delta_1] = \Pr[s_A - s_B > \delta_1],$$

$$\Pr[\beta_2(s_A - s_B) > \delta_2] = \Pr[s_A - s_B > \delta_2],$$

$$\Pr[\beta_3(s_B - s_A) > \delta_3] = \Pr[5 * (s_B - s_A) > \delta_3].$$

A.3.1 Case 1: $\bar{\beta}$ Inside of (c, d)

In this example, consider a setting where the support of δ includes values greater and less than the absolute value of $\bar{\beta} = 5$. Letting $c = -10$ and $d = 10$, consider the best response of candidate A if B proposes $s_B = 0$. A's expected vote count is

$$\Pr[s_A - 0 > \delta_1] + \Pr[s_A - 0 > \delta_2] + \Pr[5 * (0 - s_A) > \delta_3].$$

If A chooses $s_A = 1$, then expected count is

$$\Pr[1 > \delta_1] + \Pr[1 > \delta_2] + \Pr[-5 > \delta_3].$$

Given the bounds $c = -10$ and $d = 10$ and the uniform CDF (Eq. (A.3)), A's expected count is

$$\frac{1 + 10}{10 + 10} + \frac{1 + 10}{10 + 10} + \frac{-5 + 10}{10 + 10} = 11/20 + 11/20 + 5/20 = 27/20.$$

If, instead, A chooses $s_A = 0$, then the expected count is

$$\Pr[0 > \delta_1] + \Pr[0 > \delta_2] + \Pr[0 > \delta_3]$$
$$= \frac{0 + 10}{10 + 10} + \frac{0 + 10}{10 + 10} + \frac{0 + 10}{10 + 10} = 10/20 + 10/20 + 10/20 = 3/2.$$

A's best response to $s_B = 0$ is $s_A = 0$ because $27/20 < 3/2$.

Now consider the best response of A if B proposes $s_B = 1$. A's expected vote count is

$$\Pr[s_A - 1 > \delta_1] + \Pr[s_A - 1 > \delta_2] + \Pr[5 * (1 - s_A) > \delta_3].$$

If A chooses $s_A = 1$, then the expected count is

$$\Pr[1 - 1 > \delta_1] + \Pr[1 - 1 > \delta_2] + \Pr[5 * (1 - 1) > \delta_3].$$
$$\frac{0 + 10}{10 + 10} + \frac{0 + 10}{10 + 10} + \frac{0 + 10}{10 + 10} = 3/2.$$

If A chooses $s_A = 0$, then the expected count is

$$\Pr[-1 > \delta_1] + \Pr[-1 > \delta_2] + \Pr[5 > \delta_3]$$

$$= \frac{-1+10}{10+10} + \frac{-1+10}{10+10} + \frac{5+10}{10+10} = 9/20 + 9/20 + 15/20 = 33/20.$$

A's best response to $s_B = 1$ is $s_A = 0$ because $3/2 < 33/20$.

To establish the equilibrium $s^* = 0$, we now must consider the best response of B. Since A's best response to either of B's proposals is $s_A = 0$, I consider B's best response to $s_A = 0$. B's expected vote count, noting that $\Pr(B) = 1 - \Pr(A)$, is

$$= 1 - \Pr[s_A - s_B > \delta_1] + 1 - \Pr[s_A - s_B > \delta_2]$$

$$+ 1 - \Pr[5 * (s_B - s_A) > \delta_3],$$

$$= 3 - \left(\Pr[0 - s_B > \delta_1] + \Pr[0 - s_B > \delta_2] + \Pr[5 * (s_B - 0) > \delta_3] \right).$$

If B chooses $s_B = 1$, then B's expected vote count is

$$3 - \left(\Pr[0 - 1 > \delta_1] + \Pr[0 - 1 > \delta_2] + \Pr[5 * (1 - 0) > \delta_3] \right)$$

$$= 3 - \left(\frac{-1+10}{10+10} + \frac{-1+10}{10+10} + \frac{5+10}{10+10} \right)$$

$$= 3 - 9/20 - 9/20 - 15/20 = 60/20 - 33/20 = 27/20.$$

If B chooses $s_B = 0$, then B's expected vote count is

$$3 - \left(\Pr[0 - 0 > \delta_1] + \Pr[0 - 0 > \delta_2] + \Pr[5 * (0 - 0) > \delta_3] \right)$$

$$= 3 - \left(\frac{0+10}{10+10} + \frac{0+10}{10+10} + \frac{0+10}{10+10} \right)$$

$$= 3 - 3/2 = 3/2.$$

As $27/20 < 3/2$, B's best response to $s_A = 0$ is $s_B = 0$, which is a mutual best response. Therefore, $s^* = 0$ when $c = -10$, $d = 10$, and $\bar{\beta} = 5$.

This numeric example shows why Lemma A.1 holds. With stochastic voting, candidates can be more certain of their policy proposal winning the vote of a high-intensity than of a low-intensity voter. In other words, the elasticity of vote choice to policy is stronger for high-intensity voters. Depending upon the relative magnitude of intensity and the distribution in the electorate, a higher elasticity of vote choice to policy for the minority can lead candidates to frustrate the majority and propose policy with the minority even though they know with certainty the majority's contrary preference.

A.3.2 Case 2: $\bar{\beta}$ Outside of $[c, d]$

For the second numeric example, consider a setting where the support of δ does not include the absolute value of $\bar{\beta} = 5$, by letting $c = -3$ and $d = 3$. In this setting, the vote of a voter who cares intensely ($\beta_i = \bar{\beta}$) is only stochastic when the two candidates propose the same policy. When $s_A \neq s_B$, a high-intensity voter selects deterministically the candidate proposing their preferred policy because no value of the election shock would be large enough to sway their vote.

Consider the best response of candidate A if B proposes $s_B = 0$. A's expected vote count is

$$\Pr[s_A - 0 > \delta_1] + \Pr[s_A - 0 > \delta_2] + \Pr[5 * (0 - s_A) > \delta_3].$$

If A chooses $s_A = 1$, then the expected count is

$$\Pr[1 > \delta_1] + \Pr[1 > \delta_2] + \Pr[-5 > \delta_3].$$

Given the bounds $c = -3$ and $d = 3$ and the uniform CDF (Eq. (A.3)), A's expected count is

$$\frac{1+3}{2+2} + \frac{1+3}{3+3} + 0 = 4/6 + 4/6 + 0 = 8/6 = 4/3.$$

If A chooses $s_A = 0$, then, the expected count is

$$\Pr[0 > \delta_1] + \Pr[0 > \delta_2] + \Pr[0 > \delta_3]$$
$$= \frac{0+3}{3+3} + \frac{0+3}{3+3} + \frac{0+3}{3+3} = 3/6 + 3/6 + 3/6 = 3/2.$$

A's best response to $s_B = 0$ is $s_A = 0$ because $3/2 > 4/3$.

Consider the best response of candidate A if B proposes $s_B = 1$. A's expected vote count is

$$\Pr[s_A - 1 > \delta_1] + \Pr[s_A - 1 > \delta_2] + \Pr[5 * (1 - s_A) > \delta_3].$$

If A chooses $s_A = 1$, then the expected count is

$$\Pr[1 - 1 > \delta_1] + \Pr[1 - 1 > \delta_2] + \Pr[5 * (1 - 1) > \delta_3].$$
$$\frac{0+3}{3+3} + \frac{0+3}{3+3} + \frac{0+3}{3+3} = 3/6 + 3/6 + 3/6 = 3/2.$$

If A chooses $s_A = 0$, then the expected count is

$$\Pr[-1 > \delta_1] + \Pr[-1 > \delta_2] + \Pr[5 > \delta_3]$$
$$= \frac{-1+3}{3+3} + \frac{-1+3}{3+3} + 1 = 2/6 + 2/6 + 1 = 10/6 = 5/3.$$

A's best response to $s_B = 1$ is $s_A = 0$ because $5/3 > 3/2$.

To establish existence of an equilibrium $s^* = 0$, we now must consider the best response of B. B's expected vote count, noting that $Pr(B) = 1 - Pr(A)$, is

$$1 - Pr[s_A - s_B > \delta_1] + 1 - Pr[s_A - s_B > \delta_2] + 1 - Pr[5 * (s_B - s_A) > \delta_3],$$
$$= 3 - \left(Pr[0 - s_B > \delta_1] + Pr[0 - s_B > \delta_2] + Pr[5 * (s_B - 0) > \delta_3]\right).$$

Consider the best response of candidate B if A proposes $s_A = 0$. If B chooses $s_B = 1$, then B's expected vote count is

$$3 - \left(Pr[0 - 1 > \delta_1] + Pr[0 - 1 > \delta_2] + Pr[5 * (1 - 0) > \delta_3]\right)$$
$$= 3 - \left(\frac{-1 + 3}{3 + 3} + \frac{-1 + 3}{3 + 3} + 1\right)$$
$$= 3 - 2/6 - 2/6 - 1 = 18/6 - 4/6 - 6/6 = 8/6 = 4/3.$$

If B chooses $s_B = 0$, then B's expected vote count is

$$3 - \left(Pr[0 - 0 > \delta_1] + Pr[0 - 0 > \delta_2] + Pr[5 * (0 - 0) > \delta_3]\right)$$
$$= 3 - \left(\frac{0 + 3}{3 + 3} + \frac{0 + 3}{3 + 3} + \frac{0 + 3}{3 + 3}\right)$$
$$= 3 - 3/6 - 3/6 - 3/6 = 3/2.$$

B's best response to $s_A = 0$ is $s_B = 0$ because $3/2 > 4/3$.

$s_A = s_B = 0$ is a mutual best response. Therefore, $s^* = 0$ when $c = -3$, $d = 3$, and $\bar{\beta} = 5$.

A.3.3 Case 3: Asymmetric Distribution on δ

In this example, I consider an asymmetric distribution of the election shock δ, i.e., $-c \neq d$. Substantively, this represents a situation where one of the two candidates is favored by the non-policy conditions of the election. The example demonstrates that Lemma A.1 holds in this setting.

Let $c = -8$ and $d = 12$ such that candidate B is favored in the election. Consider the best response of candidate A if B proposes $s_B = 0$. A's expected vote count is

$$Pr[s_A - 0 > \delta_1] + Pr[s_A - 0 > \delta_2] + Pr[5 * (0 - s_A) > \delta_3].$$

If A chooses $s_A = 1$, then the expected count is

$$Pr[1 > \delta_1] + Pr[1 > \delta_2] + Pr[-5 > \delta_3].$$

Given the bounds $c = -8$ and $d = 12$ and the uniform CDF (Eq. (A.3)), A's expected count is

$$\frac{1+8}{12+8} + \frac{1+8}{12+8} + \frac{-5+8}{12+8} = 9/20 + 9/20 + 3/20 = 21/20.$$

If instead A chooses $s_A = 0$, then the expected count is

$$\Pr[0 > \delta_1] + \Pr[0 > \delta_2] + \Pr[0 > \delta_3]$$

$$= \frac{0+8}{12+8} + \frac{0+8}{12+8} + \frac{0+8}{12+8} = 8/20 + 8/20 + 8/20 = 24/20.$$

A's best response to $s_B = 0$ is $s_A = 0$ because $21/20 < 24/20$.

Now consider the best response of A if B proposes $s_B = 1$. A's expected vote count is

$$\Pr[s_A - 1 > \delta_1] + \Pr[s_A - 1 > \delta_2] + \Pr[5 * (1 - s_A) > \delta_3].$$

If A chooses $s_A = 1$, then the expected count is

$$\Pr[1 - 1 > \delta_1] + \Pr[1 - 1 > \delta_2] + \Pr[5 * (1 - 1) > \delta_3].$$

$$\frac{0+8}{12+8} + \frac{0+8}{12+8} + \frac{0+8}{12+8} = 8/20 + 8/20 + 8/20 = 24/20.$$

If A chooses $s_A = 0$, then the expected count is

$$\Pr[-1 > \delta_1] + \Pr[-1 > \delta_2] + \Pr[5 > \delta_3]$$

$$= \frac{-1+8}{12+8} + \frac{-1+8}{12+8} + \frac{5+8}{12+8} = 7/20 + 7/20 + 13/20 = 27/20.$$

A's best response to $s_B = 1$ is $s_A = 0$ because $24/20 < 27/20$.

To establish the equilibrium $s^* = 0$, we now must consider the best response of B. Since A's best response to either of B's proposals is $s_A = 0$, I consider B's best response to $s_A = 0$. B's expected vote count, noting that $\Pr(B) = 1 - \Pr(A)$, is

$$1 - \Pr[s_A - s_B > \delta_1] + 1 - \Pr[s_A - s_B > \delta_2] + 1 - \Pr[5 * (s_B - s_A) > \delta_3],$$

$$= 3 - \left(\Pr[0 - s_B > \delta_1] + \Pr[0 - s_B > \delta_2] + \Pr[5 * (s_B - 0) > \delta_3]\right).$$

If B chooses $s_B = 1$, then B's expected vote count is

$$3 - \left(\Pr[0 - 1 > \delta_1] + \Pr[0 - 1 > \delta_2] + \Pr[5 * (1 - 0) > \delta_3]\right)$$

$$= 3 - \left(\frac{-1+8}{12+8} + \frac{-1+8}{12+8} + \frac{5+8}{12+8}\right)$$

$$= 3 - 7/20 + 7/20 + 13/20 = 60/20 - 27/20 = 33/20.$$

If B chooses $s_B = o$, then B's expected vote count is

$$3 - \left(\Pr[o - o > \delta_1] + \Pr[o - o > \delta_2] + \Pr[5 * (o - o) > \delta_3]\right)$$
$$= 3 - \left(\frac{o + 8}{12 + 8} + \frac{o + 8}{12 + 8} + \frac{o + 8}{12 + 8}\right)$$
$$= 3 - 24/20 = 36/20.$$

As $33/20 < 36/20$, B's best response to $s_A = o$ is $s_B = o$, which is a mutual best response. Therefore, $s^* = o$ with $c = -8$, $d = 12$, and $\bar{\beta} = 5$. Symmetry is not a necessary condition for Lemma A.1.

A.4 MATHEMATICAL MODEL WITH INTENSITY UNKNOWN

In this section, I consider the second feature of intensity theory, that intensity of preference is difficult to observe. In the previous sections, I showed how frustrated majorities can result when candidates have full knowledge of voter intensities and a minority cares sufficiently more than a majority. What happens when the candidates do not know how much each voter cares about policy?

To analyze the consequences of unobserved intensity, I modify the mathematical model so that each voter intensity β_i is known to the voter but to no others. I also allow voters to choose to take costly political actions observed by the candidates and of net cost to the voters who take them.

I now turn to presentation and analysis of this more complicated model. I continue with the three-voter electorate used in Section 4.1. See analysis of an electorate of arbitrary minority size in Section B.2.

A.4.1 Primitives and Payoffs

The game is the same as above with two vote-seeking candidates, A and B, binary policy s, and an electorate of three voters with preference $\tau = o$ or $\tau = 1$. Voter policy preference is common knowledge with $\tau_i = 1$ for $i = \{1, 2\}$ and $\tau_3 = o$. Voter intensity is $\beta_i \in \{1, \bar{\beta}\}$, $\bar{\beta} > 2$.

Departing from the model with intensity common knowledge, intensity β_i is private knowledge for each voter i. That is, neither candidates nor other voters know how intensely each voter cares about policy s. There are, however, common beliefs about how likely any individual voter cares intensely, represented by the prior rate q. The rate q is the prior probability

TABLE A.1. *Payoffs and actions to the game*

Players	Voter 1	Voter 2	Voter 3	Candidate A	Candidate B
Actions	λ_1	λ_2	λ_3	s_A	s_B
Payoffs, A wins:	$\beta_1 s_A - \lambda_1$	$\beta_2 s_A - \lambda_2$	$\beta_3(1 - s_A) - \lambda_3$		
Payoffs, B wins:	$\beta_1 s_B - \lambda_1$	$\beta_2 s_B - \lambda_2$	$\beta_3(1 - s_B) - \lambda_3$		

that any individual i cares intensely, $\Pr(\beta_i = \bar{\beta}) = q$ and $\Pr(\beta_i = 1) = 1 - q$, $q \in [0, 1]$, $i \in (1, 2, 3)$. If q is near one, candidates and voters believe that most voters care intensely about the policy. If q is near zero, candidates and voters believe that most voters care only modestly about the policy.

A.4.2 Actions

Candidates each propose a policy platform, s_A and $s_B \in \{0, 1\}$. In this model, voters take two actions. At the election, voters make a vote choice given $\tau_i, \beta_i, s_A, s_B$, and δ_i, with δ following the same distributional assumptions as in Section A.1.

Voters' second action is choice over magnitude of political actions of (net) cost $\lambda_i \in \mathbb{R}_+$. These actions are inherently costly in that the voter must pay certain costs without knowing that they will subsequently receive benefits that outweigh those costs. Through a diversity of available costly actions, voters choose continuous $\lambda_i > 0$ or choose no costly action, $\lambda_i = 0$. Table A.1 summarizes players, actions, and payoffs in this version of the game.

A.4.3 Timing

1. Nature independently draws each β_i, $i \in 1, 2, 3$ from $\{1, \bar{\beta}\}$ given q.
2. Voters privately observe β_i and then simultaneously choose pre-election actions $\lambda \equiv (\lambda_1, \lambda_2, \lambda_3)$.
3. Candidates observe λ then propose policy platforms s_A and s_B.
4. Nature independently draws each δ_i, election held, and votes realized.
5. Payoffs realized.

A.4.4 Strategies and Beliefs

At the election, vote choice is a stochastic function of the weakly dominant strategy to select the candidate proposing the preferred platform. I therefore focus on voter strategies over λ, which is a function $\sigma_v(\beta_i, \tau_i)$: $\{1, \bar{\beta}\} \times \{0, 1\} \rightarrow \mathbb{R}_+$ mapping intensity and policy preference into political action λ_i.

Define $\lambda \equiv (\lambda_1, \lambda_2, \lambda_3)$ and $\beta \equiv (\beta_1, \beta_1, \beta_1)$. For both candidates, a strategy is a function $\sigma_p(\lambda) : \mathbb{R}^3_+ \rightarrow \{0, 1\}$, $p \in \{A, B\}$, mapping observed political actions λ into a policy platform s_p.

Candidates learn about intensity by the costly actions taken by each voter and use Bayes' rule to update beliefs about β. For candidate $p \in \{A, B\}$, beliefs are

$$h_p : \mathbb{R}^3_+ \rightarrow \Delta(\{1, \bar{\beta}\}^3), \tag{A.6}$$

where $\Delta(\{1, \bar{\beta}\}^3)$ is the set of lotteries over voter intensities.

I use perfect Bayesian equilibrium (PBE) as the solution concept. For a PBE, each candidate's policy strategy must be a best response given the other candidate's policy strategy and candidate beliefs about β. Candidate beliefs are consistent and updated by Bayes' rule. The voter strategy must be a best response given candidate strategies and beliefs and that other voters are also playing best responses. I focus on equilibria in pure strategies.

A.4.5 Candidate Best Responses When Intensity Unknown

Although the candidates are now uncertain about the intensity of each voter, the results of Lemma A.1 hold in a PBE for candidate *beliefs* about each voter's type, as stated in Lemma A.3.

Lemma A.3 (Candidate best responses when intensity unknown). When uncertain about the intensity of each voter, the best response for each candidate is set $s_p = 0$ when $\hat{\beta}_1 + \hat{\beta}_2 \leq \hat{\beta}_3$ else $s_p = 1$, where $\hat{\beta}_i$ is the candidates' belief about the intensity of Voter i after observing λ.

Proof Recall the vote-seeking objective function for Candidate A from Eq. (A.2)

$$V^A = \left([\beta_1 + \beta_2][s_A - s_B] + \beta_3[s_B - s_A]\right)/(d - c) - 3c/(d - c).$$

Define A's beliefs about the intensities of each voter with the vector $\hat{\beta}^A = (\hat{\beta}_1, \hat{\beta}_2, \hat{\beta}_3)$ and note that the parameters c and d are fixed.

Suppose $\hat{\beta}^A$ indicated that Candidate A should propose $s_A = 0$ per Lemma A.1. This would imply the belief $\hat{\beta}_1 + \hat{\beta}_2 \leq \hat{\beta}_3$. If Candidate A followed Lemma A.1 and proposed policy $s_A = 0$, the value of their objective function (setting aside c and d) would be

$$(\hat{\beta}_1 + \hat{\beta}_2)(0 - 0) + \hat{\beta}_3(0 - 0) = 0 \text{ because } s_B^* = 0.$$

If, instead, Candidate A did not follow belief $\hat{\beta}^A$ and proposed policy $s_A = 1$, the value of their objective function would be

$$\hat{\beta}_1 + \hat{\beta}_2 - \hat{\beta}_3 \text{ because } s_B^* = 0.$$

Because candidate policy $s^* = 0$ follows if, and only if, $\beta_3 \geq \beta_1 + \beta_2$, the expected value of Candidate A's objective function is greater (zero) when acting on beliefs $\hat{\beta}^A$ than when not $(\hat{\beta}_1 + \hat{\beta}_2 - \hat{\beta}_3)$.

It is straightforward to apply the same approach to the alternative setting where $\hat{\beta}^A$ implies $s^* = 1$ per Lemma A.1 and compare Candidate A's objective function following and not following their beliefs.

Finally, because Candidate B's beliefs are equivalent and the expected vote is symmetric to Candidate A's, their incentives to follow their best beliefs $\hat{\beta}^B$ are equivalent to the incentives of A.   □

A.4.6 Voters Prefer That Candidates Believe They Care Intensely

Lemma A.4 (Voters prefer that candidates believe they care intensely). When candidates are uncertain about the intensity of each voter, a high-intensity voter strictly prefers that the candidates believe they care intensely ($\hat{\beta}_i = \bar{\beta}$ for voter i) and a low-intensity voter weakly prefers the candidates believe they care intensely.

Proof Lemma A.3 shows that candidate policy proposals are weakly related to beliefs about the intensities of each voter.

Majority Voters 1 and 2 strictly prefer $s^* = 1$ to $s^* = 0$. Equilibrium platform $s^* = 1$ is guaranteed when either $\hat{\beta}_1 = \bar{\beta}$ or $\hat{\beta}_2 = \bar{\beta}$. They are indifferent if $\hat{\beta}_3 = 1$ because policy is at $s^* = 1$ regardless of candidate beliefs about majority intensity. But they are strictly better off if $\hat{\beta}_3 = \bar{\beta}$ because when $\hat{\beta}_1 = \bar{\beta}$ or $\hat{\beta}_2 = \bar{\beta}$, policy platforms are $s^* = 1$ rather than $s^* = 0$. Therefore, majority Voters 1 and 2 weakly prefer that candidates believe they care intensely when low-intensity, and strictly when high-intensity.

Minority Voter 3 strictly prefers $s^* = 0$ to $s^* = 1$. Equilibrium platform $s^* = 0$ occurs if, and only if, $\hat{\beta}_1 = \hat{\beta}_2 = 1$ and $\hat{\beta}_3 = \bar{\beta}$. Voter 3 is strictly better off with $\hat{\beta}_3 = \bar{\beta}$ when $\hat{\beta}_1 = \hat{\beta}_2 = 1$ and indifferent when $\hat{\beta}_1 = \bar{\beta}$

or $\hat{\beta}_2 = \bar{\beta}$. Therefore, minority Voter 3 weakly prefers that candidates believe they care intensely whether high- or low-intensity. □

A.5 PROPOSITION A.1: MINORITY POLICY REPRESENTATION THROUGH POLITICAL ACTION

When $\bar{\beta} < 2$, equilibrium policy is $s^* = 1$ per Lemma A.1 because always $\beta_1 + \beta_2 > \beta_3$. We are interested in a setting where candidates might propose policy with the minority and so I make the assumption $\bar{\beta} > 2$. See Section B.1 for an equilibrium with $\bar{\beta} < 2$.

A strategy for a voter is a function $\sigma_v(\beta_i) : \{1, \bar{\beta}\} \to \mathbb{R}_+$ mapping intensity into political action $\lambda_i \geq 0$. Beliefs for a candidate, $p \in \{A, B\}$, are a function $h_p(\lambda_1, \lambda_2, \lambda_3) : \mathbb{R}_+^3 \to \Delta(\{1, \bar{\beta}\}^3)$ mapping observed political action into lotteries over voter intensity types. A strategy for a candidate, $p \in \{A, B\}$, is a function $\sigma_p(\lambda_1, \lambda_2, \lambda_3) : \mathbb{R}_+^3 \to \{0, 1\}$ mapping observed political action into policy platform s_p.

Consider an equilibrium magnitude of political action, λ^*, and a prior rate of intensity, q, satisfying

$$1 \leq \lambda^* \leq \bar{\beta},$$
$$q \in (0, 1 - \sqrt{2}/2). \tag{A.7}$$

Combining beliefs and equilibrium magnitude of political action in Eq. (A.7) leads to Proposition A.1.

Proposition A.1 (Minority policy representation through political action). For $q < 1 - \sqrt{2}/2$ and $1 \leq \lambda^* \leq \bar{\beta}$, there exists $B > 2$ such that $\bar{\beta} \geq B$ implies an equilibrium in which Voter 3, and only Voter 3, chooses costly action λ^* when high-intensity and abstains from costly action when low-intensity. In this equilibrium, the players' strategies are

$$\sigma_1^*(1) = \sigma_2^*(1) = \sigma_1^*(\bar{\beta}) = \sigma_2^*(\bar{\beta}) = 0,$$
$$\sigma_3^*(1) = 0, \ \sigma_3^*(\bar{\beta}) = \lambda^*,$$
$$\sigma_A^*(\lambda) = \sigma_B^*(\lambda) = \begin{cases} 0 & \text{if } \lambda_3 = \lambda^* \\ 1 & \text{if } \lambda_3 = 0. \end{cases}$$

Furthermore, candidate beliefs $h_A^*(\lambda)$ and $h_B^*(\lambda)$, $\lambda \equiv (\lambda_1, \lambda_2, \lambda_3)$, assign probability 1 to $\beta_3 = 1$ when $\lambda_3 < \lambda^*$ and probability 1 to $\beta_3 = \bar{\beta}$ when $\lambda_3 \geq \lambda^*$. Regardless of λ, $h_A^*(\lambda)$ and $h_B^*(\lambda)$ assign probability q to $\beta_1 = \bar{\beta}$, probability q to $\beta_2 = \bar{\beta}$, probability $1 - q$ to $\beta_1 = 1$, and probability $1 - q$ to $\beta_2 = 1$.

Proof   Claim: there is a perfect Bayesian equilibrium $(\sigma_1^*, \sigma_2^*, \sigma_3^*, \sigma_A^*, \sigma_B^*,$
$h_A^*, h_B^*)$ in which

$$h_p^*(\lambda_1) \to \Pr(\beta_1 = \bar{\beta}) = q, \ \Pr(\beta_1 = 1) = 1 - q, \ p \in \{A, B\}, \ \forall \lambda_1 \in \mathbb{R}_+,$$
$$h_p^*(\lambda_2) \to \Pr(\beta_2 = \bar{\beta}) = q, \ \Pr(\beta_2 = 1) = 1 - q, \ p \in \{A, B\}, \ \forall \lambda_2 \in \mathbb{R}_+,$$
$$h_p^*(\lambda_3 < \lambda^*) \to \beta_3 = 1, \ p \in \{A, B\},$$
$$h_p^*(\lambda_3 \geq \lambda^*) \to \beta_3 = \bar{\beta}, \ p \in \{A, B\},$$
$$\sigma_i^*(1) = \sigma_i^*(\bar{\beta}) = 0, \ i \in \{1, 2\},$$
$$\sigma_3^*(1) = 0, \ \sigma_3^*(\bar{\beta}) = \lambda^*,$$
$$\sigma_A^*(\lambda) = \sigma_B^*(\lambda) = 0 \iff \lambda_3 \geq \lambda^*,$$
$$\text{else } \sigma_A^*(\lambda) = \sigma_B^*(\lambda) = 1. \tag{A.8}$$

Suppose voters and candidates follow Eq. (A.8). Then, when candidates observe $\lambda_3 \geq \lambda^*$, they assign probability one that $\beta_3 = \bar{\beta}$. Candidates assign probability q that $\beta_i = \bar{\beta}$ for both Voters 1 and 2, and $1 - q \ \beta_i = 1$.

Policy $s^* = 0$ occurs when candidates believe $\beta_1 + \beta_2 \leq \beta_3$. When candidates have assigned probability one to $\beta_3 = \bar{\beta}$, there is probability $(1 - q)^2$ that $\beta_1 + \beta_2 \leq \beta_3$ and probability $1 - (1 - q)^2$ that $\beta_1 + \beta_2 > \beta_3$. The policy equilibrium in pure strategies is $s^* = 0$ when

$$(1 - q)^2 \geq 1 - (1 - q)^2,$$
$$1 - 4q + 2q^2 \geq 0,$$

which occurs when $q < 1 - \sqrt{2}/2 \approx 0.3$. Proposing policy $s^* = 0$ if, and only if, $\lambda_3 \geq \lambda^*$ else $s^* = 1$ is therefore optimal on the equilibrium path when $q < 1 - \sqrt{2}/2$.

Turning to the voters, begin with minority Voter 3. If $\beta_3 = 1$, then $\sigma_3^*(1) = 0$ and Voter 3's expected benefit is zero because this choice guarantees $s^* = 1$ per Eq. (A.8). The expected payoff from deviating and choosing $\lambda_3 = \lambda^*$ is $1 - \lambda^*$. Given $1 \leq \lambda^*$ Eq. (A.7), Voter 3 does not benefit from this deviation.

Now, consider $\beta_3 = \bar{\beta}$. $\sigma_3^*(\bar{\beta}) = \lambda^*$ yields an expected benefit of $\bar{\beta} - \lambda^*$. Deviation from the strategy to $\lambda_3 = 0$ has an expected benefit of zero. The equilibrium strategy is optimal if $\bar{\beta} - \lambda^* \geq 0$, which follows from the bounds presented in Eq. (A.7).

There are two majority voter types, high-intensity and low-intensity. Without loss of generality to Voter 2, consider Voter 1. When $\beta_1 = 1$, $\sigma_1^*(1) = 0$ with an expected payoff of $(1 - q)(\beta_1)$, the probability that Voter 3 is low-intensity and therefore abstains from costly action multiplied by Voter 1's payoff to policy $s = 1, \beta_1 = 1$. Because of candidate beliefs $h_A^* = h_B^*$, deviating and choosing $\lambda_I = \lambda^*$ has an expected payoff of $(1 - q)(\beta_I) - \lambda^*$. Because $\lambda^* \geq 0$, the low-intensity majority voter does not benefit from deviating.

Finally, when $\beta_I = \bar{\beta}$, $\sigma_I^*(\bar{\beta}) = 0$ has an expected payoff of $(1 - q)\bar{\beta}$. Because of candidate beliefs $h_A^* = h_B^*$, deviating and choosing $\lambda_I = \lambda^*$ has an expected payoff of $(1 - q)(\bar{\beta}) - \lambda^*$. Because $\lambda^* \geq 0$, the high-intensity majority voter does not benefit from deviating. Majority voters do not deviate as long as $0 \leq \lambda^*$.

A *Minority policy representation through political action* equilibrium holds with the strategies and beliefs presented in Eq. (A.8) when $q < 1 - \sqrt{2}/2$ and when λ^* follows the bounds $1 \leq \lambda^* \leq \bar{\beta}$. □

A.6 PROPOSITION A.2: REPRESENTATION THROUGH SEPARATING POLITICAL ACTION

When $\bar{\beta} < 2$, equilibrium policy is $s^* = 1$ per Lemma A.1 because always $\beta_I + \beta_2 > \beta_3$. We are interested in a setting where candidates might propose policy with the minority and so I make the assumption $\bar{\beta} > 2$. See Section B.1 for an equilibrium with $\bar{\beta} < 2$.

A strategy for a voter is a function $\sigma_V(\beta_i) : \{1, \bar{\beta}\} \to \mathbb{R}_+$ mapping intensity into political action $\lambda_i \geq 0$. Beliefs for a candidate, $p \in \{A, B\}$, are a function $h_p(\lambda_I, \lambda_2, \lambda_3) : \mathbb{R}_+^3 \to \Delta(\{1, \bar{\beta}\}^3)$ mapping observed political action into lotteries over voter intensity types. A strategy for a candidate, $p \in \{A, B\}$, is a function $\sigma_p(\lambda_I, \lambda_2, \lambda_3) : \mathbb{R}_+^3 \to \{0, 1\}$ mapping observed political action into policy platform s_p.

Consider an equilibrium magnitude of political action, λ^*, and a prior rate of intensity, q, satisfying

$$(1 - q)^2 \leq \lambda^* \leq \bar{\beta}(1 - q - (1 - q)^2) \text{ if } q < 1/2,$$

$$1 - q - (1 - q)^2 \leq \lambda^* \leq \bar{\beta}(1 - q)^2 \text{ if } q \geq 1/2,$$

$$q \in (1/(\bar{\beta} + 1), \bar{\beta}/(\bar{\beta} + 1)). \tag{A.9}$$

Combining beliefs and equilibrium magnitude of political action leads to Proposition A.2.

Proposition A.2 (Representation through separating political action). For any $q \in (1/(\bar{\beta} + 1), \bar{\beta}/(\bar{\beta} + 1))$, there exists $B > 2$ such that $\bar{\beta} \geq B$ implies a separating equilibrium. In this equilibrium, the players' strategies are

$$\sigma_i^*(\mathrm{I}) = \mathrm{o}, \ \sigma_i^*(\bar{\beta}) = \lambda^*, \ i \in \{\mathrm{I}, 2, 3\}$$

$$\sigma_A^*(\lambda) = \sigma_B^*(\lambda) = \begin{cases} \mathrm{o} & \text{if } \lambda_\mathrm{I} = \lambda_2 = \mathrm{o}, \lambda_3 = \lambda^* \\ \mathrm{I} & \text{otherwise.} \end{cases}$$

and λ^* respects the bounds

$$(\mathrm{I} - q)^2 \le \lambda^* \le \bar{\beta}(\mathrm{I} - q - (\mathrm{I} - q)^2) \text{ if } q < \mathrm{I}/2,$$
$$\mathrm{I} - q - (\mathrm{I} - q)^2 \le \lambda^* \le \bar{\beta}(\mathrm{I} - q)^2 \text{ if } q \ge \mathrm{I}/2.$$

Furthermore, candidate beliefs $h_A^*(\lambda)$ and $h_B^*(\lambda)$, $\lambda \equiv (\lambda_\mathrm{I}, \lambda_2, \lambda_3)$, assign probability I to $\beta_i = \mathrm{I}$ when $\lambda_i < \lambda^*$ and probability I to $\beta_i = \bar{\beta}$ when $\lambda_i \ge \lambda^*$ for all $i \in \{\mathrm{I}, 2, 3\}$.

Proof Claim: there is a perfect Bayesian equilibrium $(\sigma_\mathrm{I}^*, \sigma_2^*, \sigma_3^*, \sigma_A^*, \sigma_B^*, h_A^*, h_B^*)$ in which

$$h_p^*(\lambda_i < \lambda^*) \to \beta_i = \mathrm{I}, \ i \in \{\mathrm{I}, 2, 3\}, \ p \in \{A, B\}$$

$$h_p^*(\lambda_i \ge \lambda^*) \to \beta_i = \bar{\beta}, \ i \in \{\mathrm{I}, 2, 3\}, \ p \in \{A, B\}$$

$$\sigma_i^*(\mathrm{I}) = \mathrm{o}, \ \sigma_i^*(\bar{\beta}) = \lambda^*, \ i \in \{\mathrm{I}, 2, 3\},$$

$$\sigma_A^*(\lambda) = \sigma_B^*(\lambda) = \mathrm{I} \text{ if}$$

$$\mathrm{I}[\lambda_\mathrm{I} \ge \lambda^*] + \mathrm{I}[\lambda_2 \ge \lambda^*] \ge \mathrm{I}[\lambda_3 \ge \lambda^*]$$

$$\text{and } \sigma_A^*(\lambda) = \sigma_B^*(\lambda) = \mathrm{o} \text{ otherwise,} \qquad (A.\mathrm{Io})$$

where $\mathrm{I}[\cdot]$ is the indicator function.

Suppose voters and candidates follow Eq. (A.10). Then, candidates believe $\beta_\mathrm{I} + \beta_2 \ge \beta_3$ with probability one when observing λ such that $\mathrm{I}[\lambda_\mathrm{I} \ge \lambda^*] + \mathrm{I}[\lambda_2 \ge \lambda^*] \ge \mathrm{I}[\lambda_3 \ge \lambda^*]$ and form the belief that $\beta_\mathrm{I} + \beta_2 \ge \beta_3$ with probability zero when λ is otherwise. Given these beliefs and Lemma A.1, the candidate strategy Eq. (A.10) is optimal on the equilibrium path.

Turning to the voters, begin with minority Voter 3. If $\beta_3 = \mathrm{I}$, then $\sigma_3^*(\mathrm{I}) = \mathrm{o}$ and Voter 3's expected benefit is o because this choice guarantees $\mathrm{I}[\lambda_\mathrm{I} \ge \lambda^*] + \mathrm{I}[\lambda_2 \ge \lambda^*] \ge \mathrm{I}[\lambda_3 \ge \lambda^*]$ and $s^* = \mathrm{I}$. The expected payoff from deviating and choosing $\lambda_3 = \lambda^*$ is the probability that neither majority voter chooses λ^* times the benefit of policy $s = \mathrm{o}$ less the cost λ^*, or $(\mathrm{I} - q)^2(\beta_3) - \lambda^*$. Given $\beta_3 = \mathrm{I}$ and $(\mathrm{I} - q)^2 \le \lambda^*$ Eq. (A.9), Voter 3 does not benefit from this deviation.

Now, consider $\beta_3 = \bar{\beta}$. $\sigma_3^*(\bar{\beta}) = \lambda^*$ yields an expected benefit of $\bar{\beta}(\mathrm{I} - q)^2 - \lambda^*$. Deviation from the strategy to $\lambda_3 = \mathrm{o}$ has an expected benefit of zero as it guarantees the candidates choose $s = 1$. The equilibrium strategy is optimal if $\bar{\beta}(1 - q)^2 - \lambda^* \geq 0$, which follows from the bounds presented in Eq. (A.9).

Majority Voters 1 and 2 have the same payoffs, beliefs, and actions, so the proof for Voter 1 is the same as for 2.[2] The postulated strategy when $\beta_1 = 1$ is $\sigma_1^*(1) = 0$ with an expected payoff of $(q + (1 - q)^2)(\beta_1)$, the probability that Voter 2 is high-intensity and chooses costly action plus the probability that both Voter 2 and Voter 3 are low-intensity, each multiplied by Voter 1's payoff to policy $s = 1$, $\beta_1 = 1$. Deviating and choosing $\lambda_1 = \lambda^*$ has an expected payoff of $\beta_1 - \lambda^*$ because whenever either majority voter chooses costly action, policy is set at the majority preference. Voter 1 does not deviate if $1 - \lambda^* \leq q + (1 - q)^2$, which holds by the bounds in Eq. (A.9).

Finally, if $\beta_1 = \bar{\beta}$, then following the postulated strategy $\sigma_1^*(\bar{\beta}) = \lambda^*$ has an expected payoff of $\bar{\beta} - \lambda^*$. Deviating with $\lambda_1 = 0$ yields $\bar{\beta}(q + (1 - q)^2)$ and Voter 1 does not deviate if $\bar{\beta}(q + (1 - q)^2) \leq \bar{\beta} - \lambda^*$, which follows the bounds in Eq. (A.9).

A separating equilibrium holds with the strategies and beliefs presented in Eq. (A.10) and when λ^* follows the bounds $\max\{(1 - q)^2, 1 - q - (1 - q)^2\} \leq \lambda^* \leq \min\{\bar{\beta}(1 - q)^2, \bar{\beta}(1 - q - (1 - q)^2)\}$. The equilibrium lower bound on λ^* follows the lower bound of minority Voter 3 $(1 - q)^2$ when

$$(1 - q)^2 > 1 - q - (1 - q)^2,$$
$$1 > 3q - 2q^2 \rightarrow (1 - 2q)(1 - q) > 0,$$

which obtains if, and only if, $q < 1/2$. It follows, then, that the equilibrium holds when λ^* is within the bounds

$$(1 - q)^2 \leq \lambda^* \leq \bar{\beta}(1 - q - (1 - q)^2) \text{ if } q < 1/2,$$
$$1 - q - (1 - q)^2 \leq \lambda^* \leq \bar{\beta}(1 - q)^2 \text{ if } q \geq 1/2.$$

Finally, q must be consistent with the bounds in Eq. (A.9):

$$\text{If } q < 1/2 : (1 - q)^2 \leq \bar{\beta}(1 - q - (1 - q)^2)$$
$$(1 - q)/q \leq \bar{\beta} \quad \rightarrow \quad 1/(1 + \bar{\beta}) \leq q.$$
$$\text{If } q \geq 1/2 : 1 - q - (1 - q)^2 \leq \bar{\beta}(1 - q)^2$$
$$q(1 + \bar{\beta}) \leq \bar{\beta} \rightarrow q \leq \bar{\beta}/(\bar{\beta} + 1).$$

---

[2] Hill (2022a) shows there is an asymmetric equilibrium where one of the majority voters takes costly action when high-intensity and the other majority voter always abstains.

A *Representation through separating political action* equilibrium holds with the strategies and beliefs presented in Req. A.10 when $q \in (1/(\bar{\beta}+1), \bar{\beta}/(\bar{\beta}+1))$ and when λ^* follows the bounds in Req. A.9. □

When q is near one or near zero, candidates are likely to propose majority policy because, when near one, a majority voter is likely to be high-intensity with probability approaching one and, when near zero, the minority voter is likely to be low-intensity with probability approaching one. In the three-voter model here, "near zero" is less than $1/(\bar{\beta}+1)$ and "near one" is greater than $\bar{\beta}/(\bar{\beta}+1)$, but these values would differ for different balances of majority and minority.

The logic in the previous paragraph holds across equilibria, including the minority-only equilibrium. Note that when q is very low, the candidates believe it unlikely the minority voter is high-intensity and so are likely to propose policy with the majority. But this is exactly why the minority voter incurs costly action at low values of q in the minority-only equilibrium. Their costly action communicates to the candidates, "I know this is rare, but I really do care intensely!"

In the separating equilibrium, each voter chooses to incur costly political action when high-intensity and to abstain when low-intensity. Costly action communicates intensity to candidates. Candidates frustrate the majority with equilibrium policy platforms $s_A^* = s_B^* = 0$ if, and only if, both majority voters abstain and the minority voter takes action.

A.7 COMPARING MAGNITUDES OF COSTLY ACTION

In this section, I compare the magnitude of equilibrium costly political action λ^* required in the two equilibria of interest. The bounds on λ^* are

$1 \le \lambda^* \le \bar{\beta}$ (Prop A.1),

$(1-q)^2 \le \lambda^* \le \bar{\beta}(1 - q - (1-q)^2)$ if $q < 1/2$, and

$1 - q - (1-q)^2 \le \lambda^* \le \bar{\beta}(1-q)^2$ if $q \ge 1/2$ (Prop A.2).

Because $B(1-q)^2 < B$ and $B(1-q-(1-q)^2) < B$ for $B = 1$ and $B = \bar{\beta}$, both bounds of Proposition A.2 are strictly less than the corresponding bounds of Proposition A.1.

Appendix B

Formalities of Chapter 5

In this appendix, I present mathematical analysis underlying the model extensions presented in Chapter 5. Other versions of this analysis are published in Hill (2022a), originally published by the University of Chicago Press and reprinted with permission.

I first show that intensity theory can generate frustrated majorities and costly political action no matter the size of the minority. The analysis describes how the intensity of the minority must vary with the size of the minority for candidates to choose to set policy with the minority (Section B.1). I then show that the two equilibria of Chapter 4 do not depend on an electorate of three voters. Instead, both equilibria hold with small, medium, or large minority sizes (Section B.2).

Next I present a utilitarian welfare analysis of the second equilibrium from Chapter 4. I start by deriving the Bethamite social optimum policy (Section B.3). I then derive the parameter values required for social welfare to be improved with costly political action and frustrated majorities (Section B.4).

B.1 CANDIDATE POLICY CHOICE WITH MINORITY OF ARBITRARY SIZE

Lemma A.1 derives the conditions where vote-seeking candidates propose policy with the minority when standing for election before three voters. In this section, I extend that model to examine prospects for frustrated majorities and costly political action when varying the size of the minority relative to the majority. The results show that candidates side with the minority as long as the minority's intensity is sufficiently greater than the intensity of the majority. The difference in intensity required to generate non-majoritarian policy in equilibrium depends on the size of the minority. The smaller the minority, the larger its intensity must be to frustrate majorities. The larger the minority, the smaller its intensity must be to frustrate majorities.

The model again has two vote-seeking candidates, A and B. Instead of an electorate of three voters, the electorate is of arbitrary size, finite, with two policy types. The minority of size $p \in (0, 0.5)$ prefers $s = 0$ and the majority of size $(1 - p)$ prefers that policy $s = 1$. Minority size p is common knowledge.

The average intensities of minority and majority are $(\beta_0, \beta_1) \in \{1, \bar{\beta}\}^2$, common knowledge. The election result depends upon the policy platforms of the candidates, s_A and s_B, the size of the minority p, average intensities β_0 and β_1, and independent stochastic election shocks δ_0 and δ_1. Election shocks are drawn independently according to the uniform distribution with upper and lower bounds c and d, common knowledge, with $c < -\bar{\beta}$ and $\bar{\beta} < d$ so that the votes of both minority and majority are stochastic.

With the uniform error distribution, A's expected vote share is

$$
\begin{aligned}
\pi^A &= (p)(\beta_0[s_B - s_A] - c)/(d - c) + (1 - p)(\beta_1[s_A - s_B] - c)/(d - c) \\
&= (d - c)^{-1}(p\beta_0[s_B - s_A] + (1 - p)(\beta_1[s_A - s_B]) - c) \\
&= (d - c)^{-1}(s_B[p\beta_0 - \beta_1 + p\beta_1] + s_A[\beta_1 - p\beta_0 - p\beta_1] - c). \quad \text{(B.1)}
\end{aligned}
$$

B's expected vote share is the complement, $1 - \pi^A$.

B.1.1 Candidate Policy Best Responses

The proof of Lemma B.1 follows closely that of Lemma A.1.

Lemma B.1 (Candidate policy best responses by size of minority). The best response for both candidates is to propose the policy preferred by the minority, $s^* = 0$, when $p \geq \beta_1/(\beta_0 + \beta_1)$, otherwise to propose the policy preferred by the majority, $s^* = 1$.

Proof Given the statement of expected vote share in Eq. (B.1), Candidate A's best response to $s_B = 0$ is $s_A = 0$ when

$$
U^A(0|s_B = 0) \geq U^A(1|s_B = 0),
$$
$$
(d - c)^{-1}(-c) \geq (d - c)^{-1}(\beta_1 - p\beta_0 - p\beta_1 - c),
$$
$$
0 \geq \beta_1 - p\beta_0 - p\beta_1,
$$
$$
p\beta_0 + p\beta_1 \geq \beta_1 \Rightarrow p \geq \beta_1/(\beta_0 + \beta_1).
$$

Candidate A's best response to $s_B = 1$ is $s_A = 0$ when

$$U^A(0|s_B = 1) \geq U^A(1|s_B = 1),$$

$$(d - c)^{-1}(p\beta_0 - \beta_1 + p\beta_1 - c) \geq (d - c)^{-1}$$
$$\times (p\beta_0 - \beta_1 + p\beta_1 + \beta_1 - p\beta_0 - p\beta_1 - c),$$

$$0 \geq \beta_1 - p\beta_0 - p\beta_1,$$

$$p\beta_0 + p\beta_1 \geq \beta_1 \Rightarrow p \geq \beta_1/(\beta_0 + \beta_1).$$

Likewise, Candidate B's best response to $s_A = 0$ is $s_B = 0$ when

$$U^B(0|s_A = 0) \geq U^B(1|s_A = 0),$$

$$1 - (d - c)^{-1}(-c) \geq 1 - (d - c)^{-1}(p\beta_0 - \beta_1 + p\beta_1 - c),$$

$$0 \geq -p\beta_0 + \beta_1 - p\beta_1,$$

$$p\beta_0 + p\beta_1 \geq \beta_1 \Rightarrow p \geq \beta_1/(\beta_0 + \beta_1).$$

Candidate B's best response to $s_A = 1$ is $s_B = 0$ when

$$U^B(0|s_A = 1) \geq U^B(1|s_A = 1),$$

$$1 - (d - c)^{-1}(\beta_1 - p\beta_0 - p\beta_1 - c) \geq 1 - (d - c)^{-1}(p\beta_0 - \beta_1 + p\beta_1 + \beta_1$$
$$- p\beta_0 - p\beta_1 - c),$$

$$0 \geq -p\beta_0 + \beta_1 - p\beta_1,$$

$$p\beta_0 + p\beta_1 \geq \beta_1 \Rightarrow p \geq \beta_1/(\beta_0 + \beta_1).$$

Therefore, the best response for both candidates is to propose the policy preferred by the minority, $s_A^* = s_B^* = 0$ if, and only if, $p \geq \beta_1/(\beta_0 + \beta_1)$. □

Lemma B.1 shows that the probability that candidates choose to frustrate the majority by proposing policy with the minority is increasing in the minority's size p, increasing in the minority's intensity β_0, and decreasing in the majority's intensity β_1. A little algebra shows that the inequality in Lemma B.1 is equivalent to the ratio of the minority's intensity to the majority's intensity greater than or equal to the ratio of the minority size to the majority size, $\beta_0/\beta_1 \geq (1 - p)/p$.[1]

B.2 ARBITRARY SIZE OF MINORITY, INTENSITY PRIVATE INFORMATION

Lemma B.1 presents candidate best responses when candidates have complete information about the intensities of minority and majority. I now

---

[1] $p \geq \beta_1/(\beta_0 + \beta_1) \to (\beta_0 + \beta_1) \geq \beta_1/p \to \beta_0 \geq \beta_1/p - \beta_1 p/p \to \beta_0/\beta_1 \geq (1 - p)/p.$

consider the setting where intensity is private information and the minority is of arbitrary size. Consider a game of incomplete information where voters may use costly action λ to signal to candidates their intensity and where candidates use Bayes' rule to update beliefs.

I adopt all notation and assumptions of the model in Section A.4 except for the assumption of three voters. Instead, assume there is a majority and minority of arbitrary proportions $1 - p$ and p, $p \in (0, 0.5)$.

There are two equilibria of interest. The first is an equilibrium where the minority incurs costly action $\lambda_0 = \lambda_0^* > 0$ when high-intensity $\beta_0 = \bar{\beta}$ and $\lambda_0 = 0$ when low-intensity, $\beta_0 = 1$.

The second equilibrium is a separating equilibrium where there exists a $\lambda^* > 0$ where both the majority and the minority choose $\lambda_i = \lambda^*$ when $\beta_i = \bar{\beta}$ and $\lambda_i = 0$ when low-intensity, $\beta_i = 1$. The second separating equilibrium may occur at a different range of parameters than the first equilibrium because the majority has different incentives to communicate than the minority.

By definition of an equilibrium, the following set of inequalities must hold for each player.

$$U^P(s_P = \tau_i | \lambda_i = \lambda^*) \geq U^P(s_P = 1 - \tau_i | \lambda_i = \lambda^*), \; P \in \{A, B\},$$

$$U^i(\lambda_i = \lambda^* | \beta_i = \bar{\beta}) \geq U^i(\lambda_i = 0 | \beta_i = \bar{\beta}) \text{ and,}$$

$$U^i(\lambda_i = 0 | \beta_i = 0) \geq U^i(\lambda_i = \lambda^* | \beta_i = 0), \; i \in \{0, 1\}. \quad \text{(B.2)}$$

In the first, minority action equilibrium, the inequalities must apply only to $i = 0$ for the minority. In the second, separating equilibrium, the inequalities must apply to both the minority and majority, $i \in \{0, 1\}$. I use perfect Bayesian equilibrium (PBE) as the solution concept.

B.2.1 Minority Action Equilibrium

Consider the first equilibrium where the minority takes costly action when high-intensity.

Proof Suppose an equilibrium exists where $\lambda_0 = \lambda_0^* > 0 \Rightarrow \beta_0 = \bar{\beta}$ and $\lambda_0 = 0 \Rightarrow \beta_0 = 1$ and, therefore, candidate beliefs about β_0 follow from observation of λ_0.

To establish the equilibrium, each inequality in Eq. (B.2) must hold for $i = 0$. The first inequality follows from Lemma B.1 and the definition of a PBE. When candidates observe $\lambda_0 = \lambda_0^*$, they form posterior beliefs $\hat{\beta}_0 = \bar{\beta}$ with probability one. When candidates observe $\lambda_0 = 0$, they form posterior beliefs $\hat{\beta}_0 = 0$ with probability one.

The second inequality requires that a high-intensity minority weakly prefers choosing costly action to the off-equilibrium action abstain $\lambda = 0$. Recalling that $q \in (0, 1)$ is the common knowledge prior probability that the majority is high-intensity, the minority's expected benefit from the equilibrium when high-intensity is

$$(q)U^\circ(\lambda_0 = \lambda_0^*|\beta_0 = \bar{\beta}, \beta_1 = \bar{\beta}) + (1-q)U^\circ(\lambda_0 = \lambda_0^*|\beta_0 = \bar{\beta}, \beta_1 = 1)$$

$$= (q)(-\lambda_0^*) + (1-q)(\bar{\beta} - \lambda_0^*)$$

$$= (1-q)\bar{\beta} - \lambda_0^*.$$

The minority's expected benefit from deviation (not choosing costly action) when high-intensity is

$$U^\circ(\lambda_0 = 0|\beta_0 = \bar{\beta}) = 0$$

because when the candidates believe the minority low-intensity, they always propose policy with the majority (Lemma B.1).

A high-intensity minority does not deviate from the equilibrium when $0 \leq (1-q)\bar{\beta} - \lambda_0^*$ or $\lambda_0^* \leq (1-q)\bar{\beta}$.

The third inequality requires that a low-intensity minority weakly prefers choosing no costly action to the off-equilibrium action abstain $\lambda = 0$. The minority's expected benefit from the equilibrium when low-intensity is

$$U^\circ(\lambda_0 = 0|\beta_0 = 1) = 0,$$

again per Lemma B.1. The minority's expected benefit from deviation (choosing costly action) when low-intensity is

$$(q)U^\circ(\lambda_0 = \lambda_0^*|\beta_0 = 1, \beta_1 = \bar{\beta}) + (1-q)U^\circ(\lambda_0 = \lambda_0^*|\beta_0 = 1, \beta_1 = 1)$$

$$= (q)(-\lambda_0^*) + (1-q)(1 - \lambda_0^*)$$

$$= 1 - q - \lambda_0^*.$$

A low-intensity minority does not deviate from the equilibrium when $1 - q - \lambda_0^* \leq 0$ or $1 - q \leq \lambda_0^*$.

Combining these results, the minority equilibrium holds when $1 - q \leq \lambda_0^* \leq (1-q)\bar{\beta}$, which holds always because $\bar{\beta} > 1$ and $\lambda \geq 0$. □

B.2.2 Separating Equilibrium

The second, separating equilibrium requires the constraints from the first equilibrium described in the section above plus the majority taking costly action when high-intensity. I describe this additional requirement in this section, leading to a statement of the separating equilibrium.

Proof Begin with the results of the first equilibrium, with the requirement that $1 - q - \lambda_o^* \le o$ or $1 - q \le \lambda_o^*$. For a separating equilibrium, there must exist a λ^* where the majority also chooses costly action when high-intensity but chooses no action when low-intensity.

Suppose a separating equilibrium exists where $\lambda_I = \lambda^* > o \Rightarrow \beta_I = \bar\beta$ and $\lambda_I = o \Rightarrow \beta_I = 1$ and, therefore, candidate beliefs about β_I follow from their observation of λ_I.

To establish existence of the separating equilibrium, each inequality in Eq. (B.2) must hold for the majority $i = 1$. The first inequality follows from Lemma B.1 and the definition of a PBE.

The second inequality requires that a high-intensity majority weakly prefers choosing costly action to the off-equilibrium action abstain $\lambda = o$. The majority's expected benefit from the equilibrium when high-intensity is

$$U^I(\lambda_I = \lambda^* | \beta_I = \bar\beta) = \bar\beta - \lambda^*$$

because when the candidates believe the majority high-intensity, they always propose policy with the majority (Lemma B.1).

The majority's expected benefit from deviation (not choosing costly action) when high-intensity is

$$(q)U^I(\lambda_I = o | \beta_I = \bar\beta, \beta_o = \bar\beta) + (1 - q)U^I(\lambda_I = o | \beta_I = \bar\beta, \beta_o = 1)$$
$$= (q)(o) + (1 - q)(\bar\beta)$$
$$= \bar\beta - q\bar\beta.$$

A high-intensity majority does not deviate from the equilibrium when $\bar\beta - q\bar\beta \le \bar\beta - \lambda^*$ or $\lambda^* \le q\bar\beta$.

The third inequality requires that a low-intensity majority weakly prefers choosing no costly action to the off-equilibrium action costly action. The majority's expected benefit from the equilibrium when low-intensity is

$$U^I(\lambda_I = o | \beta_I = 1) = (q)U^I(\lambda_I = o | \beta_I = 1, \beta_o = \bar\beta)$$
$$+ (1 - q)U^I(\lambda_I = o | \beta_I = 1, \beta_o = 1)$$
$$= 1 - q.$$

The majority's expected benefit from deviation (choosing costly action) when low-intensity is

$$U^I(\lambda_I = \lambda^* | \beta_I = 1) = 1 - \lambda^*.$$

A low-intensity majority does not deviate from the equilibrium when $1 - \lambda^* \leq 1 - q$ or $q \leq \lambda^*$.

Combining, the separating equilibrium holds when $1 - q \leq \lambda^* \leq (1 - q)\bar{\beta}$ (for the minority) and when $q \leq \lambda^* \leq q\bar{\beta}$ (for the majority), both of which hold because $\bar{\beta} > 1$.   □

These two proofs show that the key constraint on the equilibrium with costly signaling and arbitrary minority size p is not the expected rate high-intensity q but the relationship between p and $\bar{\beta}$ described by Lemma B.1. For these election dynamics to hold, the minority must either be relatively large with intensity of modest magnitude or relatively small with large-magnitude intensity.

B.3 BENTHAMITE SOCIAL OPTIMUM

In this section, I derive the Benthamite social optimum policy. This optimum is the policy that would be set were there a benevolent social planner whose only goal was to maximize the utility of the full electorate.

With the voter utility function represented in Eq. (A.1), $v_i(s, \beta_i)$, the Benthamite social optimum policy rule is

$$s^*(\beta_1, \beta_2, \beta_3) = \begin{cases} 0, & \text{if } \beta_1 + \beta_2 \leq \beta_3 \\ 1, & \text{otherwise.} \end{cases} \tag{B.3}$$

Proof follows simply by noting the benevolent central planner solves the maximization problem

$$\underset{s \in \{0,1\}}{\operatorname{argmax}} \ (\beta_1 s + \beta_2 s + \beta_3(1 - s)) = \underset{s \in \{0,1\}}{\operatorname{argmax}} \ (\beta_1 + \beta_2 - \beta_3)s,$$

which is maximized by Eq. (B.3).

This result reproduces the generic finding from the probabilistic voting literature that electoral competition delivers the utilitarian optimum policy.

B.4 PROOF TO PROPOSITION B.1: SOCIAL WELFARE WITH COSTLY POLITICAL ACTION

What are the welfare implications of frustrated majorities and costly political action? In this section, I evaluate utilitarian welfare under two different settings of electoral competition. The two settings share three voters with (common knowledge) heterogeneous preferences and (private information) heterogeneous intensity. In the first setting, individual intensity is not communicated to the candidates for office and so candidates choose policy based only on prior beliefs about the distribution of intensity (Setting 1). In the second setting, I consider a mechanism as in the separating equilibrium of Proposition A.2, where voters might incur costly political action to communicate their private-information intensity (Setting 2).

B.4.1 Notation and Definitions

Voters There are three voters, Voter 1, Voter 2, and Voter 3.

Candidates There are two candidates, A and B.

Decision One mutually-exclusive decision s must be made from the pair $\{0, 1\}$.

Preferences Individuals have preferences over decisions represented by a utility function $v_i(s, \beta_i) : \{0, 1\} \times \{1, \bar{\beta}\} \rightarrow \{0, 1, \bar{\beta}\}$. The function v_i returns a value $\beta_i \in \{1, \bar{\beta}\}$ when $s = \tau_i$, zero otherwise, where τ_i describes the voter's preference over policy.

Information Utility functions v and policy preference τ are common knowledge to all voters and candidates. Intensity type β is private information to each voter i. Prior beliefs about β_i are common knowledge, $\Pr(\beta_i = \bar{\beta}) = q$, $\Pr(\beta_i = 1) = 1 - q$ for all i.

Actions Each voter casts one vote for either Candidate A or Candidate B at an election and each candidate proposes a policy platform $s_p \in \{0, 1\}$, $p \in \{A, B\}$. In Setting 2, each voter selects a magnitude of costly political action $\lambda_i \in \mathbb{R}_+$ of certain cost.

Welfare Welfare for voter i, w_i, is $v_i(s, \beta_i) - \lambda_i$. Social welfare, W, is the sum of individual welfare, $\sum_i w_i$.

I compare the expected value of W between two settings of policy choice. In both settings, electoral competition determines policy. In Setting 1, candidate strategies are independent of voter actions λ and voter strategies are independent of voter intensity. Candidates choose policy based only on prior beliefs about intensity (q). Setting 2 analyzes welfare under the separating equilibrium in Proposition A.2.

Welfare is improved when voters have the opportunity to engage in costly political action when the policy benefit for high-intensity voters is sufficiently large, as stated in Proposition B.1:

Proposition B.1 (Social welfare with costly political action). The separating equilibrium from Proposition A.2 leads to higher expected electorate welfare than in a setting without costly political action if, and only if, $\bar{\beta} > 5$.

Proof **Setting 1** In Setting 1, candidate strategies are independent of voter signals λ and voter strategies σ_v are independent of voter intensities β.

Lemma A.1 shows that in equilibrium $s^* = 0$ when $\hat{\beta}_1 + \hat{\beta}_2 \leq \hat{\beta}_3$, else $s^* = 1$. In Setting 1, candidate beliefs about β follow from q. $\beta_1 + \beta_2 \leq \beta_3$ only obtains when $\beta = \{1, 1, \bar{\beta}\}$, which occurs with probability $(1-q)(1-q)(q)$. Thus, with probability $1 - (1-q)(1-q)(q)$, the candidates' best response is $s^* = 1$. As $1 - (1-q)(1-q)(q)$ is strictly greater than $(1-q)(1-q)(q)$ for all $q \in (0, 1)$, the pure strategy equilibrium in Setting 1 is $s_A^* = s_B^* = 1$.

Social welfare when $s_A^* = s_B^* = 1$ depends upon the distribution of intensities for Voters 1 and 2. With probability q^2, both are high-intensity and receive $\bar{\beta}$. With probability $q(1-q) + (1-q)q$ one is high- and the other low-intensity, and with probability $(1-q)^2$ both are low-intensity. This generates social welfare in Setting 1 of

$$
\begin{aligned}
W &= q^2(2\bar{\beta}) + 2q(1-q)(\bar{\beta} + 1) + 2(1-q)^2(1), \\
&= q^2(2\bar{\beta}) + (2q)(\bar{\beta} + 1) - (2q^2)(\bar{\beta} + 1) + 2(1 - 2q + q^2), \\
&= 2q\bar{\beta} - 2q + 2. \tag{B.4}
\end{aligned}
$$

Setting 2 Setting 2 is the separating equilibrium of Proposition A.2 where Voters 1 and 2 choose $\lambda_i = \lambda^*$ when $\beta_i = \bar{\beta}$, else $\lambda_i = 0$. Whenever either incurs costly action λ^*, $s^* = 1$. Welfare is

$$
\begin{aligned}
w_1 &= (q)v_1(s = 1, \beta_1 = \bar{\beta}) + (1-q)v_1(s = 1, \beta_1 = 1), \\
&= \underbrace{(q)(\bar{\beta} - \lambda^*)}_{\beta_1 = \bar{\beta}} + \underbrace{(1-q)(q)(1)}_{\beta_2 = \bar{\beta}} + \underbrace{(1-q)(1-q)(1-q)(1)}_{\beta = \{1,1,1\}} \\
&\quad + \underbrace{(1-q)(1-q)(q)(0)}_{\beta = \{1,1,\bar{\beta}\}},
\end{aligned}
$$

$$
w_2 = (q)v_2(s = 1, \beta_2 = \bar{\beta}) + (1-q)v_2(s = 1, \beta_2 = 1).
$$

$$
\begin{aligned}
w_1 + w_2 &= 2(q)(\bar{\beta} - \lambda^*) + 2(1-q)(q)(1) + 2(1-q)(1-q)(1-q)(1), \\
&= 2q\bar{\beta} - 2q\lambda^* + 2q - 2q^2 + 2(1 - 2q + q^2 - q + 2q^2 - q^3), \\
&= 2 + 2q\bar{\beta} - 2q\lambda^* - 4q + 4q^2 - 2q^3.
\end{aligned}
$$

Voter 3 chooses $\lambda_3 = \lambda^*$ when $\beta_3 = \bar{\beta}$, else $\lambda_3 = 0$. When $\lambda_3 = \lambda^*$, $s^* = 0$ with probability $(1-q)^2$ and $s^* = 1$ with probability $1 - (1-q)^2$. Welfare for Voter 3 in Setting 2 is

$$w_3 = (q)(1-q)^2 v_3(s=0, \beta_3 = \bar{\beta}) + (q)(1-(1-q)^2)v_3(s=1, \beta_3 = \bar{\beta})$$
$$+ (1-q)(v_3(s=1, \beta_1 = 1)),$$
$$= (q)(1-q)^2(\bar{\beta} - \lambda^*) + (q)(1-(1-q)^2)(0 - \lambda^*),$$
$$= q(1-q)^2(\bar{\beta}) - q\lambda^*.$$

Social welfare under Setting 2 is

$$W = 2 + 2q\bar{\beta} - 2q\lambda^* - 4q + 4q^2 - 2q^3 + q(1-q)^2(\bar{\beta}) - q\lambda^*,$$
$$= 2 + (2q + q(1-q)^2)(\bar{\beta}) - 3q\lambda^* - 4q + 4q^2 - 2q^3. \qquad (B.5)$$

Welfare comparison Electoral competition with costly political action (Setting 2) produces greater social welfare than no-communication electoral competition (Setting 1) when

$$2 + (2q + q(1-q)^2)(\bar{\beta}) - 3q\lambda^* - 4q + 4q^2 - 2q^3$$
$$> 2q\bar{\beta} - 2q + 2,$$
$$(1-q)^2(\bar{\beta}) - 2(1-2q+q^2) > 3\lambda^*,$$
$$\lambda^* < (1-q)^2(\bar{\beta} - 2)/3. \qquad (B.6)$$

Suppose λ^* follows its lower bound from Proposition A.2, providing the easiest case for the left hand side to be less than the right. The lower bound of λ^* is $(1-q)^2$ when $q < 1/2$ and $1 - q - (1-q)^2$ otherwise (Proposition A.2).

If $q < 1/2$, substituting $(1-q)^2$ for λ^* in Eq. (B.6), Setting 2 produces greater welfare than Setting 1 when

$$(1-q)^2 < (1-q)^2(\bar{\beta} - 2)/3,$$
$$1 < (\bar{\beta} - 2)/3,$$

which holds if, and only if, $\bar{\beta} > 5$.

If $q \geq 1/2$, substituting $1 - q - (1-q)^2$ for λ^* in Eq. (B.6), Setting 2 produces greater welfare than Setting 1 when

$$1 - q - (1-q)^2 < (1-q)^2(\bar{\beta} - 2)/3,$$
$$q - q^2 < (1 - 2q + q^2)(\bar{\beta} - 2)/3,$$
$$2 - q - q^2 < (1 - 2q + q^2)(\bar{\beta}),$$
$$(2 + q)/(1 - q) < (\bar{\beta}),$$

which holds if, and only if, $\bar{\beta} > 5$ and requires increasing $\bar{\beta}$ with increasing q.

Setting 2 produces greater welfare than Setting 1 at all q when $\bar{\beta}$ is at least 5. $\qquad\square$

Appendix C

Supplementary Information for Chapter 8

This appendix presents supplementary information for the data collection, experiment, and analysis of vote choice in the 2016 American presidential election in Chapter 8.

C.1 DETAILS OF EXPERIMENT

Professor Carlson and I (Carlson and Hill, 2021) used the survey platform Lucid to recruit a nationally representative sample of 3,253 US adults in January of 2019.[1] We selected others from the set of ANES respondents who had both reported voting for either Clinton or Trump and had been validated to have turned out to vote in the November 2016 election. Each participant received about each other four pieces of information selected at random from the set race, gender, income, state, party identification, and free-response report of the most important problem facing the nation. We manually screened out and removed responses that included profanity, explicit racism, or were incomprehensible. We did not correct grammatical or spelling errors.

Table C.1 presents a summary of the inputs we used, examples, and how they were presented to participants. Altogether, we elicited more than 50,000 probabilities. Participants reported beliefs about 14,312 unique combinations of characteristics.

---

[1] This chapter includes material sourced from Carlson and Hill (2021), published by Cambridge University Press and reprinted with permission.

TABLE C.1. *Example informational inputs for experiment*

Example categories	As presented to participants
Race: Asian, Black, Hispanic, Native American, White	Person A's self-reported race/ethnicity is Black
Gender: Male, Female	Person A's self-reported gender is Female
Income: Under 5,000; 5,000–9,999; 10,000–12,499; ... 250,000 or more	Person A's self-reported annual household income is between $80,000–$89,999
State: Alabama, Alaska, Arizona, ... Wyoming	Person A lives in Minnesota
Party Identification: Democrat, Independent who leans toward the Democratic Party, Independent, Independent who leans toward the Republican Party, Republican	Person A generally thinks of him/herself as an Independent who leans toward the Republican Party
Most Important Problem: Trade, too much poverty, too much hatered [sic] and racism, too much debt, too many people on welfare, threats from abroad, those wanting free entitlements, ISIS	When asked what the single most important problem this country faces is, Person A wrote: 'the national debt'

Participants could earn $0.10 for each of 20 beliefs via the crossover scoring method. One-third of our respondents were randomly assigned to receive a flat-rate bonus of $1.50 instead of $0.10 per probability estimate per round. These participants were instead told that they could win "points" using the same crossover scoring method. I pool together for analysis, as we found only small differences in behavior.

Appendix D

Supplementary Information for Chapter 9

This appendix presents supplementary information for the analysis of the institution of Democracy Vouchers in Chapter 9.

TABLE D.1. *Summary statistics, Seattle Democracy Vouchers*

Statistic	N	Mean	Median	Min	Max
Monetary donations	109,163	151.2	25.0	−7275.5	331755.0
Monetary donations (top-coded)	109,163	136.9	25.0	−7275.5	10000.0
Vouchers returned	60,326	3.8	4.0	1.0	4.0
Vouchers redeemed	60,326	2.6	4.0	0.0	4.0
Year	124,780	2017.0	2017	2011	2019
Seattle resident	124,780	0.8	1	0	1

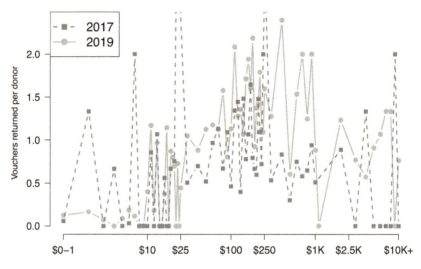

FIGURE D.1 Non-smoothed version of Figure 9.2

Note: Each point is the number of vouchers returned divided the number of donors in bins of contribution amounts.

Appendix E

Supplementary Information for Chapter 10

This appendix presents supplementary information for the analysis of primary election reform in Chapter 10.

E.1 PRIMARY CLASSIFICATION

Table E.1 documents how I have classified primary election institutions to the three categories used in Chapter 10, namely, costly, less costly, and non-partisan.[1]

E.2 DETAILS ON CONTRIBUTION AGGREGATION FROM DIME DATABASE

To create sums of individual contributions in each state, party, and election cycle, I select all individual contributions from DIME's contribution database (Bonica, 2019) with transaction codes 15, 15E, 16J, 22Y, 15S, or 15L, excluding refunds greater than $2,500, from elections 1992 through 2014. I aggregate these individual transactions to the party of recipient, state of contributor, and election cycle. For candidate receipts, I use the DIME recipient database and aggregate recipient receipts to the party of recipient, state of recipient, and election cycle.

---

[1] This chapter includes material sourced from Hill (2022b), published by Cambridge University Press and reprinted with permission.

TABLE E.1. *Categorization of primary institutions by costliness*

Costs	Closed	Partial closed	Partial open	Open to unaffiliated	Open	Top-two, blanket
Register prior to election?	Y	Y	?	?	N	N
Publicly affirm party?	Y	?	Y	?	N	N
Choose party ballot?	Y	Y	Y	Y	Y	N
Complex crossover incentives?	N	N	N	N	N	Y
Classification	Costly	Costly	Costly	Less costly	Less costly	Non-partisan, ambiguous cost

E.3 EVALUATION OF PARALLEL TRENDS

One concern with any observational study aiming to uncover causal relationships is that treatment and control groups have unobserved heterogeneity. In the DID context, the assumption necessary for identification is parallel trends. In this case, we want to believe that states that implement reform were not trending differently in political competition or contributions such that differences in state political environments, rather than primary reform itself, led to changes in outcomes.

Evaluating parallel trends is challenging in the context of this study for two reasons. First, there are few regime changes in the McGhee et al. (2014) data set and only 11 elections even in my extension of observations. Second, state-parties move into and out of treatment at different times, and I include two different treatment variables, complicating any simple graphical evaluation. McGhee et al. (2014) do not evaluate parallel trends.

I follow the recommendation of Angrist and Pischke (2009, p. 237) and add lag and lead of treatment to the DID regression model used in the main text. The idea of the test is that non-parallel trends that are correlated with treatment assignment would show up in an indicator that reform is implemented in the next election (lead on treatment). The lag term is of substantive interest to see if any initial effect decays or increases in the election following the first election under reform (lag on treatment) but does not evaluate parallel trends per se (Angrist and Pischke, 2009, p. 237).

Recent research, however, suggests that in a setting like that here with dynamic treatment assignment in multiple periods, the lead-lag test of Angrist and Pischke (2009) might be inappropriate. Sun and Abraham (2021) find that the lead and lag estimates can be biased by dynamic treatments. So the test here should be interpreted with some caution.

In Table E.2, I reproduce Table 10.2 with one lead and one lag for each primary reform variable. Sample size does not provide extensive statistical power and cases are lost due to lag and lead values outside of 1992 and 2014. There is some evidence of non-parallel trends for non-partisan primary reforms as amount of contributions, number of contributions, and number of contributors appear to increase in the election prior to non-partisan reform. The findings of Sun and Abraham (2021) make it unclear how to interpret these leads.

The percent of contributions classified in primary elections, however, is smaller prior to reform than in the reform year, indicating that the reform had primary-specific consequences. Evidence in less-costly primaries is more ambiguous. Hill (2022b) presents evidence that the parallel trends assumption holds for turnout and competition in primary elections, suggesting the reforms were exogenous to these factors of primary elections. In total, some caution is warranted given these results, particularly given smaller sample sizes.

E.4 PRIMARY REFORM AND ELECTORAL COMPETITION

An alternative explanation for increases in campaign contributions following primary reform is that primary reform increased competition in primary elections. That is, primary reform might have changed the political context (more candidates, higher salience, greater competition), which led to increased contributions rather than need of high-intensity voters for new costly political action.

In Table E.3, I present DID estimates of the effect of primary reform on three measures of political competition. Column one estimates the effect of primary reform on the percentage of House seats for each state-party with at least two (non-write-in) candidates, i.e., a contested seat. Column

TABLE E.2. *Difference-in-difference effects of primary reform on individual campaign contributions with dynamic lead and lag*

	(1) Sum of contributions (1000s)	(2) Log sum contributions	(3) Count of contributions	(4) Log count contributions	(5) Count of contributors	(6) Log count contributors	(7) Percent contributions in primary
Less costly nominating institution	9,649**	0.26*	44,174*	−0.046	12,271**	−0.12	3.19
	(3,060)	(0.11)	(18,769)	(0.12)	(3,836)	(0.14)	(4.00)
Non-partisan nominating institution	176	−0.094	22,780	−0.28*	68.4	−0.32*	2.61
	(3,304)	(0.11)	(19,988)	(0.11)	(2,148)	(0.13)	(2.25)
Non-partisan nominating institution lag t−1	8,533	0.0100	74,590	0.025	10,422	−0.0043	−0.64
	(7,026)	(0.07)	(65,297)	(0.07)	(7,853)	(0.07)	(2.24)
Less costly nominating institution lag t−1	−4,522	−0.14	11,631	0.090	1,781	0.052	4.52
	(3,034)	(0.12)	(15,049)	(0.13)	(4,035)	(0.14)	(3.26)
Non-partisan nominating institution lead t+1	26,863*	0.31	115,372	0.35*	23,818*	0.32*	−6.32*
	(11,127)	(0.18)	(80,015)	(0.14)	(11,929)	(0.14)	(2.85)
Less costly nominating institution lead t+1	12,584	−0.064	55,223	0.36*	14,806	0.31*	0.27
	(7,830)	(0.16)	(42,680)	(0.14)	(8,142)	(0.14)	(3.90)
Observations	1,100	1,100	1,100	1,100	1,100	1,100	1,100
R-squared	0.321	0.838	0.306	0.815	0.399	0.767	0.590
Number of Party-state	100	100	100	100	100	100	100
Party-state FEs	Yes	Yes	Yes	Yes	Yes	Yes	Yes
Election cycle FEs	Yes	Yes	Yes	Yes	Yes	Yes	Yes

**$p < 0.01$, *$p < 0.05$.
OLS coefficients with robust standard errors clustered on state-party in parentheses.
Monetary dependent variables in thousands of dollars.
Excluded category is institutions most costly for individual participation.

TABLE E.3. *Difference-in-differences effects of primary reform on competition in House primary elections*

	(1) Percentage house primaries contested	(2) Number house primary candidates	(3) Log primary candidates	(4) Average winning margin (percent)
Less costly nominating institution	−4.9 [−15 to 5.2]	−2.9* [−5.5 to −0.4]	−0.2 [−0.5 to 0.02]	12 [−0.2 to 24]
Non-partisan nominating institution	0.9 [−6.4 to 8.2]	−2.1 [−5.0 to 0.9]	−0.08 [−0.2 to 0.02]	14* [2.7 to 25]
Observations	1,093	1,093	1,093	969
R-squared	0.069	0.109	0.086	0.039
Number of party-state	99	99	99	98
Party-state FEs	Yes	Yes	Yes	Yes
Election cycle FEs	Yes	Yes	Yes	Yes

$**p < 0.01, *p < 0.05$.
OLS coefficients with robust 95% confidence interval clustered on state-party.
Contested primary defined as more than one non-write-in candidate.
Excluded category is institutions most costly for individual participation.

two estimates the effect on the number of primary candidates, and three the log of number candidates. Column four estimates the average margin over second place of the winning candidate. Increasing competition would suggest positive effects in columns one, two, and three, and a negative effect in column four.[2]

Point estimates in columns one, two, and three are near zero with five of six in the direction suggesting decreased competition. Confidence intervals exclude effects of reform on percent primaries contested greater than 8 percent. Coefficient estimates in column four are politically important *in the wrong direction*, suggesting primary reform increases the average winning margin. In total, Table E.3 suggests against primary reform increasing political competition at primary elections and, thus, against competition as the factor driving increased contributions.

[2] Further details of this analysis can be found in Hill (2022b).

E.5 DETAILS ON SURNAME AGGREGATION

I aggregate turnout histories from the voter files and individual contributions from DIME to the surname-state-year. I then merge average turnout in the most recent four primaries for individuals to sums and counts of contributions on surname, state, and election year. For example, in 2008 in California, I sum for each individual registrant turnout in the 2008 presidential, 2008 congressional, 2006 congressional, and 2004 presidential primaries and then take the average of those sums across all registrants with the same surname. From the DIME data, I sum and count contributions made in 2007 and 2008 for each surname with a reported address in California. These two records are then merged to create the combined data set.

I purge surname of all spaces and special characters, which leads to 87.8 percent of surnames in the contributor data matching a surname in the voter files. I locate at least one contribution for the surname of 82.5 percent of registrants in the voter files.

Turnout can vary by large magnitudes in primary elections, so I do not interact the reform indicator with average turnout. Instead, for each state-year, I classify previous primary turnout into the top quartile, third quartile, and bottom half. This categorizes state-surname-election observations into three groups: surnames that participated to the highest degree in closed primaries (top quartile), middling degree (third quartile), or lowest degree (bottom half).

Bibliography

Achen, Christopher H. and Larry M. Bartels (2016). *Democracy for Realists: Why Elections Do Not Produce Responsive Government.* Princeton, NJ: Princeton University Press.

American National Election Studies (2016a). *ANES 2016 Time Series Study [dataset].* Stanford, CA: Stanford University, the University of Michigan [producers, and distributors].

(2016b). *The American National Election Studies (www.electionstudies.org) TIME SERIES CUMULATIVE DATA FILE [dataset].* Stanford, CA: Stanford University, the University of Michigan [producers, and distributors].

American Presidency Project (2020). *The American Presidency Project at the University of California, Santa Barbara.* www.presidency.ucsb.edu/.

Angrist, Joshua D. and Jorn-Steffen Pischke (2009). *Mostly Harmless Econometrics: An Empiricist's Companion.* Princeton, NJ: Princeton University Press.

Ansolabehere, Stephen, Benjamin Ginsberg, Theodore J. Lowi, and Kenneth A. Shepsle (2018). *American Government: Power and Purpose.* Fifteenth. New York: W.W. Norton.

Ansolabehere, Stephen and Philip Edward Jones (2010). "Constituents' Responses to Congressional Roll-Call Voting". *American Journal of Political Science* 54.3, pp. 583–597.

Ansolabehere, Stephen, Jonathan Rodden, and James M. Snyder (2008). "The Strength of Issues: Using Multiple Measures to Gauge Preference Stability, Ideological Constraint, and Issue Voting". *American Political Science Review* 102.2, pp. 215–232.

Anzia, Sarah F. (2012). "The Election Timing Effect: Evidence from a Policy Intervention in Texas". *Quarterly Journal of Political Science* 7.3, pp. 209–248. http://dx.doi.org/10.1561/100.00011056.

Anzia, Sarah F. and Terry M. Moe (2015). "Public Sector Unions and the Costs of Government". *Journal of Politics* 77.1, pp. 114–127.

Arnold, R. Douglas (1990). *The Logic of Congressional Action.* New Haven, CT: Yale University Press.

Arrow, Kenneth J. (1951). *Social Choice and Individual Values*. New York: Wiley.

Ashworth, Scott and Ethan Bueno de Mesquita (2014). "Is Voter Competence Good for Voters?: Information, Rationality, and Democratic Performance". *American Political Science Review* 108.3, pp. 565–587.

Banks, Jeffrey S. and John Duggan (2005). "Probabilistic Voting in the Spatial Model of Elections: The Theory of Office-Motivated Candidates". In: *Social Choice and Strategic Decisions: Essays in Honor of Jeffrey S. Banks*. Ed. by David Austen-Smith and John Duggan. Dallas, TX: Springer.

Barber, Michael J., Brandice Canes-Wrone, and Sharece Thrower (2017). "Ideologically Sophisticated Donors: Which Candidates Do Individual Contributors Finance?" *American Journal of Political Science* 61.2, pp. 271–288.

Baron, David P. (1994). "Electoral Competition with Informed and Uninformed Voters". *American Political Science Review* 88.1, pp. 33–47.

Barro, Robert J. (1973). "The Control of Politicians: An Economic Model". *Public Choice* 14, pp. 19–42.

Bartels, Larry M. (2008). *Unequal Democracy: The Political Economy of the New Gilded Age*. Princeton, NJ: Princeton University Press.

Bawn, Kathleen, Martin Cohen, David Karol, Seth Masket, Hans Noel, and John Zaller (2012). "A Theory of Political Parties: Groups, Policy Demands and Nominations in American Politics". *Perspectives on Politics* 10.3, pp. 571–597.

Bawn, Kathleen and Gregory Koger (2008). "Effort, Intensity and Position Taking". *Journal of Theoretical Politics* 20.1, pp. 67–92.

Berelson, Bernard R., Paul F. Lazarsfeld, and William N. McPhee (1954). *Voting: A Study of Opinion Formation in a Presidential Campaign*. Chicago, IL: University of Chicago Press.

Berinsky, Adam J. (2018). "Telling the Truth about Believing the Lies? Evidence for the Limited Prevalence of Expressive Survey Responding". *Journal of Politics* 80.1, pp. 211–224.

Besley, Timothy and Stephen Coate (1997). "An Economic Model of Representative Democracy". *Quarterly Journal of Economics* 112.1, pp. 85–114.

Black, Duncan (1958). *The Theory of Committees and Elections*. New York: Cambridge University Press.

Bombardini, Matilde and Francesco Trebbi (2011). "Votes or Money? Theory and Evidence from the US Congress". *Journal of Public Economics* 95, pp. 587–611.

Bonica, Adam (2013). "Ideology and Interests in the Political Marketplace". *American Journal of Political Science* 57.2, pp. 294–311.

(2019). *Database on Ideology, Money in Politics, and Elections: Public Version 3.0 [Computerfile]*. Stanford, CA: Stanford University Libraries.

Bouton, Laurent, Paola Conconi, Francisco Pino, and Maurizio Zanardi (2021). "The Tyranny of the Single-Minded: Guns, Environment, and Abortion". *Review of Economics and Statistics* 103.1, pp. 48–59.

Brady, Henry E., Sidney Verba, and Kay Lehman Schlozman (1995). "Beyond SES: A Resource Model of Political Participation". *American Political Science Review* 89.2, pp. 271–294.

Broockman, David E. and Christopher Skovron (2018). "Bias in Perceptions of Public Opinion among Political Elites". *American Political Science Review* 112.3, pp. 542–563.

Brown, Clifford W., Roman Hedges, and Lynda W. Powell (1980). "Belief Structure in a Political Elite: Contributors to the 1972 Presidential Candidates". *Polity* 13.1, pp. 134–146.

Brown, Clifford W., Lynda W. Powell, and Clyde Wilcox (1995). *Serious Money: Fundraising and Contributing in Presidential Nomination Campaigns*. Cambridge: Cambridge University Press.

Bueno De Mesquita, Bruce, Alastair Smith, Randolph M. Siverson, and James D. Morrow (2003). *The Logic of Political Survival*. Cambridge, MA: MIT Press.

Bullock, John G., Alan S. Gerber, Seth J. Hill, and Gregory A. Huber (2015). "Partisan Bias in Factual Beliefs about Politics". *Quarterly Journal of Political Science* 10.4, pp. 519–578.

Bullock, Will and Joshua D. Clinton (2011). "More a Molehill than a Mountain: The Effects of the Blanket Primary on Elected Officials' Behavior from California". *Journal of Politics* 73.3, pp. 915–930.

Bush, George W. (2001). "President Discusses Stem Cell Research". *White House releases*.

— (2006). "President Discusses Stem Cell Research Policy". *White House releases*.

California Democratic Party et al. v. Jones, 530 U.S. 567 (2000).

California Secretary of State (2004). *2004 Official Voter Information Guide*. Sacramento, CA: California Secretary of State.

Calvert, Randall L. (1985). "Robustness of the Multidimensional Voting Model: Candidate Motivations, Uncertainty, and Convergence". *American Journal of Political Science* 29.1, pp. 69–95.

Campbell, Angus, Philip E. Converse, Warren E. Miller, and Donald E. Stokes (1960). *The American Voter*. New York: Wiley.

Canes-Wrone, Brandice, Michael C. Herron, and Kenneth W. Shotts (2001). "Leadership and Pandering: A Theory of Executive Policymaking". *American Journal of Political Science* 45.3, pp. 532–550.

Carlson, Taylor N. and Seth J. Hill (2021). "Accuracy of Beliefs about the Politics of Others". *Journal of Experimental Political Science* 9.2, pp. 241–254. DOI: https://doi.org/10.1017/XPS.2021.2.

Carnes, Nicholas (2018). *The Cash Ceiling: Why Only the Rich Run for Office– and What We Can Do about It*. Princeton, NJ: Princeton University Press.

Casella, Alessandra (2005). "Storable Votes". *Games and Economic Behavior* 51, pp. 391–419.

City of Lubbock (n.d.). *City of Lubbock, Texas, Public Meeting Journals*. https://ci.lubbock.tx.us/departments/city-secretary/council-minutes.

City of Reno (n.d.). *City of Reno, Nevada, Public Meeting Journals*. https://renocitynv.iqm2.com/Citizens/Calendar.aspx.

Cohen, Marty, David Karol, Hans Noel, and John Zaller (2008). *The Party Decides: Presidential Nominations Before and After Reform*. Chicago, IL: University of Chicago Press.

Congress.gov (2013). *S.649- Safe Communities, Safe Schools Act of 2013: Amendments.* www.congress.gov/bill/113th-congress/senate-bill/649/amendments?searchResultViewType=expanded.

Conover, Pamela Johnston, Virginia Gray, and Steven Coombs (1982). "Single-Issue Voting: Elite-Mass Linkages". *Political Behavior* 4.4, pp. 309–331.

Converse, Philip E. (1964). "The Nature of Belief Systems in Mass Publics". In: *Ideology and Discontent.* Ed. by David Apter. New York: Free Press.

Coughlin, Peter and Shmuel Nitzan (1981). "Electoral Outcomes with Probabilistic Voting and Nash Social Welfare Maxima". *Journal of Public Economics* 15, pp. 113–121.

Dahl, Robert A. (1956). *A Preface to Democratic Theory.* Chicago, IL: University of Chicago Press.

Davis, Otto A. and Melvin J. Hinich (1966). "A Mathematical Model of Policy Formation in a Democratic Society". In: *Mathematical Applications in Political Science.* Dallas, TX: Southern Methodist University Press, pp. 175–208.

—— (1968). "On the Power and Importance of the Mean Preference in a Mathematical Model of Democratic Choice". *Public Choice* 5, pp. 59–72.

Democratic Party v. Wisconsin ex rel. La Follette, 450 U.S. 107 (1981).

Disch, Lisa (2011). "Toward a Mobilization Conception of Democratic Representation". *American Political Science Review* 105.1, pp. 100–114.

Dixit, Avinash and John Londregan (1996). "The Determinants of Success of Special Interests in Redistributive Politics". *Journal of Politics* 58.4, pp. 1132–1155.

Downs, Anthony (1957). *An Economic Theory of Democracy.* New York: Harper Collins.

Einstein, Katherine Levine, David M. Glick, and Maxwell Palmer (2019). *Neighborhood Defenders: Participatory Politics and America's Housing Crisis.* New York: Cambridge University Press.

Enelow, James M. and Melvin J. Hinich (1984). *The Spatial Theory of Voting: An Introduction.* New York: Cambridge University Press.

Fearon, James D. (1999). "Electoral Accountability and the Control of Politicians: Selecting Good Types versus Sanctioning Poor Performance". In: *Democracy, Accountability, and Representation.* Ed. by Adam Przeworski, Susan Stokes, and Bernard Manin. New York: Cambridge University Press.

Federalist 57 (1788). "Federalist No. 57: 'The Alleged Tendency of the New Plan to Elevate the Few at the Expense of the Many Considered in Connection with Representation'". *New York Packet.*

Fenno, Richard F. (1978). *Home Style: House Members in Their Districts.* Boston, MA: Little, Brown.

Ferejohn, John (1986). "Incumbent Performance and Electoral Control". *Public Choice* 50.1, pp. 5–25.

Fiorina, Morris P. (1974). *Representatives, Roll Calls, and Constituencies.* Lexington, MA: Heath.

—— (1981). *Retrospective Voting in American National Elections.* New Haven, CT: Yale University Press.

Fiorina, Morris P. and Samuel J. Abrams (2009). *Disconnect: The Breakdown of Representation in American Politics*. Norman, OK: University of Oklahoma Press.

Fiorina, Morris P., Paul E. Peterson, Bertram D. Johnson, and William G. Mayer (2011). *The New American Democracy*. Seventh. New York: Pearson.

Fournier, Patrick, André Blais, Richard Nadeau, Elisabeth Gidengil, and Neil Nevitte (2003). "Issue Importance and Performance Voting". *Political Behavior* 25.1, pp. 51–67.

Fowler, Anthony (2020). "Partisan Intoxication or Policy Voting?" *Quarterly Journal of Political Science* 15, pp. 141–179.

Fowler, Anthony, Seth J. Hill, Jeff Lewis, Chris Tausanovitch, Lynn Vavreck, and Christopher Warshaw (n.d.). *Moderates*, Working paper, University of Chicago.

Fox, Justin and Richard Van Weelden (2015). "Hoping for the Best, Unprepared for the Worst". *Journal of Public Economics* 130, pp. 59–65.

Francia, Peter L., John C. Green, Paul S. Herrnson, Clyde Wilcox, and Lynda W. Powell (2003). *The Financiers of Congressional Elections: Investors, Ideologues, and Intimates*. New York: Columbia University Press.

Gallup (2020). *Gallup Historical Trends: Guns*. https://news.gallup.com/poll/1645/guns.aspx.

Gause, LaGina (2022). *The Advantage of Disadvantage: Legislative Responsiveness to Collective Action by the Politically Marginalized*. New York: Cambridge University Press.

(2022). "Revealing Issue Salience via Costly Protest: How Legislative Behavior following Protest Advantages Low-Resource Groups". *British Journal of Political Science*, 52.2, pp. 259–279.

Gerber, Alan S., Gregory A. Huber, David Doherty, and Conor M. Dowling (2011). "Citizens' Policy Confidence and Electoral Punishment: A Neglected Dimension of Electoral Accountability". *Journal of Politics* 73.4, pp. 1206–1224.

Gerber, Elisabeth R. and Jeffrey B. Lewis (2004). "Beyond the Median: Voter Preferences, District Heterogeneity, and Political Representation". *Journal of Political Economy* 112.6, pp. 1364–1383.

Gerber, Elisabeth R. and Rebecca B. Morton (1998). "Primary Election Systems and Representation". *Journal of Law, Economics, & Organization* 14.2, pp. 304–324.

Gilens, Martin (2005). "Inequality and Democratic Responsiveness". *Public Opinion Quarterly* 69.5, pp. 778–796.

Gordon, Sanford C. and Catherine Hafer (2005). "Flexing Muscle: Corporate Political Expenditures as Signals to the Bureaucracy". *American Political Science Review* 99.2, pp. 245–261.

Griffin, John D. and Brian Newman (2008). *Minority Report: Evaluating Political Equality in America*. Chicago, IL: University of Chicago Press.

Groseclose, Tim (2001). "A Model of Candidate Location When One Candidate Has a Valence Advantage". *American Journal of Political Science* 45.4, pp. 862–886.

Grossman, Gene M. and Elhanan Helpman (1994). "Protection for Sale". *American Economic Review* 84.4, pp. 833–850.

— (1996). "Electoral Competition and Special Interest Politics". *Review of Economic Studies* 63, pp. 265–86.

Hacker, Jacob S. and Paul Pierson (2011). *Winner-Take-All Politics: How Washington Made the Rich Richer – and Turned Its Back on the Middle Class*. New York: Simon & Schuster.

— (2020). *Let them Eat Tweets: How the Right Rules in an Age of Extreme Inequality*. New York: Liveright.

Hanretty, Chris, Benjamin E. Lauderdale, and Nick Vivyan (2020). "A Choice-Based Measure of Issue Importance in the Electorate". *American Journal of Political Science* 64.3, pp. 519–535.

Hertel-Fernandez, Alex (2019). *State Capture: How Conservative Activists, Big Businesses, and Wealthy Donors Reshaped the American States – and the Nation*. New York: Oxford University Press.

Hertel-Fernandez, Alex, Matto Mildenberger, and Leah C. Stokes (2019). "Legislative Staff and Representation in Congress". *American Political Science Review* 113.1, pp. 1–18.

Hill, Seth J. (2014). "A Behavioral Measure of the Enthusiasm Gap in American Elections". *Electoral Studies* 36, pp. 28–38.

— (2015). "Institution of Nomination and the Policy Ideology of Primary Electorates". *Quarterly Journal of Political Science* 10.4, pp. 461–487.

— (2017a). "Changing Votes or Changing Voters: How Candidates and Election Context Swing Voters and Mobilize the Base". *Electoral Studies* 48, pp. 131–141.

— (2017b). "Learning Together Slowly: Bayesian Learning about Political Facts". *Journal of Politics* 79.4, pp. 1403–1418.

— (2022a). "A Theory of Intensity, Electoral Competition, and Costly Political Action". *Journal of Politics*, 84.1, pp. 291–303.

— (2022b). "Sidestepping Primary Reform: Political Action in Response to Institutional Change". *Political Science Research and Methods* 10.2, pp. 391–407.

Hill, Seth J. and Gregory A. Huber (2017). "Representativeness and Motivations of the Contemporary Donorate: Results from Merged Survey and Administrative Records". *Political Behavior* 39.1, pp. 3–29.

— (2019). "On the Meaning of Survey Reports of Roll Call 'Votes'". *American Journal of Political Science* 63.3, pp. 611–625.

Hill, Seth J. and Thad Kousser (2016). "Turning Out Unlikely Voters? A Field Experiment in the Top-Two Primary". *Political Behavior* 38.2, pp. 413–432.

Hill, Seth J., James Lo, Lynn Vavreck, and John Zaller (2013). "How Quickly We Forget: The Duration of Persuasion Effects from Mass Communication". *Political Communication* 30.4, pp. 521–547.

Hirano, Shigeo, James M. Snyder, Jr., Stephen Ansolabehere, and John Mark Hansen (2010). "Primary Elections and Partisan Polarization in the U.S. Congress". *Quarterly Journal of Political Science* 5, pp. 169–191.

Howell, William G. and Terry M. Moe (2020). *Presidents, Populism, and the Crisis of Democracy*. Chicago, IL: University of Chicago Press.

Huber, Gregory A. and Kevin Arceneaux (2007). "Uncovering the Persuasive Effects of Presidential Advertising". *American Journal of Political Science* 51.4, pp. 961–981.

Huber, Gregory A., Seth J. Hill, and Gabriel S. Lenz (2012). "Sources of Bias in Retrospective Decision Making: Experimental Evidence on Voters' Limitations in Controlling Incumbents". *American Political Science Review* 106.4, pp. 720–741.

Ingham, Sean (2019). *Rule by Multiple Majorities: A New Theory of Popular Control*. New York: Cambridge University Press.

Israel, Steve (2018). "The Missing Catalyst: Voter Intensity". *Newsday*. www .newsday.com/opinion/commentary/the-missing-catalyst-voter-intensity-1.16885468.

Iyengar, Shanto, Kyu S. Hahn, Jon A. Krosnick, and John Walker (2008). "Selective Exposure to Campaign Communication: The Role of Anticipated Agreement and Issue Public Membership". *Journal of Politics* 70.1, pp. 186–200.

Jacobson, Gary C. and Jamie L. Carson (2015). *The Politics of Congressional Elections*. Lanham, MD: Rowman and Littlefield.

James P. Brady et al. v. Diana J. Ohman, 105 F.3d 726 (1998). www.ca10 .uscourts.gov/opinions/97/97-8081.pdf.

Jervis, Robert (1970). *The Logic of Images in International Relations*. Princeton, NJ: Princeton University Press.

Johnson, James (2018). "Formal Models in Political Science: Conceptual, Not Empirical". *Journal of Politics*, 81.1, pp. e6–e10.

Karni, Edi (2009). "A Mechanism for Eliciting Probabilities". *Econometrica* 77.2, pp. 603–606.

Kernell, Samuel H., Gary C. Jacobson, Thad Kousser, and Lynn Vavreck (2019). *The Logic of American Politics*. Ninth. Washington, DC: CQ Press.

Key, V.O. (1961). *Public Opinion and American Democracy*. New York: Knopf. (1966). *The Responsible Electorate*. New York: Random House.

Klar, Samara and Yanna Krupnikov (2016). *Independent Politics: How American Disdain for Parties Leads to Political Inaction*. Cambridge: Cambridge University Press.

Kousser, Thad (2015). "The Top-Two, Take Two: Did Changing the Rules Change the Game in Statewide Contests?" *California Journal of Politics and Policy* Online only.

Kousser, Thad, Justin H. Phillips, and Boris Shor (2018). "Reform and Representation: A New Method Applied to Recent Electoral Changes". *Political Science Research and Methods* 6.4, pp. 809–827.

Kramer, Gerald H. (1971). "Short-Term Fluctuations in U.S. Voting Behavior, 1896–1964". *American Political Science Review* 65.1, pp. 131–143.

Krehbiel, Keith (1998). *Pivotal Politics: A Theory of U.S. Lawmaking*. Chicago, IL: University of Chicago Press.

Krosnick, Jon A. (1990). "Government Policy and Citizen Passion: A Study of Issue Publics in Contemporary America". *Political Behavior* 12.1, pp. 59–92.

Lacombe, Matthew J. (2021). *Firepower: How the NRA Turned Gun Owners into a Political Force*. Princeton, NJ: Princeton University Press.

Lalley, Steven P. and E. Glen Weyl (2018). "Quadratic Voting: How Mechanism Design Can Radicalize Democracy". *American Economic Association Papers and Proceedings*, 108, pp. 33–37.

Lax, Jeffrey R. and Justin H. Phillips (2012). "The Democratic Deficit in the States". *American Journal of Political Science* 56.1, pp. 148–166.

Leighley, Jan E. and Jonathan Nagler (2014). *Who Votes Now?* Princeton, NJ: Princeton University Press.

Lengell, Sean (2013). "Leaks Hurt Gun Control, Sen. Pat Toomey Says". *The Washington Times*.

Lenz, Gabriel S. (2012). *Follow the Leader?: How Voters Respond to Politicians' Policies and Performance*. Chicago, IL: University of Chicago Press.

Lindbeck, Assar and Jorgen W. Weibull (1987). "Balanced-Budget Redistribution as the Outcome of Political Competition". *Public Choice* 52.3, pp. 273–297.

Lohmann, Susanne (1993). "A Signalling Model of Informative and Manipulative Political Action". *American Political Science Review* 87.2, pp. 319–333.

Lohr, Sharon L. (2019). *Sampling Design and Analysis*. Second. Boston, MA: Chapman & Hall.

Luker, Kristin (1985). *Abortion and the Politics of Motherhood*. Berkeley, CA: University of California Press.

Masket, Seth (2016). *The Inevitable Party*. New York: Oxford University Press.

Mayhew, David R. (1974). *Congress: The Electoral Connection*. New Haven, CT: Yale University Press.

Mayo, Henry B. (1960). *An Introduction to Democratic Theory*. New York: Oxford University Press.

McDonald, Michael P. (2019). "1980–2014 State Turnout Rates". *United States Election Project*.

McGhee, Eric, Seth Masket, Boris Shor, Steven Rogers, and Nolan McCarty (2014). "A Primary Cause of Partisanship? Nomination Systems and Legislator Ideology". *American Journal of Political Science* 58.2, pp. 337–51.

McGhee, Eric and Boris Shor (2017). "Has the Top Two Primary Elected More Moderates?" *Perspectives on Politics* 15.4, pp. 1053–1066.

McKelvey, Richard D. (1976). "Intransitivities in Multidimensional Voting Models and Some Implications for Agenda Control". *Journal of Economic Theory* 12, pp. 472–482.

McKelvey, Richard D. and John W. Patty (2006). "A Theory of Voting in Large Elections". *Games and Economic Behavior* 57, pp. 155–180.

Meirowitz, Adam (2005). "Polling Games and Information Revelation in the Downsian Framework". *Games and Economic Behavior* 41, pp. 464–489.

Menger, Andrew and Robert M. Stein (2020). "Choosing the Less Convenient Way to Vote: An Anomaly in Vote by Mail Elections". *Political Research Quarterly* 73.1, pp. 196–207.

Merriam, Charles Edward and Louise Overacker (1928). *Primary Elections*. Chicago, IL: University of Chicago Press.

Mildenberger, Matto and Dustin Tingley (2017). "Beliefs about Climate Beliefs: The Importance of Second-Order Opinions for Climate Politics". *British Journal of Political Science* 49.4, pp. 1279–1307.

Miller, Warren E. and Donald E. Stokes (1963). "Constituency Influence in Congress". *American Political Science Review* 57.1, pp. 45–56.

Mueller, John (1999). *Capitalism, Democracy, and Ralph's Pretty Good Grocery*. Princeton, NJ: Princeton University Press.

National Conference of State Legislatures (2012). *NCSL: Initiative, Referendum and Recall*. www.ncsl.org/research/elections-and-campaigns/ initiative-referendum-and-recall-overview.aspx.

National Institutes of Health (2020). *Stem Cell Basics*. https://stemcells.nih.gov/.

Nisbet, Matthew C. and Amy B. Becker (2014). "The Polls – Trends: Public Opinion about Stem Cell Research, 2002 to 2010". *Public Opinion Quarterly* 78.4, pp.1003–1022.

Obama, Barack (2009). "Remarks on Signing of Stem Cell Executive Order". *White House speeches and remarks*.

  (2013). "Statement by the President". *White House speeches and remarks*. https://obamawhitehouse.archives.gov/the-press-office/2013/04/17/state ment-president.

Olson, Mancur (1965). *The Logic of Collective Action*. Cambridge, MA: Harvard University Press.

Orr, Lilla V. and Gregory A. Huber (2020). "The Policy Basis of Measured Partisan Animosity in the United States". *American Journal of Political Science* 64.3, pp. 569–586.

Page, Benjamin I. and Martin Gilens (2017). *Democracy in America?: What Has Gone Wrong and What We Can Do about It*. Chicago, IL: University of Chicago Press.

Palfrey, Thomas R. and Howard Rosenthal (1985). "Voter Participation and Strategic Uncertainty". *American Political Science Review* 79.1, pp. 62–78.

Patty, John W. (2002). "Equivalence of Objectives in Two Candidate Elections". *Public Choice* 112.1, pp. 151–166.

  (2016). "Signaling through Obstruction". *American Journal of Political Science* 60.1, pp. 175–189.

Patty, John W. and Elizabeth Maggie Penn (2019). "Are Moderates Better Representatives than Extremists? A Theory of Indirect Representation". *American Political Science Review* 113.3, pp. 743–761.

Pew Research Center (2013). *In Gun Control Debate, Several Options Draw Majority Support*. www.pewresearch.org/politics/2013/01/14/in-gun-control-debate-several-options-draw-majority-support/.

Posner, Eric A. and E. Glen Weyl (2018). *Radical Markets: Uprooting Capitalism and Democracy for a Just Society*. Princeton, NJ: Princeton University Press.

ProPublica (n.d.). *ProPublica Nonprofit Explorer: National Rifle Association*. https://projects.propublica.org/nonprofits/organizations/530116130.

R Core Team (2020). *R: A Language and Environment for Statistical Computing*. R Foundation for Statistical Computing. Vienna, Austria. www.R-project.org/.

Rabinowitz, George and Stuart Elaine Macdonald (1989). "A Directional Theory of Issue Voting". *American Political Science Review* 83.1, pp. 93–121.

Rahn, Wendy M. (1993). "The Role of Partisan Stereotypes in Information Processing about Political Candidates". *American Journal of Political Science* 37.2, pp. 472–496.

RePass, David E. (1971). "Issue Salience and Party Choice". *American Political Science Review* 65.2, pp. 389–400.

Reno Realty blog (2021). *Reno-Sparks, NV Historical Median Home Sale Data.* https://renorealtyblog.com/resources/historical-median-sold-data.

Riker, William H. (1982). *Liberalism against Populism*. San Francisco, CA: Waveland Press.

Riker, William H. and Peter C. Ordeshook (1968). "A Theory of the Calculus of Voting". *American Political Science Review* 62.1, pp. 25–42.

Rivers, Douglas (1988). "Heterogeneity in Models of Electoral Choice". *American Journal of Political Science* 32.3, pp. 737–757.

Schattschneider, E.E. (1935). *Politics, Pressures and the Tariff*. Hamden, CT: Archon Books.

 (1960). *The Semisovereign People: A Realist's View of Democracy in America.* New York: Holt, Rinehart and Winston.

Schnakenberg, Keith E. and Ian R. Turner (2019). "Signaling with Reform: How the Threat of Corruption Prevents Informed Policymaking". *American Political Science Review* 113.3, pp. 762–777.

Sears, David O., Richard R. Lau, Tom R. Tyler, and Harris M. Allen Jr. (1980). "Self-Interest vs. Symbolic Politics in Policy Attitudes and Presidential Voting". *American Political Science Review* 74, pp. 670–684.

Seattle Democracy Voucher Program data (2020). *Seattle Democracy Voucher Program Data*. www.seattle.gov/democracyvoucher/program-data.

Seattle Ethics and Elections Commission Data (2020). *Seattle Ethics and Elections Commission List of Contributors*. http://web6.Seattle.gov/ethics/elections/lists.aspx.

Shotts, Kenneth W. (2006). "A Signaling Model of Repeated Elections". *Social Choice Welfare* 27, pp. 251–261.

Sinclair, Betsy (2012). *The Social Citizen: Peer Networks and Political Behavior.* Chicago, IL: University of Chicago Press.

Skocpol, Theda (2013). *Diminished Democracy: From Membership to Management in American Civic Life*. Norman, OK: University of Oklahoma Press.

Sniderman, Paul (2000). "Taking Sides: A Fixed Choice Theory of Political Reasoning". In: *Elements of Reason: Cognition, Choice, and the Bounds of Rationality*. Ed. by Arthur Lupia, Mat McCubbins, and Samuel Popkin. New York: Cambridge University Press.

Sniderman, Paul and John G. Bullock (2004). "A Consistency Theory of Public Opinion and Political Choice: The Hypothesis of Menu Dependence". In: *Studies in Public Opinion: Attitudes, Nonattitudes, Measurement Error, and Change.* Ed. by Willem E. Saris and Paul M. Sniderman. Princeton, NJ: Princeton University Press.

Spence, Michael (1973). "Job Market Signaling". *Quarterly Journal of Economics* 87, pp. 355–374.

Stolberg, Sheryl Gay (2006). "Democrats Hope to Divide G.O.P. Over Stem Cells". *The New York Times.*

Sun, Liyang and Sarah Abraham (2021). "Estimating Dynamic Treatment Effects in Event Studies with Heterogeneous Treatment Effects". *Journal of Econometrics* Online first. https://doi.org/10.1016/j.jeconom.2020.09.006.

Tausanovitch, Chris (n.d.). *Measuring Preference Intensity.* Working paper, UCLA.

Thomsen, Danielle M. (2014). "Ideological Moderates Won't Run: How Party Fit Matters for Partisan Polarization in Congress". *Journal of Politics*, 76.3, pp. 786–797.

de Toqueville, Alexis (1835 [2013]). *Democracy in America.* The Project Gutenberg EBook of Democracy In America. www.gutenberg.org/files/815/815-h/815-h.htm.

Tullock, Gordon (1967). "The Welfare Costs of Tariffs, Monopolies, and Theft". *Western Economic Journal* 5.3, pp. 224–232.

Vavreck, Lynn (2009). *The Message Matters: The Economy and Presidential Campaigns.* Princeton, NJ: Princeton University Press.

Verba, Sidney, Kay Lehman Schlozman, and Henry E. Brady (1995). *Voice and Equality: Civic Voluntarism in American Politics.* Cambridge, MA: Harvard University Press.

Ware, Alan (2002). *The American Direct Primary: Party Institutionalization and Transformation in the North.* New York: Cambridge University Press.

Wasow, Omar (2020). "Agenda Seeding: How 1960s Black Protests Moved Elites, Public Opinion and Voting". *American Political Science Review* 114.3, pp. 638–659.

Wawro, Gregory J. and Eric Schickler (2006). *Filibuster: Obstruction and Lawmaking in the U.S. Senate.* Princeton, NJ: Princeton University Press.

Weingast, Barry R., Kenneth A. Shepsle, and Christopher Johnsen (1981). "The Political Economy of Benefits and Costs: A Neoclassical Approach to Distributive Politics". *Journal of Political Economy* 89.4, pp. 642–664.

Wilson, James Q. (1995). *Political Organizations.* Princeton, NJ: Princeton University Press.

Witko, Christopher, Jana Morgan, Nathan J. Kelly, and Peter K. Enns (2021). *Hijacking the Agenda: Economic Power and Political Influence.* New York: Russell Sage Foundation.

Zaller, John (1992). *The Nature and Origins of Mass Opinion.* New York: Cambridge University Press.

(2003). "Coming to Grips with V.O. Key's Concept of Latent Opinion". In: *Electoral Democracy*. Ed. by Michael B. MacKuen and George Rabinowitz. Ann Arbor, MI: University of Michigan Press.

Zaller, John and Stanley Feldman (1992). "A Simple Theory of the Survey Response: Answering Questions versus Revealing Preferences". *American Journal of Political Science* 36.3, pp. 579–616.

Index

For EU product safety concerns, contact us at Calle de José Abascal, 56–1°,
28003 Madrid, Spain or eugpsr@cambridge.org.

www.ingramcontent.com/pod-product-compliance
Ingram Content Group UK Ltd.
Pitfield, Milton Keynes, MK11 3LW, UK
UKHW010250140625
459647UK00013BA/1772